EVERYMAN'S
BIBLE
COMMENTARY

ROMANS

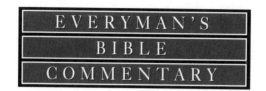

EVERYMAN'S
BIBLE
COMMENTARY

ROMANS

Alan F. Johnson

MOODY PRESS
CHICAGO

To Peter, Erin, and Nolan Magary;
Ian, Erik, Alysa, and Ashley Rodgers;
Adam, Austin, and Marie Baker;
Dane, Madelyn, and Skylar Brewer,
children of my children,
bright stars in my life
and in God's firmament

CONTENTS

PREFACE

Since the first appearance of this commentary (1974), a number of events have occurred that made the first revised edition (1985) and now this new revision desirable. Although the Word of God does not change, our understanding and hearing do change with advances in the knowledge of Scripture and changes in the world and in the church where we live out our Christian lives. The intervening years have seen the publication of a number of monumental commentaries on Romans. C. E. B. Cranfield's two-volume work (1975, 1979—see selected bibliography) set a new standard for careful, conservative, historical, and theological exegesis of the letter that in my opinion has not been surpassed. I have incorporated his materials extensively throughout this commentary.

Ernst Käsemann's German Lutheran commentary has been translated into English (1980), and though not entirely conservative, it nevertheless sets forth Paul's main theme as justification by faith and contains a wealth of exegetical and theological help on the epistle. I have likewise referred to this work, though not as extensively as Cranfield.

More recently we have fortunately seen the publication of a number of large, extensive, and significant commentaries on

Romans. Leon Morris (1988), a prince of interpreters, has given us again a reliable, more traditional but perceptive, expository–exegetical treatment of the book with a great deal of sound judgments. The extensive Word Biblical Commentary Series now contains the detailed two-volume work of British scholar James D. G. Dunn (1988), which is the first major-length, more conservative commentary to adopt with modifications the "new perspective" on Paul (see below).

Three significant exegetical commentaries on Romans have been published in the nineties. J. A. Fitzmyer (1993) of Duke Divinity School gives us not only a Roman Catholic perspective but also a fine, detailed, and perceptive treatment. Two massive evangelical exegetical commentaries have appeared recently, Douglas J. Moo (1996), and Thomas R. Schreiner (1998). Both have interacted extensively with contemporary discussions, including the new perspective on Paul. I have included the views of these latter two especially throughout this commentary. Finally, mention should be made of the fine expository treatment of the book by British evangelical statesman John Stott (1994), who understands the modern issues well but has focused on the message of Romans.

The *New International Version* (1973, 1978, 1984) has become the most widely read English translation and is now the translation used throughout this work. Another recent event that has aided interpreters is the publication of the initial volumes in the new series, *Ancient Christian Commentary on Scripture, The New Testament* (1998). Fortunately for us, Romans was one of the first published. I have included quotes throughout from the early church fathers, which has enriched the commentary beyond the original edition.

The world and the Christian community have also changed in the past two to three decades. Some issues remain, such as the resurgence of Islamic fundamentalism, the continuing problem of peace in the Middle East, the abortion problem, the threat to the church of being co-opted by excessive identification with partisan politics or by affluence. Other things have changed, such as the disappearance of the Moral Majority or the looming threat of nuclear holocaust. Today we are faced with an unchecked, worldwide AIDS crisis and a time of unparalleled prosperity on Wall Street where the computer and the Internet are changing our culture profoundly.

More telling is the continued slide into ideological pluralism, relativism, and forms of postmodernism. The areas of truth and moral absolutes in particular are increasingly held as suspect or even oppressing, which results in the weakening of the uniqueness of Christ and the gospel as we face the public encounter with pluralists whose agenda often attempts to reduce all religions to equal relative value and truth content. Do not all of these developments intensify our need for a deeper understanding and obedience to the revealed truth in Romans?

THE NEW PERSPECTIVE ON PAUL

Finally, a monumental study of first-century Judaism has now produced a watershed in the way Paul is understood. Scholars are calling it the "new perspective" on Paul. This event was the publication of E. P. Sanders's *Paul and Palestinian Judaism* (1977). In a nutshell, what Sanders did was to examine all the available Jewish writings of the Christian and pre-Christian period to establish insofar as possible what Jews of the time actually thought about the law, grace, meritorious works, and salvation. His conclusion was that Pharisaical Judaism did not actually believe in a works or merit salvation or justification by law works as traditionally taught by Christian scholars up to the present time. Instead Jews in Paul's day held to a "covenant nomism." One comes into right relationship to God and enters the covenant by grace alone and faith. Once in the covenant, obedience to the Law of Moses maintains one in good standing before God. According to Sanders, Paul and Romans must be reread in this light and not through the lens of Luther and his battle with Roman Catholic works salvation.

Various responses to Sanders's watershed study have occurred, ranging from warm embrace to respectful rejection. Whatever one's position, it is now necessary for modern scholars (including evangelicals) to interact and evaluate these discoveries and ideas to see if they help or hinder our understanding of Paul's thought. My own response in brief is mixed. Some of Sanders certainly needs to be brought into the background of those who opposed Paul's gospel. Other ideas are unacceptable, such as his belief that Paul's views on the law were confused and contradictory. In my opinion, there remains an element of "legalism" (meritorious works for salvation) in the opponents Paul addresses in Romans that cannot be evaded.

I hope those who have found the previous editions of this commentary helpful will find this new and extensive revision even more satisfying.

HOW TO READ AND USE THIS BOOK

Every book must be read in view of its intended purpose if the author's efforts are to be found helpful. This book is not the book of Romans. At best it is a brief attempt to explain and comment on some of Paul's main themes in the letter. As such, it must not be used as a substitute for Paul's own letter, which is far more important than anything we could say about it. You must read and reread the book of Romans itself as you use this commentary. Readers should have open before them the actual letter of Paul and first read each paragraph section of Romans and then consult the suggested explanation.

These notes are human, fallible, and subject to revision. The aim is not sermonic or devotional but a fresh interpretation of the ageless letter in the light of our contemporary age and it's needs.

Though the main body of the book has the college student and the concerned layperson in mind, the more important exegetical and theological problems are briefly addressed in the endnotes. Thus there are two books in one, an introductory explanation for serious beginners and also suggestions for the more advanced students and scholars.

It has been an inexpressible experience of joy and learning for me to have spent these many hours pouring over the rich truths found in Paul's letter to the Romans. This epistle has changed my life. What I have learned of God and myself from the book has definitely affected the whole quality of my life. If even some small spark of this enthusiasm and joy can reach across these pages to the reader, I shall be deeply grateful.

FREEDOM

"Public freedom at last depends on spiritual freedom, and spiritual freedom is not in human nature but in its redemption."

P. T. Forsyth

THE BOOK OF ROMANS IN ONE SENTENCE

"Who are we? We are God's creatures; Yes, but we are God's image, and through the misuse of our God-bestowed freedom, we are God's shame and we are God's problem; But by that incredible strategy of the cross, God makes it possible for us to become the Creator's children; And we may become the Creator's co-laborers, and we, finite humans, may become the friends of an infinite and all-holy God; And ultimately we may be, if we will have it so, God's glory."

Vernon C. Grounds (adapted with permission)

INTRODUCTION

IMPORTANCE OF ROMANS

Since the content of the book of Romans is weighty and without much practical personal application until chapter 12, I would like at the outset to stress the great significance of the book lest discouragement over mastering its content turn you away too soon from its inspiring pages.[1]

A few quotations will help put Romans into perspective. Coleridge said of Romans that it was "the profoundest work in existence." Luther remarked that it was "the chief part of the New Testament and the perfect Gospel." "If a man understands it," Calvin stated, "he has a sure road open for him to the understanding of the whole Scripture." Godet referred to it as the "Cathedral of Christian Faith." More recently the notable Princeton scholar Bruce Metzger has called Romans the "Constitution of Universal Christianity." The German scholar, Peter Stuhlmacher, refers to the letter as "The sum and crown of the Pauline gospel."

Great intellects like Augustine, Luther, Calvin, and Edwards have studied Romans only to discover depths beyond their depths. George Wilson of Scotland, the distinguished poet, biographer, and scientist, received Christian instruction from his friend, Dr. John Cairns, who wrote to him of Romans: "The Gospel tide nowhere forms so many deep, dark pools where the neophyte may drown. . . . You will have something like a glimpse of the divine depth and richness of that despised old textbook, the New Testament."[2]

It may be because Romans is the greatest treatise on God that has ever been written that the letter has figured prominently in every significant evangelical renaissance in history.[3] Such was the case with Augustine, Luther, and John Wesley. Although not a full return to evangelical faith, the more recent work of Karl Barth on Romans (*Romerbrief,* 1919) broke the stranglehold of liberal theology on the scholarly world and brought some significant return to a biblical theology.

A book that has been so used by God in days past might also in our day play a role in the awakening of God's people from their slumber. That such a need exists can be abundantly documented. Consider, for example, the timely words of the late Dr. John A. MacKay, president of Princeton Seminary for twenty-three years:

> It seems increasingly clear that the chief need of contemporary Christianity and of society in general in this confused and revolutionary time is an evangelical renaissance. By that I mean a rediscovery of the Evangel, the Gospel, in its full dimension of light and power, together with the elevation of the Gospel to the status that belongs to the Gospel in the thought, life, and activity of all persons and organizations that bear the name "Christian."[4]

Or consider the startling words of missioner-theologian, C. Rene Padilla of Buenos Aires, Argentina, who, a number of years ago in reviewing three books on missions in *Christianity Today,* suggested that the important questions they raise can all be reduced to one: "What is the Gospel?"[5]

With Luther we may today as well recognize that Romans is among those biblical books "which show you Christ and teach everything that is blessed and necessary for you to know, even though you never again see or hear any other book or doctrine."[6]

With these important historical precedents in mind, we can well afford to apply ourselves to the careful study of Paul's letter, expecting that God may in some small measure kindle anew our love and devotion to Him and perhaps enable us to be a part of a new evangelical renaissance in our day.

Author, Date, and Place of Writing

So conclusive is the argument for Pauline authorship of this epistle that no serious scholar doubts that it comes from the noted apostle to the Gentiles. Not only in the great theme of the grace of God, but in the evidence that the person who wrote the letter was without doubt a Jew who was thoroughly familiar with Pharisaical Judaism (Acts 23:6), as well as one who was burdened to minister to the Gentiles (Acts 13:47; Gal. 2:2, 8; see Rom. 11:13), we have further support for the letter's authorship by Paul.

Although Paul no doubt could identify with the Greco-Roman culture in which he was raised at Tarsus (Acts 22:3) and bear the impress of responsibilities of Roman citizenship (Acts 22:25), the greatest influence on his life was his rabbinic, Pharisaical Jewish background (Rom. 11:1; Gal. 1:13–14; Phil. 3:5–6). Today scholars are increasingly convinced that Paul's Jewish background places him squarely in the mainstream Judaism of his day. He was not a cheap or second-class Jew.[7]

Other important influences on Paul's life were his acceptance of Jesus as Messiah and Lord (Gal. 1:15–16), his contact with the Christian tradition before him (Rom. 1:3–4; Gal. 1:18), and his missionary-apostleship calling (Gal. 1:16).

Romans was most probably written in Corinth in the house of Gaius during Paul's last visit, which lasted about three months, in the spring of A.D. 57 or 58 (Acts 20:1–3).[8] This date depends upon internal references to the apostle's circumstances as they relate to information in the book of Acts. A key factor in the actual year date involves Proconsul Gallio, who heard charges against Paul at Corinth on Paul's second missionary journey (Acts 18:12–18). According to an inscription found at Delphi, Gallio was installed as proconsul at Corinth about A.D. 52. Calculating from this date until Paul finally left Corinth for the last time would involve another five years (Acts 20:1–3).

Recognizing the early date of the book of Romans as probably occurring before any of the written Gospels adds importance to its portrait of Christ and of early first-century Christianity.

OCCASION AND PURPOSE

Paul apparently had finished his work in the east, and after depositing the collection for the poor saints in Jerusalem, he planned to visit Rome on his way to Spain (15:22–28). The apostle, in hopes that the important Roman church might be an aid to his missionary endeavors in the far west, therefore wanted to introduce himself and give a sample of his message to the saints in Rome before he arrived. But does this reason alone account for the lengthy and intricate explanation of his gospel message that the letter contains? Why not send a brief note through Phoebe (16:1) and indicate that he would give a full verbal statement of his message when he arrived in Rome?

One explanation of the long, weighty letter might be that he expected trouble in Jerusalem that could prevent him from ever reaching Rome. The treatise, then, would provide a preparation for his defense at Jerusalem as well as a final memorial to his ministry and a basis for the Roman church to evangelize the west in his absence.[9] A variation of this view would expect Paul to meet resistance to his gospel in Jerusalem on the part of Jewish Christians who were quite zealous to keep the Mosaic Law and even to require Gentiles who accepted Christ to do the same (Acts 21:17–25). The letter would then clarify just what Paul actually preached in distinction to hearsay.

Another intriguing view involves an attempted historical reconstruction of the church situation in Rome in A.D. 57. Both from Acts 18:2 and external evidence, we know that the emperor Claudius issued an edict evicting all the Jews from Rome in A.D. 49 due to disturbances over Christ (see note 10 in chapter 1). The thirteen or so Jewish synagogues in Rome at the time lacked any central leadership, and the members were quite culturally diverse. When the Christian mission came to Rome, some synagogues were receptive, whereas others were not. In the aftermath of the clash between synagogues over the Christ issue, the whole Jewish population (40–50,000) was required to leave Rome. This marked the end temporarily of the Jewish-Christian presence in Rome. At that time (A.D. 49), house churches were formed so that the Christians could meet apart from the synagogue. During the five years the edict was in effect (until the beginning of Nero's reign), the house churches did not have Jewish Christians. However, when the Jews returned to Rome, they found the church different from the way they knew it in the synagogue context. There was now a Gentile majority, and the Gentiles were in leadership. The book of Romans, then, in this view was written to the Gentile majority to exhort them to welcome and to live together in one congregation with the Jewish-Christian minority.[10]

More certain is the fact that there is a strong emphasis in the letter on Paul's view of salvation versus certain legalistic (meritorious works for salvation) Jewish and/or Jewish Christian concepts ("the works of the law" see 3:20, 28) and the integrity of his gospel over against alleged charges of moral permissiveness. Paul must have expected to find in Rome and perhaps in Jerusalem such objections to the gospel as he customarily preached it.[11] In any event, Romans provides us, as well as the ancient Italians, with an introduction to some of the main currents in Paul's theological thoughts.

THE ROMAN CHURCH

There is considerable speculation both as to the origin of the church in Rome and its constituency. Nothing is known with certainty, but some general directions may be suggested. Concerning the Roman Catholic view of Peter founding the church, there is no historical evidence. Furthermore, Peter was still in Jerusalem at the time of the Jerusalem Council (Acts 15, ca. A.D. 50), yet it is almost certain that Christians were gathering in church homes in Rome before this time (Rom. 1:7).[12] It is difficult to imagine Paul writing to the church at Rome as he did if Peter indeed had founded it, or to guess why he should omit reference to Peter anywhere in the letter if the fisherman was the apostle in residence in Rome.

A further suggestion explains the church's arising from Roman Jews who were present in Jerusalem on the Day of Pentecost and, having been converted, returning to establish the church (Acts 2:10). However, there is no evidence that any Roman Jews were in fact among the converted at Pentecost. Furthermore, the word "staying" in Acts 2:5 could also refer to permanent residents living in Jerusalem.

Another view, which likewise has no certainty, is that the church was founded by various converts of Paul who had heard his preaching in other parts of the world and were converted and then traveled to Rome for various reasons. Paul certainly knew by name a large number of people at Rome (Rom. 16:3–15)—which might support this view. On the other hand, if this is the correct explanation, it is difficult to see why Paul was so anxious to go to Rome to preach the gospel to those who had already heard him before.

Concerning the constituency of the church in Rome, it seems quite evident from the internal references that it consisted mainly of Gentiles with some Jewish intermixture (1:5–8; 1:12–14; 6:19; 11:13; 11:28–31). Cranfield best summarizes the evidence: "The truth would seem to be that it is impossible to decide with anything like absolute certainty whether at the time Paul wrote to them the majority of the Roman Christians were Gentiles or Jews, and that we ought therefore to leave this question open."[13] It is estimated that the Roman church must have grown to considerable size during Paul's time.[14] This growth may account for the multiple meeting places referred to in the letter (16:5; 14–16). The frequency of the names mentioned in chapter 16 in the catacombs and other early Roman inscriptions is well documented by C. H. Dodd in his *Epistle to the Romans*.[15]

THEME AND CHIEF CHARACTERISTICS

The theme of Romans can be stated in different ways depending on which part of the book is emphasized. Some prefer to call it "salvation as the revelation of God's righteousness"; others, "the righteousness of God by faith"; or "justification by grace through faith"; and "God saving men in Christ"; or "God's righteousness in Christ for the salvation of the entire world" (Stuhlmacher). It is all but universally agreed that the theme of Romans finds brief statement in the words of Romans 1:16–17: "I am not ashamed of the gospel, because it is the power of God for the salvation of everyone who believes: first for the Jew, then for the Gentile. For in the gospel a righteousness from God is revealed, a righteousness that is by faith from first to last, just as it is written: "'The righteous will live by faith.'"

This theme of salvation as the righteous act of God accomplished in Jesus Christ's death and resurrection and proclaimed in the gospel message is set forth meticulously in Paul's exposition. He first shows the desperate need of all people before God for this salvation. Gentiles are seen as notoriously given over to idolatry and various perversions that prove their rebellion against the Creator (1:18–32), while Jews and Christian Jews are no better off for their religious heritage when they pervert God's covenant grace into self-righteousness (2:1–3:20). Only God's mighty act of grace and love accomplished in Jesus Christ's death and resurrection and received freely on the basis of faith can effect the pardon and reconciliation of persons who are under God's condemnation (chaps. 3–4).

Next, Paul unfolds the truth that this new standing before God also brings into existence a new being realized in the Christian experience of joy and certainty (chap. 5) and in the progressive defeat of the rule of sin in one's life through the power of the indwelling Spirit of Christ (6–8). After treating the historical problem of Israel's rejection of the Messiah and His gospel and Gentile apathy and ignorance (9–11), he turns to general exhortations concerning specific areas of Christian living—personal, societal, political, and fraternal (12:1–15:13).

Among the chief characteristics of the letter are its long introduction, the unusual number of personal greetings at the close of the letter, more extensive use of the Old Testament in quotations (about 57 times) than all his other letters combined, and the rich theological emphasis, especially on God Himself. The most common words in the letter are "God" (153 times), "law" (72 times), "Christ" (65 times), "sin" (48 times), "Lord" (43 times), and "faith" (40 times).

INTEGRITY OF THE LETTER

The chief critical questions relate to the nature of chapter 16 and the different textual traditions at points in the letter. The benediction ("the grace of our Lord Jesus be with you") is placed in chapter 16 either at the end of verse 20 (most witnesses), or at verse 24 (some), or after verse 27 (some). The position of the doxology (16:25–27) constitutes the greatest textual problem. We can only summarize the facts and state our conclusion in brief. More interested students should consult lengthier treatments.[16]

Though the doxology appears in many manuscripts after 14:23, and in one early witness after 15:33, and in several texts both after 14:23 and at 16:25, the weight of early evidence favors placing it at 16:25–27.[17] Certainly the doxology is Pauline and relates in content to the epistle of Romans. No serious attention should be given to theories such as the Ephesian destination of chapter 16, or that the original letter ended at 14:23 or 15:33, or to the recent view that chapter 16 was the original ending of Mark's gospel.[18] The theory that traces the varied history of the textual tradition of chapters 15 and 16 to the influence of the early heretic Marcion is probably least open to dispute.[19]

OUTLINE OF ROMANS

I. The Opening (1:1–17)
   A. The Apostle's Greeting (1:1–7)
   B. Paul and the Romans (1:8–15)
   C. The Theme of His Letter (1:16–17)

II. The Doctrinal Foundation of Christianity: The Gospel According to Paul (1:18–11:36)
   A. Humanity's Condition: Under the Judgment of God (1:18–3:20)
      1. Persons Without the Knowledge of the Bible (1:18–32)
      2. Persons with the Knowledge of the Bible (2:1–3:8)
      3. Conclusion: The True Moral Guilt of the Whole World (3:9–20)
   B. The Good News: God's Righteousness by Faith (3:21–4:25)
      1. God's Provision: Justification Through Christ by Faith (3:21–31)
      2. Abraham and Justification by Faith (4:1–25)
   C. The New Situation: Freedom from the Wrath of God (5:1–21)
      1. The Benefits Stemming from Freedom from the Wrath of God (5:1–11)
      2. Adam and Christ (5:12–21)
   D. The New Situation: Freedom from Sin's Captivity (6:1–23)
      1. Union with Christ in His Death and Resurrection (6:1–14)
      2. Bondage to Righteousness (6:15–23)
   E. The New Situation: Freedom from the Mosaic Law's Domination (7:1–25)
      1. The Marriage Analogy (7:1–6)
      2. The True Nature of the Law (7:7–25)
   F. The New Life of the Spirit (8:1–39)
      1. The Indwelling Spirit and the New Moral Life (8:1–16)
      2. The Indwelling Spirit and Authentic Hope in Suffering (8:17–27)
      3. The Plan of God (8:28–30)

NOTES

1. For a thorough discussion of all the introductory questions pertaining to Romans, among the best sources are Donald Guthrie, *New Testament Introduction*, 3d ed., rev. (Downers Grove, Ill.: InterVarsity, 1970), 393ff.; Everett F. Harrison, *Introduction to the New Testament* (Grand Rapids: Eerdmans, 1964), 280ff.; Paul Feine and Johannes Behm, *Introduction to the New Testament*, ed. Werner G. Kümmel, trans. A. J. Matthill Jr. (Nashville: Abingdon, 1966), 216ff.; C. E. B. Cranfield, *A Critical and Exegetical Commentary on the Epistle to the Romans* 2 vols., The International Critical Commentary (Edinburgh: T. and T. Clark, 1975, 1979). This last work contains a model study on the history of interpretation of the epistle (1:30–44).

2. Cited by A. Skevington Wood, *Life by the Spirit* (Grand Rapids: Zondervan, 1963), 8.

3. Leon Morris, "The Theme of Romans," in *Apostolic History and the Gospel*, ed. Ward Gasque and Ralph Martin (Grand Rapids: Eerdmans, 1970), 263.

4. John A. MacKay, "Toward an Evangelical Renaissance," Christianity Today 16, no. 9 (4 February 1972): 6–8.

5. C. Rene Padilla, "What Is the Gospel?" *Christianity Today* 17 (20 July 1973): 1106.

6. See Richard N. Longenecker, *Paul, Apostle of Liberty* (Grand Rapids: Baker, 1976); also W. D. Davies, *Paul and Rabbinic Judaism*, rev. ed. (New York: Harper, 1955).

7. Guthrie, *New Testament Introduction*, 25.

8. Ibid., 25.

9. Harrison, *Introduction to the New Testament*, 286.

10. Wolfgang Wiefel, "The Jewish Community in Ancient Rome and the Origins of Roman Christianity," in *The Romans Debate*, ed. Karl P. Donfried (Peabody, Ma.: Hendrickson, 1991), 85–101; similarly Krister Stendahl, "Paul and the Introspective Conscience of the West," in *Paul Among Jews and Gentiles* (Philadelphia: Fortress, 1976), 78–96. For a masterful and thrilling historical reconstruction, see historian Paul Maier's *The Flames of Rome* (New York: Doubleday, 1981), especially chap. 7.

11. Feine and Behm, *Introduction to the New Testament*, 221–22; Guthrie, *New Testament Introduction*, 27; see also Peter Stuhlmacher, *Paul's Letter to the Romans: A Commentary* (Philadelphia: Westminster/John Knox, 1994), 6–8. For the view that Paul was also concerned about Jewish-Christian objections and distortions of his gospel, see Acts 21:20–25 and the discussion of Andrew T. Lincoln, "From Wrath to Justification: Tradition, Gospel, and Audience in the Theology of Romans 1:18–4:25" in *Pauline Theology, Vol. III, Romans*, David M. Hay and E. Elizabeth Johnson, eds. (Minneapolis: Fortress, 1995), 130–59.

12. Acts 18:2–3 implies that Aquila and Priscilla (Prisca in Rom. 16:3 NASB), who came to Corinth from Rome, were already Christians, which would further confirm the earlier existence of the church in Rome before A.D. 49.

13. Cranfield, *A Critical and Exegetical Commentary*, 1:21.

14. Guthrie, *New Testament Introduction*, 24.

15. C. H. Dodd, *Epistle to the Romans* (Naperville, Ill.: Allenson, 1932).

16. Guthrie, *New Testament Introduction*, 28–41; Cranfield, *A Critical and Exegetical Commentary*, 1:5–11; John Murray, *The Epistle to the Romans*, 2 vols. (Grand Rapids: Eerdmans, 1959), 2:262–68; Douglas Moo, *The Epistle of Romans* (Grand Rapids: Eerdmans, 1995), 6–9.

17. Murray, *Epistle to the Romans*, 2:268. Since most of the lectionary texts support the placing of the doxology at 14:23, it may be that the majority of manuscripts were influenced by this tradition.

18. Evan Powell, *The Unfinished Gospel: Notes on the Quest for the Historical Jesus* (Westlake Village, Calif.: Symposium Books, 1994).

19. Guthrie, *New Testament Introduction*, 393ff.; Donfried, *The Romans Debate*, 44–52.

1
THE OPENING

1:1–17

Ancient Greek letters in the first century, unlike ours, customarily began with the names of sender and recipient and a short greeting involving thanksgiving to God. Paul expands the usual address in an unusually long and highly significant form to express a brief statement of his Christian faith and his ministry (vv. 1–7) and to relate his genuine concern for those in Rome (vv. 8–17). Paul had not yet visited Rome. It is this fact that explains the length of the introduction—he is zealous to inform the church at Rome of his earnest desire and determination to go there. Since most of the key ideas occurring throughout the remainder of the letter are found in this introduction, we can profitably pay close attention to it in attempting to understand Paul's thought.

The following overall view of the introduction may be helpful to refer back to as the details are discussed.

Greeting — Author (1)
(1–7) —— Gospel (2–6)
— Recipients (7)

Paul and the Romans — Proof of his interest in those at Rome
(8–17) —— (8–10)
— Reasons for his interest (11–15)
— The theme of his letter (16–17)

THE APOSTLE'S GREETING
1:1–7

In verses 1–7 Paul identifies and describes himself, relates his calling, gives the essential essence of the gospel, and greets the Roman Christians. Paul, the author, describes himself in verse 1 in a threefold manner. The name Paul (Gk. *Paulos*) was his Latin surname, which became his friendly name. Paul also had the name of Saul, no doubt his Hebrew name. He possibly changed to being known most often by his Roman name as a reflection of his conversion to Jesus and his widespread ministry to Gentiles (Acts 9:1, 4; 13:1–2, 7; James D. Dunn, *Romans*, Word Biblical Commentaries, 2 vols. [Dallas: Word, 1988], 1:6–7). He is first of all a "bond-servant of Christ Jesus" (NASB). This term occurs as a frequent identification of the followers of Christ in the New Testament (Gal. 1:10; James 1:1; 2 Pet. 1:1; Jude 1 NASB). In Greek usage the word "bond-servant"— *doulos*—denotes a slave and would not be used of a Greek citizen's relationship to his ruler or divine king. Although it is possible that Paul could be thinking of serving Jesus Christ as an actual slave in the Greek or Roman sense, it is more likely that he had the Semitic idea of a slave in mind. The Hebrew kings could be served, and the highest of his ministers might be regarded as his slaves (1 Sam. 8:11–14). Distinguished members and citizens of the theocratic kingdom of Israel were also called the servants of God (2 Sam. 7:19, Amos 3:7). Paul, then, appears as an outstanding member and chief minister, or slave, of God in His new divine program.

Second, he refers to himself as (divinely) "called as an apostle" (NASB). Again, Paul's idea probably goes back to the rabbinic Jewish usage of "apostle" (Gk. *apostolos;* Heb. *shaliah*) as a term to denote one who is legally authorized to act as the representative or proxy of another and who carries the full authority of the one who commissions him.[1] Thus Paul claims direct divine authority as a validly commissioned representative of Jesus Christ Himself (Gal. 1:11–12). One should not, then, hesitate or accept the teaching of Paul as having anything less than the very authority of Christ Himself.

Third, Paul declares himself to be "set apart for the gospel of God." He may have the calling of the prophets of old in mind (Jer. 1:5) as he relates his peculiar experience of having God mark him out as a special missionary to the Gentiles (Acts 13:1–2; Gal. 1:15). He is set apart "for the gospel of God," that is, in order to proclaim it. Paul's word for gospel, *euangelion*, should be translated "good news" (i.e., something good has happened) to bring out its full sense.[2] It is this gospel, or message, of God's salvation that burdens Paul's heart throughout the whole letter (1:1, 9, 15–16).

In verses 2–6 Paul digresses briefly from his greeting to dwell upon the essential subject of the good news, "Jesus Christ our Lord" (v. 4). For his Jewish readers he is especially eager to state that this gospel has historical continuity with God's revelations to Israel in the promises given through the prophets in the Old Testament (Rom. 3:21, 31; 4:6; Luke 24:25–27, 44–47; 1 Pet. 1:10–12). "Scriptures" designates the officially recognized body of temple writings that were considered divinely originated (inspired) and thus authoritative for teaching and conduct (2 Tim. 3:15–16). "Holy" (only used here of Scripture) further emphasizes its source as distinctively *divine* revelation (Rom. 3:2; 9:17; 15:4).

Paul now proceeds to identify the substance of his gospel as that which pertains to God's Son, Jesus Christ, who as true man and true God in one mysterious Being bestows upon him whatever grace and authority he possesses (vv. 3–5). Here in two lines of antithetical parallelism (vv. 3–4) one finds a brief statement of the unique person of Jesus of Nazareth.[3]

First, in respect to His real humanity ("according to the flesh" NASB), Jesus was born a Jew (descended from Abraham) in the family line of David (Matt. 1:6; Luke 3:31; Acts 2:30; Rev. 5:5). Although Paul does not dwell upon the actual historical facts of Jesus' life on earth, it is evident that he nevertheless considered that real historical life (as the Gospels relate) to be of the utmost importance to the validity of the gospel he preaches. He taught what the Gospels later confirmed, that according to the Old Testament (2 Sam. 7:16) and Jewish belief, the Messiah would be from Davidic descent.[4]

Yet something else must be said about Jesus, not contradictory to His true humanity but complementary. "According to the flesh" (Gk. *sarx,* flesh) in verse 3 stands in parallel to "according to the Spirit" in verse 4 (NASB). Although the expression "Spirit of holiness" may be a reference to the Holy Spirit,[5] many commentators feel it is more appropriate to understand this expression as a reference either to Christ's divine personality, which would, because of the parallelism, form a complement to the previous expression about His human nature, or to His human spirit, distinguished by an exceptional holiness.

The church has always taught that though the life Jesus lived on earth was wholly human (i.e., not lived by powers or resources unavailable to us), the personality revealed was God, the Son of the Father. It must be stressed that without this truth of the dual character of Jesus, not only is our concept of God affected, but the gospel becomes pointless.[6]

The word "declared" in the Greek *(horizo)* is related to our English word "horizon," which "defines" or "delimits" the boundary between the sky and the earth. The early church Fathers taught that in God's powerful deed of raising Jesus from the dead there lies irrefutable evidence clearly to mark out or distinguish this human life as the divine Son of God and hence rightfully and solely our *Lord.* Recent interpreters argue that the expression means that by the resurrection Christ was "appointed" Son-of-God-in-power (in contrast to His being Son of God in apparent weakness and poverty in His earthly life).[7]

It is from this person that Paul claims to have received grace (gifts of enablement) and apostleship (commission as an ambassador) for the purpose of everywhere securing people to put their trust wholly in Christ and be obedient to Him. His mission for the sake of Christ's name (i.e., for Christ Himself) brings him into contact with those at Rome who are Jesus Christ's called ones like Paul himself.

Finally, in verse 7 he finishes the address by referring to the recipients in their earthly status as Romans and in their relation to God as loved by Him (for Christ's sake) and called to a life of separation unto God as saints. They are not "called to be saints," not "called because saints" but "saints (holy) because called" (Augustine). "The holiness is not primarily that of individual moral character, but that of consecration to God's service." Sainthood is "therefore ascribed to all Christians, who are, however, bound by this very consecration to personal holiness of life."[8] As "saints" they are to be separated from the world's values and consecrated wholly for God's use. "Grace" was customarily used in Greek letter addresses, whereas "peace" (Heb. *shalom*) was and still is the common greeting among Semitic peoples (Num. 6:24–26). Paul enriched these standard terms with added Christian significance.

Having now introduced his letter, himself, and his gospel (vv. 1–7), he will go on to explain further his interest in the Romans and the full meaning of God's good news.

PAUL AND THE ROMANS
1:8–15

In verses 8–17 Paul briefly relates his own genuine personal concern for those in Rome, giving proof of his feelings in his thankfulness for their faith (v. 8), in his unceasing remembrance of them in prayer (v. 9), and in his unrelieved desire to visit them and labor among them in preaching the gospel that he briefly summarizes (vv. 10–17).

Paul's thanksgiving to God (v. 8) reveals not only his own large heart of love, since many of those addressed were probably not his own converts, but also the virility of their witness to Christ in the non-Christian communities. "Your faith" would not mean "the Christian faith which you hold in common with all other Christians," but rather "the Christian faith as you hold it."[9] Their zeal for Christ and their love for one another was so manifested that others announced everywhere that something had happened to the Romans (1 Thess. 1:6–8).[10] This confirms Jesus' words that a city built on a mountain cannot be hid (Matt. 5:14).

In his prayer and earnest desire to visit them he offers another proof of his sincere concern for their welfare (vv. 9–15). Note the expression, "serve with my whole heart" (v. 9). His service consists not merely in outward activity but, more significantly, in the service of worship to God in his inner person that issues forth in the outward labor of preaching the gospel of His Son. "Now at last by God's will" (v. 10) reflects the delicate, beautiful, and important relationship between praying expectantly to God for a specific matter and at the same time recognizing a submission to the will of God, knowing that what we earnestly desire may not be His will, at least at the present. Paul desires that by his coming and ministry the Holy Spirit would so use him that the Romans would receive the benefit of the presence and power of God (v. 11), yet not themselves only but—in a beautiful touch of humility—that Paul himself also might be mutually strengthened in the practice of his faith by his interaction with them in this service (v. 12; 1 Cor. 12:7).

It may be asked why Paul, if he is so eager to go to Rome, had not gone before this. He answers by further assuring them of his love, explaining that he had repeatedly attempted to come, but saying that in each former case he had been prevented (Rom. 15:22–23). Paul was the author of his purposes but not of his circumstances (v. 13). He did not have a constant, unending series of successes!

Another reason for his burden to preach especially to the Romans relates to the universal character of the gospel message (vv. 14–15). Because of Paul's calling he is morally obligated to minister the gospel to all people without respect to their culture or social status. "Greeks . . . non-Greeks . . . wise . . . foolish" (v. 14) refers to those inhabitants of the regularly recognized Greek city-states (Greeks, "wise") and those outside these areas (non-Greeks, "foolish") such as the Gauls, Scythians, Celts, and Spaniards, who were considered by the Greeks as uncultured in that they were unable to speak Greek clearly (1 Cor. 14:11). Thus, because the relation in which we stand in Christ and His gospel is deeper and more essential than all national, racial, and personal distinctions, Paul, the Jew, stood eager and willing (if God permitted) to preach to those also in Rome, the capital of the whole world. How many of us today are ready to go (not wait for them to come to us) to the universities or to Washington, D.C., to the senators of our country as well as to the culturally and economically deprived of Chicago's South Side?

But what really is the gospel? What would Paul preach in Rome and in Jerusalem? Why should he go to such trouble?

THE THEME OF HIS LETTER
1:16–17

Initially, his first response to these questions lies in his statement in verses 16–17, and yet the whole rest of the letter does not exhaust the answers.

In the mention of Rome (v. 15), Paul no doubt is excited as he contemplates the capital and theater of the world where he would ultimately come face-to-face with the mighty power concentrated in that stronghold of heathenism and the multitudes of peoples gathered there from every nation of the Mediterranean world. He responds, "I am not ashamed of the gospel," even though for its sake he had been spitefully treated in other great cities, such as Athens, Ephesus, and even in Corinth, from which he now writes.

His confidence in spite of these hindrances lies in the true greatness of the reality discovered in the message he proclaims. *First* of all, the gospel itself is nothing less than the power of God. This expression "power [Gk. *dynamis*] of God" should not be overlooked. In Paul's usage, the power of God is often associated with the wisdom of God in contrast to human wisdom (1 Cor. 1:24; 2:4; 2 Cor. 6:7). It is also a resurrection life power (2 Cor. 13:4), always associated with God's action toward us in Jesus Christ resulting in salvation (1 Cor. 1:18) and actually manifested in some manner in contrast to mere words or ideas (1 Cor. 2:4). Beyond this, how can the decisive activity of God in the human life be analyzed? For Paul, no other expression could convey the reality of his own experience and that of others. In the gospel resides the living revelation of God Himself flowing forth to save men and women.

"Salvation" (Gk. *sōtēria*) probably conveys the thought of the widest possible inclusion of all God's benefits in Christ to believers. Although not a frequent word of Paul's, it certainly is central to his thoughts.[11] In this epistle alone, salvation includes forgiveness of sin and acceptance before God (chaps. 1–4), as well as deliverance from the future wrath of God (5:9), the present new life in the Spirit of God (chaps. 6–8), and the future resurrection of the body (8:11).

Elsewhere in the New Testament, Peter teaches that the salvation from sin and darkness to peace and fellowship with God that began in the ministry, death, and resurrection of Jesus will be completed in the future in those who believe. That future salvation is now presently at work in Christians through the power of the gospel (1 Pet. 1:3–5). To this Paul also agrees (Rom. 13:11).

The divine power in the gospel is not dependent upon any human wisdom or virtue or condition such as works done in obedience to any law or ceremony, however sacred. Paul declares that the saving power of God is effective alone by faith "to everyone who believes" (1:16, NASB). Faith can only be that response to the gospel of God's saving power that is characterized by obedient trust in the God who has decisively acted in Jesus Christ's death and resurrection to provide for us what we could never do for ourselves (v. 5). It is this attitude of turning away from all self-effort and human achievement and casting ourselves totally upon the God and Father of Jesus Christ that effects the mighty working of God's power resulting in our salvation. Salvation is something freely given rather than earned. God gives this grace without regard to merit or national origin, without regard even to special religious distinction. Why, then, "to the Jew first" (NASB)? Historically, the Jews were the first to hear from Jesus' own lips this new thing God would do through Him (Heb. 2:3), and second, unto them were committed the covenants (Acts 3:26; Rom. 3:2; 9:4), and especially the Abrahamic covenant with the promise that "through your offspring [Christ] all nations on earth will be blessed [with salvation]" (Gen. 22:18; Gal. 3:8, 16).

Second, Paul's confidence is also related to the substance of the gospel, which is spelled out more fully in verse 17. It consists in the manifestation of "a righteousness from God." It might be helpful to show the parallelism between verse 16 and verse 17 in the following manner:

Verse 16	Verse 17 (NASB)
gospel	in it (gospel)
power . . . for salvation	righteousness (life and salvation)
of God	of God
everyone who believes	faith to faith . . . the righteous . . .
	shall live by faith

In the gospel the "righteousness *[dikaiosunē]* from God" finds expression. But what is the "righteousness from God"? By the righteousness of God Paul may have meant that quality or attribute of God whereby He reveals Himself to be right or righteous and humans sinful. But, as Luther argued, this could hardly be "good news." Or it could mean the righteousness that God requires of me. But again, how is this good news to me a sinner?

In our day, three chief interpretations are advanced, based on whether the expression "the righteousness of God (NASB)" means "God's (own) righteousness" or "a righteousness from God" (NIV). Or, to state the issue differently, does "righteousness" here mean the saving activity of God or a gift and status conferred on us?

Luther argued that the righteousness of God is that righteousness imputed to us by God by which we are accounted righteous (justified). Luther quotes Augustine favorably in this definition, "The righteousness of God is that righteousness which he imparts in order to make men righteous. Just as that is the Lord's salvation by which he saves us."[12] So in this view the righteousness of God is that righteousness that He imparts or gives in order to make sinners righteous.

However, for Luther it was important that this righteousness is "alien" to us. In a fashion somewhat unlike Augustine, Luther denied that this righteousness ever becomes internal to us. It is *Christ's* righteousness and not ours. This protects his emphasis on *sola gratia* (solely by grace). On the other hand, others argue that the term "the righteousness of God"(NASB) means "God's righteousness" and should not be confused with the similar expressions "righteousness" (4:13) or "righteousness . . . from *[ex]* God" (Phil. 3:9). In the Old Testament, the righteousness of God can be seen almost as a synonym for salvation in the same way Paul parallels the two in verses 16 and 17 (see also Isa. 46:13; 51:5; Pss. 24:5 (NASB); 31:1; 98:1–2; 143:11). God's righteousness is His own covenant faithfulness and trustworthiness whereby He fulfills His promise to Abraham to bring salvation to all people (Gen. 12:3; Gal. 3:7–8). In this second view, the righteousness of God refers to God's activity in Christ by which He fulfills His covenant promises, effects the satisfaction of His own holiness in the death and resurrection of Jesus for our sins (Rom. 3:25–26), and extends to us guilty sinners a free, full pardon and restoration to Himself (justification).

A third view espoused by a number of recent commentators argues that we must combine these two above positions and see Paul's term as including both realities. So Stuhlmacher states, "According to our reflections concerning the history and meaning of the concept, one should not establish a false alternative between the two. The expression incorporates both."[14]

Although it is difficult to decide between these views, the commentary will follow the latter view of Stuhlmacher that sees both saving power and gift, at the same time recognizing there are also good reasons to adopt either of the former two views cited.

God's righteousness is "by faith from first to last" (1:17). Though a difficult expression with many interpretations, it seems best to relate this to the parallel in verse 16, "everyone who believes," and to understand the phrase to emphasize that salvation (God's righteousness) is solely (utterly) by faith.[15] Paul's quotation of Habakkuk 2:4 stresses that the Old Testament taught that this salvation came (solely) by faith, and the one who has it (the just) also lives by faith (Gal. 3:11; Heb. 10:38).[16]

These two verses contain a rich sampling of Paul's chief words: *gospel, power of God, salvation, faith, Jew, Gentile, and righteousness of God*. They have each been touched on briefly in this section, but it will be necessary to return again and again to them in this book as Paul does in his. The scope of the gospel is universal. It is God's saving power for all persons at all times. At the same time the gospel shows forth and interprets God's righteousness. It is this theme that Paul develops in Romans.

God's righteousness is experienced by those who will respond to the gospel in obedient trust in Jesus Christ.

In the following lengthy section (1:18–11:36), Paul argues out the main kernel of his gospel. He first asserts that all—regardless of race, nationality, personal distinctions, or religious heritage—are under God's judgment and stand morally guilty before the Judge of the universe (1:18–3:20). Paul then turns to the provision of the gift of salvation in the sacrificial death of Jesus, the manner in which this provision is secured by faith, and the resulting new life with its abundance (3:21–5:21). He then proceeds to answer two major questions raised by his gospel: What is the relationship between God's grace and human freedom? (6:1–8:39); and, What about God's faithfulness in light of the Jews' unbelief? (9:1–11:36).

NOTES

1. G. Kittel and G. Friedrich, eds., *Theological Dictionary of the New Testament* (Grand Rapids: Eerdmans, 1964), 1:415. (This reference is hereafter referred to as TDNT.)

2. Cranfield (*A Critical and Exegetical Commentary on the Epistle to the Romans*, 1:55) shows that the word has connections to the Old Testament, where it means either to announce good news, especially of victory (e.g., 1 Sam. 31:9), or to announce the inbreaking of God's reign, the advent of His salvation, vengeance, or vindication (e.g., Pss. 40:9; 96:2; Isa. 40:9). There are connections also to the pagan world, where the word was used of the emperor-cult to announce such events as the birth of an heir, his coming of age, and his accession. Paul's use would contrast with the latter since he speaks of the good news of God.

3. It is quite probable that in these two verses Paul is making use of an already existing Christian confessional formula (*Cranfield Critical and Exegetical Commentary,* 1:57). There are possibly three similar passages in Romans (3:24–26; 10:9–10; 16:25b–26).

4. Daily in the synagogues today the fifteenth and seventeenth benedictions of the ancient Jewish prayer known as the *Shemoneh Esreh* (Eighteen Benedictions) refers to the expectation of the coming of a Davidic Messiah: "Speedily cause the offspring of David, thy servant, to flourish . . . may our remembrance ascend . . . with the remembrance of our fathers, of Messiah the son of David thy servant. . . ." These two prayers were formulated well

before the birth of Jesus.

5. Cranfield (*Critical and Exegetical Commentary,* 1:64) holds this position and argues that the "Holy Spirit, who as given by the exalted Christ, is the manifestation of His power and majesty, and so the guarantee of His having been appointed Son of God in might." So also Moo, *Romans,* 50.

6. Donald Baillie, *God Was in Christ* (New York: Scribner's, 1948), 144ff. contains a worthwhile discussion of how the Trinitarian concept of God among Christians uniquely advances a concept of God as a God of grace. See also Arthur McGill, *Suffering: A Test of Theological Method* (Philadelphia: Westminster, 1982) chap. 4 (hailed by some as the greatest piece of theological literature in the 20th century).

7. Cranfield, *Critical and Exegetical Commentary,* 1:62.

8. E. H. Gifford, "Romans," in *The Bible Commentary: New Testament* (New York: Scribner's, 1881), 3:57.

9. C. K. Barrett, *The Epistle to the Romans* (New York: Harper & Row, 1957), 24.

10. This testimony becomes more meaningful when it is remembered that according to the Roman historian Suetonius, the emperor Claudius had by an edict forced the Jews out of Rome in A.D. 49 (Acts 18:2) because of "trouble instigated under the influence of Chrestus" (*Lives of the Twelve Caesars* [New York: Random House, Mod. Lib., n.d.], chap. 25). "Chrestus" is undoubtedly a misspelling for Christus (Christ), and the disturbances were probably caused by the agitation and rivalry between Jewish Christians and non-believing Jews in the synagogues of Rome as Christ was preached as Messiah and Lord (C. K. Barrett, ed., *The New Testament Background: Selected Documents* [New York: Macmillan, 1957], 14); Paul Maier, *The Flames of Rome,* chap. 7.

11. The noun occurs only eighteen times in Paul's letters, including five times in Romans (1:16; 11:11; 13:11). The verb form "to save" occurs more frequently (twenty-nine times), including at least eight times in Romans (5:9, 10; 8:24; 9:27; 10:1, 9, 13; 11:14, 26).

12. Martin Luther, *Luther: Lectures on Romans,* Wilhelm Pauck, ed. (Philadelphia: Westminster Press, 1961), 18.

13. For a full discussion of this point and how Paul's concept of justification should be related to the Hebrew concept of righteousness rather than (as usually) the Greek concept, see Norman M. Snaith, *The Distinctive Ideas of the Old Testament* (New York: Schocken, 1964), chaps. 4 and 8 especially.

14. Moo also argues for a "both and" view: Both divine activity and power, and also gift (*Romans*, 73–75; also Peter Stuhlmacher, *Paul's Letter to the Romans* (Philadelphia: Westminster/John Knox, 1994), 31–32. An unusual amount of attention has been focused recently on this problem. Cranfield and Käsemann favor the first view (see Cranfield, 1:92–99; Ernst Käsemann, *Commentary on Romans* [Grand Rapids: Eerdmans, 1980], 24–30). Sam K. Williams argues convincingly for the second in "The 'Righteousness of God' in Romans," JBL 99 (1980): 241–90; also see J. P. Sanders, *Paul and Palestinian Judaism* (Philadelphia: Fortress, 1977), 491–92.

15. Grammatical parallels to this construction seem to have this effect, e.g., Rom. 6:19, "lawlessness, resulting in further lawlessness" (utter lawlessness); 2 Cor. 2:16, "death to death"(NASB) (utter death); Käsemann calls it "Semitic rhetoric."

16. The NIV and NASB ("The righteous man shall live by faith") emphasizes that the just person *lives by faith,* whereas the RSV rendering ("He who through faith is righteous shall live") emphasizes that the person who *by faith is righteous* will live (both now and in the future kingdom). The former sense seems to be the meaning of the Habakkuk passage in the Hebrew, the Targum (Aramaic translation), the LXX, as well as the Qumran commentary on Habakkuk (IQpH8:1–3), Gal. 3:11, and Heb. 10:38 (supported by John Murray, *The Epistle to the Romans*, 1:33) following J. B. Lightfoot. Most modern commentators, however, follow the latter sense (RSV, NRSV), arguing that the immediate context and the structure of the epistle require this emphasis (supported by Nygren, Cranfield (1:102), Käsemann, Barrett, and Moo).

2

HUMANITY'S CONDITION: UNDER THE JUDGMENT OF GOD

1:18–3:20

Paul cannot adequately declare the significance of the manifestation of the righteousness of God (3:21–22) until he has first painted the canvas with the actual human situation in God's sight. Over against God's righteousness stands human unrighteousness (1:18–32), as well as the righteousness of our own making (2:1–3:8). Paul's burden is to show that all people have true moral guilt in the presence of a holy God. The apostle will first charge that the Gentiles, or persons who do not have God's written Word, are without excuse before a revealed Creator to whom they are responsible (1:18–32). Second, he turns toward the other major segment of humanity, those who have the written law of God, and accuses them of not keeping this law (2:1–3:8). He finds that both groups, in effect, all people, are equally under God's judgment and without hope in themselves (3:9–20).

PERSONS WITHOUT THE KNOWLEDGE OF THE BIBLE
1:18–32

In only three places in the New Testament do we find material relating to how the gospel was preached to strictly non-

Bible-oriented audiences. The first was in Lystra (Acts 14:15–17), where Paul preached to the pagan (though cultured) Lycaonians, but the message is brief and interrupted. Second, in Athens (Acts 17:16–32), Paul again confronts non-Jewish pagan philosophers (Stoics and Epicureans) with the message about Jesus. The third instance comes also from Paul and is found in Romans 1:18–32 and portions of chapter 2. Our generation has rightfully been characterized as the post-Christian age, and more recently as the postmodern world.[1] Out of many past years of biblical emphasis and knowledge, our present western culture reflects the beginning of the emergence of a society largely made up of people without knowledge of the Bible. While some, holding to a nonrational optimism, have entitled our day the "Age of Aquarius," others more realistically describe our condition as "The Twilight of Western Thought.'"[2] This fact alone makes the content and approach of this section (1:18–2:16) of great importance in understanding how to relate the gospel to our generation.

REVELATION OF GOD'S WRATH (1:18)

Having just spoken of the revelation of God's righteousness (v. 17), Paul turns to the revelation of God's wrath (v. 18). Someone might say, "Why do I need salvation?" Paul answers: "Because you are under the wrath of God." "But why am I under His wrath?" "Because you suppress the truth."

Before commenting on these questions and answers, it might be helpful to clear up the problem of the relationship between this section (v. 18) and the previous (vv. 16–17). Some see Paul taking a long digression that continues until he resumes the thought about the gospel in 3:21. This is a mistake for two reasons. First, it ignores the ordinary sense of the Greek particle "for" *(gar)* that begins verse 18 and intimately binds the thought of this verse to verse 17 (unfortunately omitted in the NIV, but see NRSV). Second, the word (and tense) "revealed" Paul uses for the wrath of God (v. 18) is identical to the word (and tense) he uses in reference to the righteousness of God (v. 17). Even though the thought is complicated, it seems to run along these lines: Just as the future salvation of believers is now in the present being revealed in the gospel of Jesus Christ and appropriated by faith, so both the past wrath of God against sin (as demonstrated in Calvary's events) as well as the future wrath of God (2:5) is now in the present revealed both in the preaching of the gospel and in the human scene and experienced by those who turn away from the truth of God (v. 29).

Whatever else, it seems clear from this connection that the true preaching of the gospel can only occur with the concurrent preaching of the real wrath of God upon all persons. This truth is lacking among many of our generation of gospel preachers.[3] Wrath is God's dynamic and personal (though never malicious) reaction against sin (3:5; 9:22), and it has cosmic significance in that it is "from heaven" (1:18).

But why is God's wrath directed toward me? Because I in my "godlessness and wickedness" suppress the truth.[4]

Paul's word for "suppress" is important but unfortunately ambiguous in the Greek *(katechō)*. It may mean, and often does, to "hold on to" something such as spiritual values (1 Thess. 5:21). In this case, Paul would be saying that in spite of our wickedness we still "hold on to" a certain basic truth about our existence.[5] On the other hand, because he is developing the thought of our refusal to acknowledge the truth of God implicit in the creation (vv. 19–20), I prefer the alternate idea in the word. We "hold back" or "resist" (see Luke 4:42; 2 Thess. 2:6–7) the truth of God as Creator so that this truth does not find expression in our lives (v. 21).[6]

REVELATION OF THE KNOWLEDGE OF GOD (1:19–20)

But how can God direct His wrath toward me for suppressing the truth of His Creatorship when I have never even heard of the God of the Bible or the gospel? The answer is that all people know certain truths about God (v. 19). How? "Since" (reason number one) God has continually in past history, as long as there has been a universe (and in the present), revealed Himself to all human beings through the created order of existence. This knowledge of God, though limited, is nevertheless real and clear ("clearly seen" NASB), even though our wicked suppression of it has dimmed or even extinguished it.

Calvin's remark is striking: "In saying that God *manifested it*, he means that the purpose for which man is created is to be the spectator of the fabric of the world; the purpose for which eyes have been given him is that by gazing on so fair an image he may be led on to its Author."[7] What is manifested to them and thus known to every person everywhere is God's "eternal power and divine nature" (v. 20)—that is, that God is God and not man. We perceive in the created existence not only our own finiteness, but because of God's revelation to us we are aware of our creatureliness. We know that we are not the autonomous (independent) center of our lives and world, but that God as Creator and Lord stands infinitely above us as the Source and Goal of our created life.[8] Therefore Paul can say of all of us: "So that men are without excuse."[9] Without excuse because we have turned our devotion to idols rather than the Creator.

I, then, may be justly visited with the wrath of God because, though I may not have heard about God in the Bible or in the gospel, I have suppressed this rudimentary truth of my creatureliness that God continually reveals to me in (or, by) "what has been made."[10] God does not reap (wrath) where He has not sown (knowledge and love).

REJECTION OF THE KNOWLEDGE OF GOD (1:21–23)

In these verses (21–23) Paul gives a second reason ("for" in v. 21) God justly visits His wrath on us. Not only do we have the possibility of knowing God through creation and history and fail to do so; Paul indicates the root of the matter is that we actually possessed a knowledge of God ("knew God"), but failed in a proper acknowledgment: "They neither glorified him as God nor gave thanks to him" (v. 21). Instead we became senseless and practiced disobedience (idolatry) and rebellion. Our failure was not so much that we failed to recognize God, but that we would not acknowledge God as *Lord* and live in grateful obedience—in fact (in Paul's view), to "believe" is to have "faith." Rather, we chose to be our own Lord ("professing [themselves] to be wise" NASB). By throwing off our obligations to God, we thought to rise above creatureliness. Instead the new gods of our own making, which we exchanged for the Creator, while for a time our servants, eventually became our masters and brought us to a more debased and lower state than before. In the end we "worshiped and served created things" (vv. 23, 25).

Five steps downward have been noted in this whole process, beginning significantly with the attitude of the heart of rebellion against lordship, in that we honored Him not, neither were we thankful, but rather we became futile in our speculations, and claiming to be wise, we exchanged the glory of God for some part of the created world (vv. 21–23): (1) practical indifference to God's truth, (2) worthless speculation about God, (3) death of the God idea, (4) pride of human reason, and (5) fetishism (devotion to occult objects). This whole description should be understood as a sort of philosophy of paganism's development in any given setting and not as an historical account of a specific religious apostasy.

Here it may be appropriate to ask a few questions about pagan religions (nontheistic) and idolatry. It has been popular since the resurgence in recent days of comparative religious studies to think of the world religions as preparatory to Christianity. In them, we are told, God is revealed in an incomplete fashion, whereas in Christianity the full revelation of God is seen. But did Paul see any divine revelation present in any of the pagan religions of his day? It seems that whatever faint glimmer of truth about the true God Paul may have acknowledged in the pagan religions (Acts 17:23, 27–28), he is clear that pagans are mostly in ignorance of the truth about God and need the proclamation of the gospel that calls them to turn away from the idolatrous and ineffective substitutes to the living God who alone through Christ can deliver us from our sins (1 Thess. 1:9–10).[11]

Although there is a general revelation of God given to every person in all the world, this revelation is generally suppressed and opposed by our sinfulness. Actually, the pagan religions of the world, which display a good bit of commonality, find their commonality not in some true knowledge of God but in a common response to the revelation of God that comes to them continually in the things that are made. *Biblical* religions (Judaism and Islam and all forms of so-called Christianity) must be evaluated in the light of the gospel of Christ revealed in the New Testament. *Nonbiblical* religions are both a willful ignorance of as well as a reaction, an answer, a resistance to, and a defense against God's true revelation in the created order. Disobedience, not obedience, is the explanation of the commonality. However, this fact does not exclude the possibility that some individuals within these systems of religion may have responded to this true revelation of God (2:14–15). So the very presence of false religion in the world is evidence of the continual revelation of God that leaves all inexcusably guilty before Him.[12] Nevertheless, the Christian attitude toward those who are adherents of different religions should never be one of superiority. The missionary D. T. Niles beautifully captured the true relationship of the Christian to others of different faiths by stating that we come to them as "one beggar telling another beggar where he found bread."

So is there idolatry in the Western world today? If idolatry begins in the mind when we pervert our idea of God into something other than what He really is, then, yes.[13] Luther said, "Whatever your heart clings to and relies on is your god." Science, reason, progress, secularism, pleasure, material acquisition, nationalism, militarism, and mysticism have become for many the new gods of the Western world.[14] To us today comes the gospel with its call to radical conversion in the midst of the modern pantheon of gods.

RESULTS OF THE REJECTION OF THE KNOWLEDGE OF GOD (1:24–32)

In these final verses of the chapter, Paul shows how the wrath of God works its way out in the concrete human situation of those who have abandoned God as Lord. Let it be repeated that this does not mean there will be no final wrath of God in all the future (2:5), but even now in history God makes His wrath operative. Paul indicates this by three times repeating the same dire expression, "God gave them over" (vv. 24, 26, 28). Not that God causes people to sin, but He abandons them to their own passions as a form of His wrath. This is an awesome truth. In modern societies, moral permissiveness, especially in its sexual perversion and inversion, can be seen as God's acts of wrath upon those who have turned away from the truth and have suppressed the acknowledgment of God as the Lord of their lives. The point is that we are really significant beings in a significant history. When we choose to abandon God and make ourselves lords, we are abandoned by God to our own lusts. Since we are not only individuals but social creatures, when we choose to leave God, we also affect others in our present society as well as our descendants.

Today's culture everywhere reflects the loneliness, despair, fragmentation, and loss of personal identity that result from the perceived sense of the loss of God in the culture. To many, God is dead, but so are we.[15] Our culture is increasingly characterized by relativism and pluralism, which teaches that all values are personal, shifting opinions; there is no objective truth or right; one moral view is as acceptable as another. Nowhere has the tendency to try to relativize absolutes become more evident than in the erosion of conscience in the moral realm.[16] One characteristic of our day is nihilism, the determined effort to destroy everything, to break down every institution, every system of thought, every abiding norm. Nihilism begins with the abandonment of God. Without a true knowledge of God there are no abiding truths, lasting principles, or norms, and humanity is cast upon a sea of speculation and skepticism and attempted self-salvation.

So Paul continues with, "God gave them over in the sinful desires of their hearts to sexual impurity for the degrading of their bodies with one another (v. 24). In their freedom from God's absolutes, they turned to perversion and even inversion of the created order. In the end their godless humanism (human-centeredness) resulted in dehumanization of each other. For "degrading" their bodies must refer not to the normal sexual relations of married heterosexual couples (which in Scripture is always pleasing to God), but, as Paul will show (vv. 26–27), to perverted sex and the inverted relations of same-sex sexual acts.

This fate came to those who "exchanged the truth of God [see v. 21] for a [Gk. "the"] lie [that humanity is absolute]" (v. 25).

Because men and women inverted the creature-Creator relationship, God visits them with the undesirable consequences of creature-creature inversion. In the rest of the chapter nothing new is added to this point until verse 32, but a number of illustrations are given of how God's abandonment of men and women to their own desires works its way out in the personal and in the social realms.

In verse 26 Paul again repeats the somber sounding, "God gave them over," that connects the moral degradation to their apostasy from God, and goes on to speak first of the perversion of the created order (natural) by women. Although male homosexual acts are clearly in Paul's mind in verse 27, some think that the female counterpart (lesbianism) is not expressly described in verse 26. Yet the "in the same way" of verse 27 seems to indicate that he is describing in verse 26 the same kind of sin in the female as he goes on to condemn in males.

Homosexual sexual acts (v. 27) among males is further evidence of the inversion of the created order ("abandoned natural relations with women"), which results in "indecent acts." Such persons are now receiving that "due penalty for their perversion" (of worshiping the creation, v. 25). What due penalty? Perhaps Paul refers to the gnawing unsatisfied lust itself, together with the dreadful physical and moral consequences of sexual promiscuity. This sin, it must be borne in mind, is not worse than other sins or one that removes us from the human race or the grace of God. Those caught up in homosexual sins need compassion like any other sinner, but homosexual activity is wrong, and the increase of this practice in today's society (as in Paul's) is further evidence of our culture's apostasy from the truth of God.[17]

Paul adds in verse 28 the reason for this debauchery: "Since they did not think it worthwhile to retain the knowledge of God, he gave them over to a depraved mind." Something of the Greek play on words is lost in the English. It goes like this: "As they found God worthless to their knowledge . . . God gave them over to a worthless [depraved] mind." Having first chosen in their wickedness to suppress God's truth as it was revealed to them, they were given over by God to a form of thinking that approves "things which are not proper" (NASB) or things not fitting in God's moral order (obscenities). How we live determines how we think as much as how we think determines our behavior. When we live a while in a particular sinful manner, our minds begin to justify and rationalize our actions.

There follows in verses 29–31 a listing of various sins that illustrate Paul's point. They almost defy classification or groupings. Among them are personal sins, social sins, sins of pride, greed, injustice, perversions. It is a picture of utmost degeneracy. A meditation on these shows at once how complete a disorientation of the life results when the creature is alienated from the Creator.

There is a species of ant that lives in some parts of Africa. It lives in subterranean tunnels many feet in the earth, where the young are sheltered and the queen is housed. The workers go on foraging trips to distant places, returning to the nest with that on which the colony feeds. It is said that if, while they are away, their queen is molested, the workers, far away, become nervous and uncoordinated. If she is killed, they become frantic, rush around aimlessly, and eventually die in the field. It is thought that the workers in the normal situation are constantly oriented to the queen by some radarlike device; if she is killed, all orientation ceases, and frenzy ensues, a frenzy that ends in death. Can we find a better parable of our human alienation from God?

Paul concludes in verse 32 with, "Although they know God's righteous decree [sentence] that those who do such things deserve death, they not only continue to do these very things [occasionally, in a more restricted way] but also approve [Gk. *syneudokeō*, "agree with" or applaud] of those who [habitually] practice them."[18] To do these things against one's sense of right is culpable, but to be in moral agreement with others who practice these obscenities (even if one does not do them) shows that the sympathies lie there and renders those persons inexcusable. That those who are without the Bible "know God's righteous decree" seems to anticipate the argument from conscience in 2:14–15.

In summation of Paul's argument dealing with those without the knowledge of the Bible (1:18–32), it may be said that (1) the visible revelation of God's wrath upon the pagan world can be seen most clearly in their moral perversions and inversions (individual and social) of the created order; (2) these perversions are the direct result of their exchanging the worship of the Creator for the creation; and (3) they are under the judgment of God and inexcusable because God has made the rudimentary knowledge of Himself continuously available to all people, yet this knowledge has been willfully suppressed.

So, why do those without the Bible's knowledge need the salvation offered in the gospel? Because they are under the wrath (judgment) of God. Why are they under the wrath of God? Because they have individually suppressed God's lordship in their lives, and they have inherited a perverted religious tradition.

What evidence is there from the human situation that God's wrath is already being manifested? Paul finds the proof in the moral degradation of societies and of the lives of those who have been abandoned to follow their whimsical lusts.

Paul has not yet brought all humans under this judgment. He must now consider the case of those who possess the knowledge of God in the Bible.

Persons with the Knowledge of the Bible
2:1–3:8

Although Paul no doubt has both the proud Jew (including Jewish Christians) and the proud cultured Gentile (Greek and Roman, including Gentile Christians) in mind in 2:1–16, he does not specifically mention the Jew until verse 17. His burden consists in showing that those who have not sunk to the depths of depravity that some in the pagan world have, because they have the light of God's will in the Bible, are nevertheless under the same judgment of God. Not the possession of the knowledge of the truth but the practice of the spirit of the truth shows who has really acknowledged the Creator. The idea that God shows no partiality (2:11) means that the proud Jew is brought to judgment on the same basis as the Gentile, as Paul will illustrate in more detail (vv. 12–16).

Turning directly to the Jews in verse 17, he accuses them of false pride in both their religious knowledge (vv. 17–24) and their religious rite of circumcision (vv. 25–29). Finally, Paul discusses the main advantages of being a Jew (3:1–4) and answers objections to his position (3:5–8).

PRINCIPLE OF GOD'S JUDGMENT: NO PARTIALITY (2:1–11)

After having just heard the detailed description of the plight of the idolatrous pagan world, a morally minded person might heartily agree with Paul's condemnation and even at this point offer an amen. But how can "good" people who are not idolaters come under Paul's sweeping thesis that all have sinned and that they can only be delivered from God's judgment by the righteousness of God in the gospel?

In our day, there are many moralistic people in and out of the churches. We generally think of them as middle- or upper-middle-class society, the "moral majority." Many of these people still attempt in principle to hold to the basic Judeo-Christian morality but have abandoned the radical biblical religious root of personal regeneration. They want the fruit of Christianity without its root, personal relationship to Jesus Christ. What of these, Paul? His answer consists of charging that the critics of others have condemned themselves, because the criticism of such sinners (1:18–32) reveals that these persons know what is right from wrong and have therefore no excuse for their own violation of God's law (vv. 1–3).

In verse 1, Paul strikes an immediate blow to the conscience of the moralist by asserting, "You, therefore [because what was true of those in 1:18–32 is also true of the self-righteous critic], have no excuse [see also 1:20 for the same word!], . . . you are condemning yourself [whether Jew or pagan moralist], because you who pass judgment do the same things."[19]

The moralist might say, "The wrath of God justly rests on the debauched, idolatrous Gentiles but not on us non-idolatrous Jews." There are two reasons that the moralist is on thin ice with respect to the judgment of God. In the first place, such persons reveal by their criticism of the heathen vices that they know God's moral requirement. They cannot plead ignorance of God's will. And yet Paul alleges that they "do the same things." Not that these people were necessarily idolaters or violent or disobedient to parents, but they were sinners (vv. 21–24, stealing, adultery, sacrilege) and broke the same law of God that the pagans violated in grosser fashion. E. J. Carnell has noted, "Self-righteous people make one of two capital mistakes: either they misunderstand the height of God's law or they misunderstand the depth of their own moral conduct."[20]

Second, behind all the sins in 1:29–32 lies the sin of idolatry, which reveals the ambition to put oneself in the place of God and so to be one's own Lord.[21] But is this not precisely what judges do when they assume the right to condemn others and then excuse themselves for the same behavior (James 4:11–12)? True, God's judgment rightly falls on the wickedness of the pagan (Rom. 2:2), but do you think *you* of all persons, *you* who know God's will can do as they do and yet get away with it ("escape," v. 3)? Anticipating his answer, Paul would say no, "God does not show favoritism" (v. 11).

Furthermore, since moralists have escaped the present wrath of God to a large extent because they have not so overtly suppressed the truth as have people without the Bible, they should not misread God's kindness to them (in not immediately visiting wrath) as if such delay were an indication that God has somehow favored them. Moralists should repent of their sin and wickedness and realize that God judges on the basis of their works or practices and not on the basis of their national or religious heritage (vv. 4–11).

These verses (4–11) touch on the vital matter of the future judgment of God. Is there a literal future hell?[22] Paul, it seems, speaks unhesitatingly in verse 5 of "the day of God's wrath, when his righteous judgment will be revealed." Moralists wrongly think that they will escape God's judgment by taking God's side and condemning the sin of unrighteous people (vv. 1–3). Further, they are also in error in thinking that because of their religious and national heritage they are excused from judg-

ment, and God is now extending special favor ("kindness, tolerance and patience," v. 4) to them.[23]

But all such thinking is wrong, because God's judgment is
completely impartial (v. 11). He judges not on the basis of who
the person is, but with respect alone to the nature of the practices that have been done (v. 6). Religious moralists (Jew, pagan,
or Christian) must recognize that God's kindness (absence of
visible judgment) is extended to them out of grace. Rather than
interpret this "tolerance" (Gk. *anochē*, restraint) as a special
favor in judgment, God's long-suffering should be viewed as a
persuasive force to try to bring us to our knees in "repentance"
and faith (v. 4).[24]

Unbelieving Jews or professing Christian Jews of Paul's day,
who were seeking justification based on Mosaic Law works,
may have thought that, because they were seeing little evidence
now of wrath from God, it must be the case that in the future
life they would have unmixed reward. In reality, Paul declares,
they were by their "unrepentant heart . . . storing up wrath" (v.
5) against themselves for the future day of judgment. This unexpected inversion by Paul clearly reminds us that a form of supposed sincerity, even before God, can be sincerely misleading
because of our sinfulness and may lead to eternal judgment.

Verses 7–9 have been a source of perplexity to many Christians. In them Paul establishes the truth that God's judgment of
all people will be on the basis of their works or practices. This
thought has led many Protestants to feel an uncomfortable tension over what appears to be a contradiction between salvation
by faith alone, without works, and Paul's teaching here. In brief,
the solution (as well as the tension) lies in understanding the
nature of the works to which Paul here makes mention.

First, Paul considers those described as receiving "eternal
life" (v. 7). Most of the translations have missed the actual
thought of Paul. Paraphrased, the Greek would mean something like this: "To those who with patient endurance in good
work (as an outward lifestyle) seek for the glory, honor, and
incorruption God alone can give (as the object of their inward
motivation), He will render eternal life." Those who by their
good works prove they seek the things that alone are God's are

contrasted in verse 8 with those who are self-seekers, who are "self-seeking and who reject the truth."[25] The self-seeker suppresses the truth in unrighteousness (v. 8); and against such the wrath and fury of God are directed (1:18).

The "doing good" in verse 7 (contrast, "does evil," v. 9) refers to the whole Christian life of righteousness through faith in Christ that Paul will develop later. The patient continuance in good works (Eph. 2:10) demonstrates that the life's source is faith in God and the gospel. The real issue is whether people see their good works as evidence that they are doing a good job for God, or whether (as in Paul's view) they see them as marks not of human meritorious achievement but of hope and trust in God.

There can be no question, then, of God's showing any special favoritism (Matt. 5:45). Each person faces an impartial Judge who will determine whether the life was lived in pursuit of God's glory or in self-seeking unrighteousness (v. 11).

GOD'S JUDGMENT AND THE KNOWLEDGE OF THE LAW (2:12–16)

"But Paul," one might interject, "you forget that Jewish people have had the privilege of God's special revelation in the Bible (law). Doesn't this give them an advantage over the pagans whom God has not so blessed?" In verses 12–16, Paul begins to break down yet another prop. The sorest point of all for the Jew was Paul's contention that there is no protection from the wrath of God in the possession of the Bible (law): "For it is not those who hear the law [listeners—Sabbath by Sabbath] who are righteous in God's sight, but it is those who obey the law who will be declared righteous" (v. 13).[26] It is performance of God's will, not possession (or knowledge) that averts the wrath of God (James 1:22). God's revelation (law) does not protect one from judgment. It is rather the instrument for a more severe reckoning with the exceeding sinfulness of sin (7:7). More knowledge brings more responsibility and greater accountability. Thus the law becomes the possessor's accuser—his destruction, not his salvation.

In order to maintain his thesis of the equality before God of both those without and those with the Bible, Paul must answer yet another objection. "If the law will be my standard of judgment," the religious moralist might object, "how can God treat pagans equally with me when they have no law to judge them? Won't the absence of the law to judge them allow pagans to escape God's wrath?" "No," Paul answers, "because though pagans are without the biblical revelation (Law of Moses), they are not thereby outside all revelation of God's will ("law for themselves," v. 14)." How do pagans without the Bible have the knowledge of God's will? More disturbingly, are pagans lost because they are without the knowledge of the Bible and Christ's gospel? In trying to answer these questions, we must be careful to note what Paul does say on this point and what he does not say.

Some quite convincingly argue that Paul is referring to Christian Gentiles in verse 14 when he says, "When Gentiles, who do not have the law, do by nature things required by the law. . . ." He would then be anticipating his argument later on about justification without the law for all (3:21–31). An objection to this view might point out that Paul says these Gentiles have no knowledge at *all* of the law, and yet they do "by nature" what the law requires—both of which characteristics would hardly be true of Gentile Christians. Yet the NASB and NIV translation of this verse is arbitrary, and the phrase in question could be equally well rendered: "When Gentiles who do not have the law by nature (i.e., by birth) do what the law requires . . ." They are doers of the law, not in the sense that they earn salvation by law-keeping or that they know it fully, but in the sense that their faith in Christ and the gift of the Spirit has put them into a positive relation to the law (or will of God) because they now have it in their hearts and desire earnestly to fulfill its moral requirements (v. 15).[27] It is difficult to decide between the two views. The following discussion will develop the alternative, more popular, view while recognizing the strength of the Gentiles-as-Christians approach.

It will help to begin with the matter of the "conscience," whose role Paul describes as "bearing witness" (v. 15). Conscience is not acquired through our environment. Rather, man finds himself already in his earliest years functioning morally as a creature made in the image of God. Dogs or other domesticated animals seem to have a conscience only because of their association with humans. Conscience in the ancient world and in the New Testament is that "uneasy awareness that one has done something wrong" (O'Donovan). It is important to note that this small voice within does not function legislatively or as a guide to good behavior but only judicially to condemn us. Conscience assumes the presence of a valid norm. It anticipates a complementary something whereby it may then govern itself. As a resident police officer, it does not make the rules but nabs us when we have done wrong in the light of the existing rules. It refuses to be normless. That conscience is innate in every human being is unquestioned; what standard it approves or disapproves is quite a different matter. The content, or norm, by which the conscience judges us is not innate, or at least not entirely innate, but is controlled by God's revelation, the creation order, the environment, and local social standards.[28] Conscience, therefore, can be educated or changed by the introduction of new norms.

Scripture refers to a dulled or calloused conscience. Through repeated ignorings of the "no" voice, the moral faculty grows numb (1 Tim. 4:2). The familiar experience of repeatedly shutting off the alarm clock in the morning and then going back to sleep illustrates in the physical-psychic realm how the conscience in the moral realm can be ignored until we no longer hear its voice. If we convince ourselves in a relativistic and pluralistic postmodern society that there are no objective universal moral norms, then will not the self-critical function of conscience deteriorate?

Paul says that there are three witnesses that agree together that pagans have a basic knowledge of wrong (a norm), even though they do not have the knowledge of the written revelation of God. They are: (1) the outward (phenomenological) or natural ("by nature," v. 14) establishment of societal laws for controlling behavior; (2) the conscience, which judges us concerning our own actions with reference to the natural norms (v. 15); and (3) alternately accusing or else excusing thoughts we have about the behaviors of others that may be publicly debated (v. 15).[29]

Pagans, by natural moral instinct, set up from time to time certain social standards that include some of the same rules as the laws of God in the Bible, such as the pursuit of lawful vocations, the procreation of offspring, filial and natural affections, the care of the poor and sick, and numerous other natural virtues required by the Mosaic Law. Paul teaches that since they do this, they are not without a law to judge them. The "things required by the law" (v. 14) that the Gentiles do naturally must mean certain things the biblical law also requires. We should not take this to mean that the whole Mosaic Law or even all the Ten Commandments are written on the hearts of pagans. Paul does not say this. Similarly, the expression "work of the Law" (v. 15 NASB) is not the law itself but the effect of the law, that is, the setting of the conscience by the knowledge of God's will. So in effect they themselves (in virtue of being human persons) become a law (norm) for themselves.

In other words, there is something, Paul argues, in the very pattern of created human existence that should (and sometimes does) lead the Gentile to an attitude of humble, grateful, dependent creatureliness. There do exist some moral standards among the heathen not identical to, but certainly similar to, certain things in the Bible.[30] This similarity, Paul says, is not simply coincidental but reflects God's revelation of His will to human beings in their conscience and in the natural or created order (1:20–21). When pagans violate this standard, they stand under the judgment of God and should in humble repentance cast themselves upon the mercy of the Creator for forgiveness. Their sin consists principally in their failure, through rebellion, to humble themselves—nevertheless, God will judge them on the basis of the specific violations of their own conscience.[31] Can they be saved by this knowledge? Paul does not answer this question directly, and the Christian tradition is divided over the correct answer. Our answer will depend on whether we believe (1) that the knowledge of God revealed to the pagan is enough for salvation, and (2) that some people do *de facto* respond positively to this revelation of God. A *no* response to either of these would, among other reasons, justify Christian missions.

So Paul concludes this section by returning in verse 16 to the thought of verse 13. We connect the words from verse 13, "not those who hear the law who are righteous in God's sight, but it is those who obey the law" with those in verse 16, "on the day when God will judge men's secrets." Yet the reference to "the secrets of men" shows that Paul also includes in this summary verse his thoughts expressed in verses 14–15—that not only our outward practices, but also our inner motivations, feelings, and thoughts will be the subject matter of God's examination in the future day of judgment. The standards of judgment will be Paul's gospel,[32] that is, the very truths he has been revealing in chapters one and two; and the agent of judgment will be Jesus Christ Himself (John 5:27; Acts 17:31).[33]

THE LAW AND JEWISH PERFORMANCE (2:17–24)

Paul now turns directly to the Jew who has the written law of God. He is still dealing with the thought of God's universal judgment on all people and the further principle that it is not the listeners to the law who are right before God but the doers of the law. Paul has already rejected the fallacy that Jews have a special privilege and advantage before God even when they do not respond appropriately (2:14–15). Now he wants to nail this down further and leave no way of escape. It was not that Jews were wrong in prizing their possession of the law and esteeming its knowledge an advantage. The problem was that they trusted in the mere knowledge and possession of the law and clung to its outward observances. But certain kinds of Jews and Jewish Christians in Paul's day did not let the law convict them of their sin and lead them into obedient faith that would result in their keeping the real intent of the law. Moralists of all kinds thus reveal their rebellion against God, not by their outward immorality and corruption, but by the hardening of their hearts (2:5) and by their refusal to repent of their bankrupt self-righteousness.

In verses 17–20 Paul sets forth the acknowledged advantage on which Jews prided themselves: They (1) "bear the name

'Jew'" (as members of the covenant people); (2) "rely upon the Law" (trusted the law for right standing before God); (3) "boast in God" (the true worship of God); (4) "know His will" (the revealed will of God); (5) "approve the things that are essential" (keen sense of moral discernment); (6) are "guide to the blind" (in spiritual insight and light for them in darkness); (7) "corrector of the foolish" (unlearned); and (8) "a teacher of the immature" (have the last word in proper parental education). Jews could do all this confidently because they had the "embodiment of knowledge and of the truth" in the biblical revelation (law) of God (v. 20 NASB).

But, Paul argues, it is not in the law one should trust, for sin reigns despite the law. "You, then, who teach others, do you not teach yourself? You who preach against stealing, do you steal? You who say that people should not commit adultery, do you commit adultery [see John 8:11]? You who abhor idols, do you rob temples?" (vv. 21–22). The great wrong in the life of these Jews was that while they prided themselves in their relationship to God, they dishonored God by "breaking the law" (v. 23) and brought God's reputation to nothing in the eyes of the Gentiles (v. 24).

CIRCUMCISION AND KEEPING THE LAW (2:25–29)

Why be a Jew at all? Truly to be a Jew is to obey God in faith from the heart (v. 29). Their outward sign (circumcision) of the covenant relationship cannot shield them from the wrath of God. Circumcision was only a visible sign of a true heart relationship to God of love and obedience (Deut. 30:6; Rom. 4:11). Some Jews mistook the sign for the reality. When they evidenced by their breaking of God's law that the reality was not there, God invalidated the sealing significance of the rite (v. 25).

On the other hand, when people do not have the sign but demonstrate by loving obedience to God and His will that they possess the inward reality, their uncircumcision by nature will be counted by God as if they were circumcised and in covenant relationship (v. 26). The word Jew means "praise" (Gen.

29:35). Paul states that the true Jew is not the one who glories and trusts in the outward appearance of circumcision or in the listening to the law and legalistically (without the Spirit and with an eye on merit) following its precepts. The true Jews are those who in their hearts have entered into a relationship with God of humble response (faith) to God's gracious love and election (Deut. 10:16). Such people look to God for His praise, and not to human beings.

Paul may not be actually arguing that Gentiles who fulfill the intent of the law become true Jews (despite much appeal to these verses to the contrary). He is speaking as a Jew to other Jews (v. 17) to the effect that the real significance of being called Jews lies in their relationship to God, and not in their nationality or religious heritage. Although it is true that Paul says, "If those who are not circumcised [Gentiles] keep the law's requirements, will they not be regarded as though they were circumcised?" (v. 26), he does not go so far here as to call Gentiles true Jews (but see Gal. 6:16 and chap. 8, note 25). "Circumcision of the heart" (v. 29) refers to true repentance before God (Jer. 4:4); "by the Spirit, not by the written code" either has reference to the Holy Spirit's work or less likely to the inward spiritual relationship to God contrasted with the mere performance of the rite (v. 30); "such a man's praise is not from men, but from God" (v. 29) picks up the thought of verse 17 ("name 'Jew'" NASB) and excludes all criticism of others based on pride of superiority. Thus the truth is established that it is the Holy Spirit enabling us to keep the law that is efficacious, not its mere outward forms and ritual performance (8:4).

THE ADVANTAGE OF THE JEW (3:1–8)

Is there then any advantage at *all* in being a Jew and having circumcision (3:1)? The answer expected from what Paul has just said might appear to be no. But rather he says, "Much in every way!" (3:2). "First" (Gk. *prōton*) anticipates a list of advantages, but Paul gives here (see 9:4–5) only the first and no doubt the most important reason: because "they were entrusted with the very words of God" (3:2). Although the "oracles" (Gk.

logia, words or pronouncements) may refer to the whole Old Testament revelation of God in the Bible, from verse 3 it may be inferred that the Abrahamic and prophetic promises of a Messiah are also prominent (see also Acts 7:38; Heb. 5:12, 1 Pet. 4:11). What Paul is saying is that this revealed salvation-history (words of God) was of tremendous advantage to the Jewish people in that it gave them a special understanding of God, our human condition, the salvation of God, His will, the promises of the coming of the Christ (Luke 24:44), and the Abrahamic promises confirmed by the prophets.[34]

There now follow three objections to Paul's thesis that the Jews do have an advantage in the Word of God given to them (3:3–8). Perhaps by listing them together with Paul's answers they can be seen more clearly:

Objection Number 1 (implied): "The Jews have disbelieved these (Abrahamic and messianic) promises."

Answer: "Will their lack of faith nullify God's faithfulness?" (vv. 3–4).

Objection Number 2: "But if our unrighteousness brings out God's righteousness . . ." (v. 5).

Answer: "Certainly not! If that were so, how could God judge the world?" (v. 6).

Objection Number 3: "If my falsehood enhances God's truthfulness and so increases His glory, why am I still condemned as a sinner?" (vv. 7–8).

Answer: "Their condemnation is deserved" (v. 8).

The first objection touches on the problem of the unbelief of Israel in the Abrahamic and prophetic promises of the Messiah that Paul later develops in detail (chaps. 9–11). How is Israel's possession of the oracles of God any advantage if they don't believe them? Israel has been and is now the trustee of the divine Word that God wills the salvation of all peoples on the basis of faith. Perhaps the words of God are not really reliable after all. Paul's answer is that the unbelief of "some" (not all) does not nullify the reliability of God's words. Nor does such unbelief cancel the great advantages to the nation of possession of the knowledge of God in the Scriptures and of being a covenant people. Can the lack of response to God's promises (unbelief) cancel out His faithfulness (and make Him a liar) to His own divine plan announced to Abraham?

In verse 4, after reacting with abhorrence to such a thought, Paul adds a further statement about the relationship of God's faithfulness to man's sin and includes a reference to Psalm 51. "Not at all![35] Let God be true, and every man a liar . . . that you may be proved right when you speak." Even if *all* (not just some) were to disbelieve God's words, it would only serve to highlight the truth and faithfulness of God. For example, David declares that his sin, rather than making God unjust for condemning him, has vindicated God's justice (Ps. 51:4). If sin does not disestablish God's justice, then neither can unbelief cancel out God's faithfulness and truthfulness.

This approach of Paul raises further objections concerning how God can be just in condemning the sinner when his sin really serves to establish the righteousness of God (v. 5).[36] Paul answers again in abhorrence of the thought and appeals to God's moral government of the world: "How could God judge the world?" (v. 6). This future judgment is for Paul an uncontestable given.

Further, it is objected, if God gets glory through sin, why not go on sinning and bring more glory to God (v. 7)? At this point, Paul dismisses the question with a rather rude slap across the cheek, "Their condemnation [judgment] is just" (v. 8 NASB)—that is, the judgment of all those who object to being judged as sinners. But he will return to these moral problems again later in the letter (chaps. 6 and 9–11).

Paul has now charged that the person with the knowledge of God in the Bible stands equally under God's wrath with the pagan. There is no advantage for either before God's judgment. Such persons demonstrate by their judgment of the pagan that they know what is wrong, yet by their own life they show that their relationship to God is all external and formal, not personal and real. The great advantage of possessing the Bible's revelation of God and His will including the promises is not invalidated by any amount of unbelief. God's promises remain true regardless of human rejection.

CONCLUSION: THE TRUE MORAL GUILT OF THE WHOLE WORLD
3:9–20

In this final paragraph of the long section dealing with mankind's condition under the judgment of God (1:18–3:20), Paul concludes by bringing both the sinner without the Bible (1:18–32) and the sinner with the Bible (2:1–3:8) together as equally "under sin" (3:9). The Jew (or moralist) is no better off than the pagan. Both are equally guilty before God. Paul appeals to the statements of the Old Testament Scriptures concerning both Jews and Gentiles (vv. 10–18) and concludes that all people are universally and totally affected by rebellion against God (vv. 19–20).[37]

THE CHARGE (3:9)

"What shall we conclude then? Are we [Jews] any better [off] [than the pagan Gentiles]? Not at all!"[38] It might be inferred from Paul's statements in verse 2 that Jews were in a better position in regard to judgment than pagans because they had the advantage of the words of God. But Paul says the opposite is true. Although Jews have a great advantage in every other way, in one respect they do not, that is, in judgment for sin. He adds that he has already "made the charge" (Gk. *proaitiaomai*) that both are "under sin." To be under sin means, as Paul has shown in 1:18–2:29, to be under God's wrath and judgment for sin (7:14; Gal. 3:22). It may also mean "under the power [dominion] of sin" (NEB, RSV). Paul is saying that all persons (no exceptions) are under the dominion of both the moral guilt and the corruption of sin.

THE PROOF (3:10–18)

Paul now turns to six selective passages from the Psalms and the book of Isaiah to demonstrate that the Bible teaches that all are unrighteous before God and do not acknowledge Him as Lord in their lives. The points he makes require little comment.

1. The *character* of humans (vv. 10–12). In five negative statements, Paul leaves no hope for our having a divine spark of righteousness in us that only needs to be fanned.

2. The *conduct* of humans (vv. 13–17). We betray the inner condition of our hearts by our speech ("throats," "tongues," "mouths," see Matt. 12:37; Mark 7:20–21) and by our actions ("feet," "paths," "path of peace" NASB). The heart blazes the way, and the mouth and feet follow.

3. The *cause* of their conduct is put last (v. 18): "There is no fear of God before his eyes" (Ps. 36:1).

THE CONCLUSION (3:19–20)

Jews, of course, might think to escape from the force of these quotations from their own Bible by insisting that they refer to pagans and not to the Jewish covenant people. Although even a careful study of the context of the quotes shows otherwise, Paul responds somewhat differently by reminding the objector that "whatever the Law says, it speaks to those who are under the Law" (NASB). This revelation in the Old Testament law (whole OT)[39] that reveals the universal sin of all people before God also declares the judgment of God equally upon both Jew and pagan.

The twofold purpose for which the Old Testament declared this judgment was: (1) that none, whether Jew or pagan, may plead before God any righteousness of their own: "That every mouth may be closed" (NASB) (Gk. *phrassō*, shut up), or as Phillips puts it: "that every excuse may die on the lips of him who makes it"; and (2) that the whole human race (world) should "become accountable to God" (NASB). The law then cannot be used as an excuse or repose. We must be silent and confess that we are sinners: "It is the straightedge of the Law that shows us how crooked we are" (PHILLIPS).

But why did the Old Testament speak in this harsh manner about us? Because God must reveal to us our true condition before Him, the Creator, that we have no righteousness of our own. Jews and Gentiles must, then, abandon law works[40] as a means of acceptance before God: "Therefore no one will be declared righteous in his sight by observing the law" (v. 20). The psalmist exclaims, "If you, O Lord, kept a record of sins, O Lord, who could stand?" (Ps. 130:3). Therefore the proper response before God is to invite God to not "bring your servant into judgment, for no one living is righteous before you" (Ps. 143:2). The first true function of the law (whether of Moses or the prophets) is to unmask us and show us that we are sinners ("knowledge of sin" NASB) and that it is impossible to be accepted before God on the basis of keeping the law. But can we accept this exposure?

According to Hans Christian Andersen's famous tale, certain clever swindlers approached an emperor offering to weave for him a rare and costly garment that would have the marvelous capacity of making known to him the fools and knaves in his realm. Because of the magical quality of the threads, the garment would be invisible to all but the wise and pure in heart. Delighted, the emperor commissioned the weaving of the royal robes at great cost, only to find, to his dismay, that he obviously was a fool and knave, for he saw nothing on the looms. On the day set for the grand parade, the clever swindlers collected their royal fee, dressed the emperor in his potbellied nakedness, and skipped out of town as the parade began. The whole populace joined the courtiers in praising the king's garments, none daring to admit that they saw nothing but the emperor's nudity, lest they be branded as self-admitted fools and knaves. The entire parade of folly collapsed, however, as the shame of sovereign and people was exposed by a child's honest remark, "The emperor has no clothes!"

Neither the ruler nor his subjects were admitting his nakedness until the boy's truth destroyed their lie, ripping away their fig leaf of common hypocrisy. Thus, everyone's pride was hurt, and everyone's shame was exposed. Likewise, so long as we live under the illusion that we are righteous in ourselves and refuse to acknowledge the folly of our sinfulness in the presence of the truth of God's revelation, there can be no appreciation of the gospel that Paul preaches. It is not enough to admit that we (emperor) have no outer clothing. We must see that whether we have the knowledge of the Bible or do not know the Bible, in the sight of God we are absolutely naked! It is not merely that we have committed sins (partially unclothed), but we must see ourselves as sinful before God and in rebellion (totally unclothed), completely incapable in ourselves of providing any acceptable clothing (righteousness) in the sight of our Creator.

We have, in rebelling, suppressed the truth of our creaturehood revealed in the external nature of our existence (vv. 20–23). We have also rebelled against God's law in our inward nature by violating our conscience (2:14–15). Sin, as Paul has explained, is basically a wrong relationship to God; it is active or passive rebellion against His lordship over our lives; it is a power controlling us. This is the Bible's concept of sin that leaves us without excuse and under the judgment and wrath of God. Our predicament renders us hopeless unless God has found some other means of accepting sinful people apart from either law works or religious rites. Will He rescue us? How will He do it and still remain just and holy?

NOTES

1. Dorothy L. Sayers, *Christian Letters to a Post-Christian World* (Grand Rapids: Eerdmans, 1969); Francis A. Schaeffer, *The God Who Is There* (Downers Grove, Ill.: InterVarsity, 1968); *Escape from Reason* (Downers Grove, Ill.: InterVarsity, 1968); *Death in the City* (Downers Grove, Ill.: InterVarsity, 1969); and Os Guinness, *The Dust of Death* (Downers Grove, Ill.: InterVarsity, 1972). On postmodernism see: Roger Lundin, *The Culture of Interpretation, Christian Faith and the Postmodern World* (Grand Rapids: Eerdmans, 1993); Thomas C. Oden, *After Modernity . . . What? Agenda for Theology* (Grand Rapids: Zondervan, 1990). This expression is, of course, relative. The present situation could be reversed at any time by a worldwide revival.

2. See book of similar title by the Dutch philosopher Hermann Dooye-weerd, *In the Twilight of Western Thought* (Philadelphia: Presb. & Ref., 1960); see especially Donald Bloesch, *The Crumbling of the Foundations* (Grand Rapids: Zondervan, 1984).

3. "There is no real preaching of the Christian gospel except in light of the fact that man is under the wrath of God" (Schaeffer, *Death in the City*, 93). It also seems evident that the true wrath of God is only seen against the background of the norm in the gospel—the righteousness of God in Jesus Christ. Cranfield remarks: "It is that we do not see the full meaning of the wrath of God in the disasters befalling sinful man in the course of history: the reality of the wrath of God is only truly known when it is seen in its revelation in Gethsemane and on Golgotha" (*A Critical and Exegetical Commentary on the Epistle to the Romans*, 1:110).

4. The terms "godlessness" and "wickedness" are best understood as an emphatic expression of one and the same thing (Anders Nygren, *Commentary on Romans* [Philadelphia: Fortress, 1949], 101). The single expression "by their wickedness" of the latter phrase seems to confirm this. Our moral condition of wickedness is never separated from religious corruption and is seen by Paul as a result of our religious apostasy.

5. Schaeffer, *Death in the City*, 102, explains Paul's thought thus: "They . . . hold some of the truth about themselves and about the universe . . . but they refuse to carry these truths to their reasonable conclusions."

6. Perhaps even "to hold imprisoned" (TDNT, 2:829).

7. John Calvin, *Epistle of Paul to the Romans,* trans. Ross MacKensie (Grand Rapids: Eerdmans, 1961), 31.

8. These verses do not argue for the Medieval Thomistic natural theology or natural religion. Paul does not have in mind deductive (Aristotelian) logical arguments that can prove God's existence, but as vv. 21–23 show, he is referring to an actual continuous revelation of God to all persons that they possess (which could not be true of logical systems leading to belief in God) but have abandoned. The traditional Thomistic logical arguments for God's existence do not prove God exists but simply show that once God is assumed, then the world can be logically and adequately explained. To say this, however, does not overlook the witness to God present in the creation that can be perceived by all persons.

9. The "so that" indicates not merely result but purpose.

10. Or "in His works." Not only in the beginning but throughout the whole history of mankind, God has made Himself known in His works (Nygren,

104). Cranfield, however, prefers the traditional sense of "things made" rather than works in general (1:115).

11. Nygren, 108; See especially, Mark Seifrid, "Natural Revelation and the Purpose of the Law in Romans" *Tyndale Bulletin* 49.1 (1998), 115–29; and Bruce W. Winter, "In Public and in Private: Early Christian Interaction with Religious Pluralism," chapter 6 in *One God, One Lord in a World of Religious Pluralism,* Andrew D. Clarke, and Bruce W. Winter, eds. (Cambridge: Tyndale House, 1991).

12. See G. C. Berkouwer, *General Revelation* (Grand Rapids: Eerdmans, 1952), chap. 7, "Revelation and Knowledge," for a full discussion of this thesis; also Dooyeweerd, "What Is Man?" in the *Twilight of Western Thought;* William M. Ramsay, "The Pauline Philosophy of History," in *The Cities of St. Paul* (Grand Rapids: Baker, 1960).

13. A. W. Tozer, *The Knowledge of the Holy* (New York: Harper & Row 1961), 11.

14. Note also the rapid increase today of occultism, oriental mysticism, and drugs, which may be a transitional stage on the road to a full-blown reversion to idolatry. See Jacques Ellul, *The New Demons* (New York: Seabury, 1975); Bloesch, *The Crumbling of the Foundations* (Grand Rapids: Zondervan, 1984); and the non-Christian Naomi R. Goldenberg, *Changing of the Gods: Feminism and the End of Traditional Religions* (Boston: Beacon, 1979).

15. Some materials on this are the books of Francis A. Schaeffer already cited; Kenneth Hamilton, *In Search of Contemporary Man* (Grand Rapids: Eerdmans, 1967); C. Stephen Evans, *Despair: A Moment or a Way of Life?* (Downers Grove, Ill.: InterVarsity, 1971); John W. Sanderson Jr., *Encounter in the Non-Christian Era* (Grand Rapids: Zondervan, 1970); Bloesch, *The Crumbling of the Foundations.*

16. By "moral realm" we mean the whole spectrum of human values including, but not limited to, sexual values.

17. The most reliable recent studies for Americans place all homosexual persons (i.e., those who practice exclusive same-sex sexual relations and identify themselves as gay or lesbian) at about 4 percent for males and 1 percent for females of the total population (see E. O. Laumann, et. al, "The Social Organization of Sexuality: Sexual Practices in the United States" The National Opinion Research Center: University of Chicago Press, 1994). The revisionist interpretation that argues that Paul is talking here about heterosexuals who practice homosexual acts or that Paul is dealing not with what we know as homosexual acts but that what he condemns is acts connected with idolatry and cult prostitution is set forth in John Boswell, *Christianity, Social Tolerance, and Homosexuality* (Chicago: Univ. of Chicago Press, 1980) and

William Countryman, *Dirt, Greed, and Sex* (Philadelphia: Fortress, 1988). These views are effectively critiqued in Richard B. Hays, "Relations Natural and Unnatural: A Response to John Boswell's Exegesis of Romans 1," *Journal of Religious Ethics* 14 (1986): 184–215; J. Glen Taylor, "The Bible and Homosexuality," *Themelios* 21 (Oct. 1995): 4–9; Donald J. Wold, *Out of Order, Homosexuality in the Bible and the Ancient Near East* (Grand Rapids: Baker, 1998). The recent appearance of a rare first-century silver goblet (known as the Warren Cup), unearthed in Palestine in 1900 and purchased by the British Museum for 2.8 million dollars with nude male figures engaged in sex (including young boys) shows the common acceptance in Greco-Roman culture of this practice (*London Times*, 5 May 1999). AIDS should not be thought of as a special judgment of God on this kind of promiscuity, but neither should it be excluded in certain instances from one of the consequences of sin. AIDS sufferers nevertheless are people who need the compassionate care of committed Christians who are called to minister loving help, regardless of how the disease may have been contracted.

18. The Greek word here translated "practice" is *prassō*, meaning "habitually practice." It is much stronger than the word "commit" (KJV). "Those who condone and applaud the vicious actions of others are actually making a deliberate contribution to the setting up of a public opinion favorable to vice, and so to the corruption of an indefinite number of other people. So, for example, to excuse or gloss over the use of torture by security forces or the cruel injustices of racial discrimination and oppression, while not being involved in them directly, is to help to cloak monstrous evil with an appearance of respectability and so to contribute most effectively to its firmer entrenchment" (Cranfield 1:135).

19. This diatribe style was common to the philosophers and preachers in Paul's day. It is not impossible that some of the arguments in this book were first worked out by Paul in actual confrontation and debate with non-Christians as they interjected remarks and received Paul's replies (3:5–8; 6:1, 15).

20. E. J. Carnell, *Christian Commitment* (Grand Rapids: Eerdmans, 1957), 202.

21. C. K. Barrett, *The Epistle to the Romans*, 44.

22. If 1:18–32 gives us some indication of the present result of the wrath of God in the loss of our humanity, then the future withdrawal of all (perhaps not *all*; even in judgment there is mercy) of God's grace and kindness from us can only be dreadfully imagined. "Deprivation," rather than the medieval imagery of burning or physical pain (e.g., Dante's *Inferno*), may depict more of the biblical concept (see C. S. Lewis, *Problem of Pain* [New York: Macmillan, 1961], 106–16).

23. These ideas can be seen in the Jewish Apocryphal book of the Wisdom of Solomon (15:14), which Paul evidently knew.

24. The Greek tense (connotative present) can signify action being attempt-ed but not successfully completed (e.g., John 13:6); in such cases "tries to" supplies a good auxiliary (F. Blass and A. Debrunner, *A Greek Grammar of the New Testament and Other Early Christian Literature*, ed. and trans. Robert W. Funk [Chicago: Univ. of Chicago, 1961], par. 319, 167). Repen-tance (Greek, *metanoia*) in the New Testament does not basically signify sorrow for sin or even remorse, but stands for the radical change in thought and will that turns a person away from himself to acknowledge God as Lord, and away from disobedience of God's will to obedience. For Paul, repentance is divinely worked (2 Cor. 7:9–11) and includes the action of faith in Jesus Christ (the latter is Paul's more common word).

25. Greek for "self-seeking" is *eritheia*, which is derived from a word mean-ing "hireling." The idea, then, is not "contentious" (KJV) but "base self-seeking" since they use their works as evidence of human achievement (see TDNT, 2:660); also Cranfield, 1:148.

26. Hypothetically at least, this seems to be the point. In Galatians 3:21 Paul argues that, if a law could have given life, then surely righteousness would have come to humans through the keeping of the Mosaic Law, but since all are sinners and transgressors of the intent of the law, God brought righteousness to us in a different manner.

27. See Cranfield for a thorough articulation of this view through verses 12–16. He cites Augustine and Ambrosiaster as early—and Barth more recent—exponents of the same view (1:156). More recently also Glenn N. Davies, *Faith and Obedience in Romans* (Sheffield: Sheffield Academic Press, 1990), 60–67. For the alternate view, see Ernst Kasemann, *Commen-tary on Romans*, 62–68.

28. This is well illustrated in the story told by a missionary to northern Brazil. He had observed a very nervous and fidgety native with sweat on his brow enter the village and seem very uneasy even in the presence of his friends. Later, the missionary learned that this fellow had just killed a man of another tribe. Although in this society it was not considered wrong to kill a member of another tribe, this man was obviously under the pressure of an uneasy awareness that he had done something wrong. While societal norms do set the conscience, there is also the witness of God in the nature of our relations with other human beings that overrides the errant social stan-dards.

29. The construction is very difficult in the Greek. Two possibilities exist here grammatically: (1) the idea of "mean while . . . one another" (KJV) (Gk. *metaxy allēlōn*) refers to mutual judgment of each other's behavior and is different from, though not unrelated to, the functioning of conscience; or (2) these words refer to their inward thoughts: "their conflicting thoughts accuse or perhaps excuse them" (RSV). It is difficult to decide, though the

KJV idea seems better. See H. P. Liddon, *An Explanatory Analysis of St. Paul's Epistle to the Romans* (Grand Rapids: Zondervan, 1961), 46–49; Nygren, 125; William Sanday and Arthur Headlam, *A Critical and Exegetical Commentary on the Epistle to the Romans* (Edinburgh: T. & T. Clark, 1900), 60. Cranfield again argues that this whole process takes place not in the present but in the future judgment, where Gentile Christians will be reminded both of their failures of complete obedience and of the fact that their thoughts have been changed through faith in Christ toward obedience (1:162).

30. C. S. Lewis states, "There have been differences between their moralities [speaking of different civilizations and ages], but these have never amounted to anything like a total difference" (*Mere Christianity* [New York: Macmillan, 1943], 5).

31. It seems that missionary as well as evangelistic effort among young people in our country should pay closer attention to this point. We may see places where others are violating *our* standards, but our point of contact with them may have to be in an area where they are actually rejecting by their lives a standard that they have committed themselves to. This is an area where they may be aware of having done wrong.

32. Not Paul's gospel in distinction to Jesus' or Peter's or John's gospel, but the gospel Paul taught as the norm and with which the other apostles were in agreement (see Gal. 2:9).

33. Although the Christian is never described by Paul or any NT writer as being saved by works but ever by faith alone, yet saving faith is never alone. Salvation involves the life we are saved to as well as the life we are saved from. We are saved to holiness and good works (Eph. 2:10). Thus, although judgment always proceeds on the basis of works (Rev. 20:12), God's salvation is never on the basis of works but always faith. Yet the outworking of this salvation produces a lifestyle characterized by good works before God, and therefore the principle of God's judgment is maintained even in the case of the believer (1 Cor. 3:11–13).

34. For a very convincing case that uppermost in Paul's mind was the Abrahamic covenant promises, which included the Messianic promise ("in you all the families of the earth shall be blessed," Gen. 12:3 NASB; see Gal. 3:8, 16), see Sam K. Williams, "The 'Righteousness of God' in Romans," 265–68. Further, Williams argues that the terms "the faithfulness of God" (v. 3), "the righteousness of God" (v. 5), and "the truth of God" (v. 7 NASB) are virtual equivalents throughout the whole epistle.

35. The expression in the Greek *(mē genoito)* literally translated means "perish the thought!" or "may it not be!" However, since in the Greek OT (LXX) this same expression is used in connection with the name of God (1 Sam. 24:6; 26:11; 1 Kings 21:3), the KJV translation, which adds the

stronger idea of God's abhorrence ("God forbid"), is to be preferred (John Murray, *The Epistle to the Romans,* 1:94 n. 1). However, this expression has been trivialized and secularized in modern usage.

36. "I am speaking in human terms" (NASB) means simply that he is adopting the diatribe method of interjecting objections opposed to his views so that he might further clarify his teaching.

37. Total depravity must not be understood to mean that all people are as bad or as depraved as they can get; or that in this condition they show no love, kindness, honesty, morality, etc., but that we are infected with rebellion against our Creator, and this rebellion has extended itself in some measure throughout our whole being. If sin were blue in color, I would be some shade of blue all over. Even in my best deeds there is a discoloration of self-centeredness instead of God-centeredness. Charles H. Spurgeon, the great English preacher, once remarked, "He who doubts total depravity had better study himself."

38. This latter sentence has two major interpretive problems in determining Paul's exact thought. The first involves the word "better" (Gr. *proechomai*), which has three possible meanings; the second involves the words "not at all" (Gr. *oy pantōs*), which has two different senses. The sense of "not in every respect" seems preferable to me as well as to others (Cranfield, 1:187–91; Käsemann, 68). Only the NEB margin seems to have this correct sense for both expressions. For the sense, "Not at all," see E. H. Gifford, "Romans," in *The Bible Commentary: New Testament,* 85; TDNT, RSV; Barrett, *The Epistle to the Romans,* 66–69.

39. The "law" (as in chaps. 2 and 3) refers not only to the Mosaic codes but also to the prophets and Psalms, i.e., the whole OT (F. F. Bruce, *The Epistle of Paul to the Romans* [Grand Rapids: Eerdmans, 1963], 99).

40. "Works of the Law" (NASB) is an expression hotly debated today. It seems best to understand this term to refer to an approach to the Mosaic Law by either unbelieving Jews or Christian Jews who put themselves under the old Mosaic covenant without the power of the indwelling Spirit for living a life pleasing to God. Such an approach is doomed to failure, as Paul shows in chapter 7.

3

THE GOOD NEWS: GOD'S RIGHTEOUSNESS BY FAITH

3:21–4:25

Thankfully, God's word of judgment is not His only or last word. "But now" (v. 21), Paul says, something utterly new has entered human history. This is the great turning point of the letter. All human accomplishment falls short of God's glory and stands justly under God's wrath. But our own need is met by God's intervention in mercy and grace through Jesus Christ. Now *God's* righteousness effecting our salvation has been revealed as a free gift to the guilty. This salvation is obtained solely on the basis of faith in Jesus Christ apart from any moralistic works (3:21–26). It comes solely by God's grace. Therefore, all meritorious boasting in works is excluded by the principle of complete trust in Jesus Christ for acceptance before God (3:27–31). This faith method of salvation taught in the good news of the gospel is in fact the very one revealed in the Old Testament and illustrated beautifully and irrefutably by the lives of Abraham and David (chap. 4).

GOD'S PROVISION: JUSTIFICATION THROUGH CHRIST BY FAITH
3:21–31

This section has been called "the heart of the epistle and of the Pauline message." In the brief span of a few verses, Paul sets forth God's finished plan and how He dealt with the sinful human condition. Since Paul compresses such a tremendous amount of truth into a brief section, we will need to examine and enlarge (from other Pauline passages) upon a number of the key words found here, such as redemption, grace, justification, faith, and propitiation. Paul's precise thought is also revealed by his use of about twenty independent prepositions and eight prepositions compounded with other words. These syntactical relationships are difficult to explain in a brief commentary, but one should be aware that there is far more in the text than the word meanings.

In short, Paul teaches that what we could not effect for ourselves (righteousness) because we are under the wrath of God, God has provided as a free gift through faith in Jesus Christ. The actual historical and public crucifixion of the young Jewish carpenter, Jesus of Nazareth, reveals God's righteousness and provides the basis for this full forgiveness and deliverance from God's wrath of all who put their trust in God's Son (1:16). Paul refers to the death of Jesus in the language of the Old Testament sacrificial system (vv. 24–25). Since God's deliverance comes to us solely by faith, there can be no place for boasting or self-congratulation (vv. 27–30).

THIS RIGHTEOUSNESS IS NOT BY THE LAW (3:21)

Paul likes to speak paradoxically: "apart from law" and yet "to which the Law and the Prophets testify."[1] It has already been shown by Paul that law-righteousness (legalism) rests upon human achievement and, because of our self-centered nature, leads to God's wrath. So God's righteousness must be manifested in a different way so as to lead to our justification. On the other hand, the law (OT) itself, if we correctly understand it, points in the same direction (3:31). In the *law*, Abraham and David (chap. 4) are illustrations of how God's gift-righteousness came to these men of old through faith. Paul has already referred to Habakkuk 2:4 from the prophets (1:17). Paul's rich use of the word *law (nomos)* should not be overlooked. Here Paul stresses that the righteousness of God comes not by legalism (law), yet the law (OT) as God's revelation witnesses to the importance of faith.

The "righteousness from God" once again comes before us. Paul has in 1:17 related this term to the gospel and the power of God working salvation to all who believe. The reader is referred to that passage for further help and to the discussion under justification (3:24).

THIS RIGHTEOUSNESS IS THE RIGHTEOUSNESS OF FAITH (3:22–23)

As in 1:17, Paul immediately links this saving activity with our faith response. Most commentators see *both* of the following expressions related to this same truth: "through faith in Jesus Christ" and "to all who believe" (v. 22). However, the two expressions so understood seem redundant. Therefore, some see the expression "through faith in Jesus Christ" as a reference to Jesus' own faithfulness to God. They translate the term as "through the faithfulness of Christ" and understand it to mean that through Christ's faithfulness and obedience, God has manifested His saving grace, which allows all nations to stand, justified by faith, before God.[2]

"There is no difference" (e.g., between Jew and Gentile, those with the knowledge of the Bible and those without the knowledge of the Bible, moralist and pornographer), "for all have sinned" (v. 23). They have sinned in the sense of Paul's concept of sin in 1:18–3:20, namely, that regardless of the differences among us in respect to the kind and intensity of our offenses against God's law, all without exception are in the category of rebellious sinners ("under sin," 3:9). We have willfully suppressed the outward and inward knowledge of God, who claims as Creator to be Lord of our lives. In doing this, we "fall short of the glory of God."

The tenses in the two verbs are important. All "have sinned" (Greek past tense)[3] and "fall short" (present tense). The historical fact of our continued sinful condition leads to our present falling short or "lack" (Gk. *hystereō*, "in need of" or "deprived of") of the "glory of God." God created us in His own image that in dependence upon Him, we might reflect the Creator's own personal and moral excellence. Sin breaks our relationship with God and fractures the full imaging activity of the creature. Jesus Christ, as a human being, perfectly reflected the invisible God (Heb. 1:3). Through Him, sinful human beings are restored to the fully intended image and glory of God (2 Cor. 3:18; Col. 3:10).

THE DIVINE PLAN OF EFFECTING THIS RIGHTEOUSNESS BY FAITH (3:24–26)

How does God actually provide this grace-gift of His saving righteousness? What role does Jesus Christ, and His death and resurrection, play in this plan? Can even God account a sinful person as being righteous? How is God's gift attained? Some comment on each of the key words in verses 24–25 may help to illuminate the apostle's thoughts on these questions.

1. *Justification* (v. 24). What does Paul mean by being justified? Considerable discussion has revolved around attempted definitions of this concept. Some regard it as the key theme of the whole epistle. The Greek verb translated "justified" *(dikaioō)* has exactly the same stem as the Greek noun for "righteousness" *(dikaiosynē)*. To justify someone, then, would logically mean to make someone righteous in the sense of infusing goodness. Although Chrysostom (A.D. 347–407) and Augustine (A.D. 396–430) and the church likewise followed this view for centuries, it is now generally held to be wrong (an exception being some Roman Catholics). Yet even from one consideration alone this ancient view is questionable. In the Epistles, frequent mention is made of Christians who are not entirely ethically good (righteous), yet are nevertheless justified (e.g., 1 Cor. 3:3; 6:11).

In place of Augustine's view is offered the rendering to "declare [or treat] as righteous" (3:20).[4] This idea suggests to some that God now views sinners as if they were righteous (good) or had never sinned. Although this rendering escapes the difficulty of asserting that in justification we are infused with ethical righteousness, it likewise flounders on linguistic and theological grounds. If God *treated* as ethically righteous those who were not morally righteous, would this not be a sort of legal fiction? Can even God pretend that black is white or that bad is good?

It is far better and more in harmony with Paul's whole teaching to understand justification to mean to *make righteous*.[5] At the same time, it is necessary to recognize that "righteous" (in this instance) has no reference to ethical goodness or virtue, but means *right, clear, acquitted* in God's court.[6] Justification, then, is God's saving activity in behalf of guilty sinners whereby He goes forth in power to *forgive* and *deliver* them in the present time from judgment by His grace, to declare a *new reality* to exist, to give them the gift of His righteousness, and to *transform* and *empower* them so that they can act to become by the power of the Holy Spirit what they are in the new reality. It is more than—but certainly includes—the mere forensic (legal acquittal, declaring) act of God. God actually works to forgive sinners (4:5), to place them in a whole radically different relationship to Himself (5:2), and to give them power through the indwelling Spirit to become righteous before God by keeping His commandments (8:4). In this new relationship we receive enablement through the Holy Spirit, who brings the lordship of Jesus Christ to bear on our lives (8:1–9), to worship and serve God in His will (holiness).[7] Calvin catches this emphasis by arguing that God justifies us by placing us "in Christ." Therefore we participate in Christ's life by the Holy Spirit.

This justification Paul further qualifies by the word "freely" (Gk. *dōrean,* "for nothing"). This same word is found in John 15:25, where Jesus says, "They hated me without reason," and in Galatians 2:21, "Christ died for nothing." It is plain, then, that by this word Paul is stressing the gift aspect of God's way of putting us right with Himself. We are acquitted (forgiven and introduced to salvation) for no cause or reason in us; that is, we have no merit or virtue, nor is any required (Phil. 3:9).

2. *Grace* (v. 24). The reason that sinners, though guilty, can be justified lies in God's grace. This is a key word of Paul's in all his epistles (he uses it 100 times). In the succeeding chapters, this element will be a primary point as he discusses the new life

imparted through justification (5:2). Grace (Gk. *charis*) is the free and unmerited favor of God. It is that aspect of God's love that leads Him to bestow on us His free forgiveness even while we are rebellious sinners (5:8; Eph. 2:8). Grace, however, is more than God's favorable attitude toward us; it includes also the activity and divine provisions for living fully in the new relationship (Rom. 5:21; 1 Cor. 15:10; 2 Cor. 12:9). When Paul wants to stress that salvation arises from God's initiative and not from ours, he uses the word *grace* (Rom. 11:6).

God's grace, although free to the sinner, cannot be made a "cheap" grace, because it cost God the tremendous price of the death of His own Son. What has cost God so much cannot be cheap for us. Costly grace confronts us with a call to relinquish our very lives and submit absolutely to the obedience of Christ.[8]

G. Campbell Morgan used to relate an experience he had while preaching this message of free forgiveness in a small mining town in the Midwest. Following the service, a miner came up and argued that this kind of salvation was too cheap. Morgan asked him how he got to work each day. The miner replied, "I walk. I live close to the mine." "How do you get down in the mine shaft?" Morgan asked. "I ride the elevator," the miner said. Morgan continued, "How much does it cost you?" "Nothing, it's free for us miners," he said. "Well," replied Morgan, "it must be a cheap operation then!" "No," said the miner, "it's free for us, but it cost the company a lot." Then suddenly, as if a light had dawned, he exclaimed, "Oh, my dear God, now I see it. Salvation's free for me, but it cost the company a lot, all that God had!"[9]

The important question here is whether grace is purely arbitrary, or whether it rests in some decisive judicial act of God that allows Him to maintain His own holy standards and yet to acquit and deliver sinners.

3. *Redemption* (v. 24). Paul's answer to this question lies in understanding the death of Jesus as a sacrificial death. Two words drawn from the Old Testament highlight this. "Redemption" (Gk. *apolytrōsis*) means basically to buy slaves in the market place in order to set them free. Additionally, this imagery draws as its primary background from both the Old Testament

concept of the redemption of the nation Israel from slavery in Egypt (Exod. 6:6; 15:13) and from the significance of the Passover lamb sacrifice (Exod. 12; 1 Cor. 5:7).

Slavery produced a human condition from which a person could not free himself. It was hopeless unless someone from outside willingly intervened and paid the price to buy and to set the slave free. For those Americans who remember the release of the Vietnam prisoners of war, the event may form a close modern parallel. The imagery depicts the evil plight in which we all find ourselves as a result of our sin. We are in a state of imprisonment from which we are powerless to break free. We are helplessly under the judgment of God. But God Himself has intervened, paid the price, and powerfully effected the release. From the reference to "blood" in verse 25, the price paid can be nothing else than the death of Christ (Mark 10:45; Gal. 3:13; 1 Pet. 1:18–19).[10] Christ's death provided the required ransom price to free us from the captivity and dominion of sin and to liberate us to do the will of God. Jesus of Nazareth is Himself the ransom (Mark 10:45; 1 Cor. 1:30; Titus 2:14).

4. *Propitiation* (v. 25). Paul immediately links the redemption effected through Christ with the concept of "a propitiation in His blood through faith" (NASB). "Sacrifice of atonement" (Gk. *hilastērion*, mercy seat)[11] must be understood in the light of the context of Paul's argument in 1:18–3:20. He has established that there is a real wrath of God that extends to all persons because of their own willful suppression of the truth of His claims as Creator and Judge. In this context, Paul shows that in the historical death of Jesus ("in His blood"), this wrath (anger) of God found adequate judicial satisfaction.

God condones nothing because of His holy and righteous nature. Since sin deserves punishment and death (1:32; 6:23), there can be no forgiveness and reconciliation without judicial moral satisfaction. It cannot be far from the truth if we see in the death of Jesus a substitution for us sinners (2 Cor. 5:21; 1 Pet. 2:24). He, the righteous One (yet fully human), suffered the just penalty (wrath) for our sins that God might still remain just and the One who can fully pardon the guilty sinner (v. 26). The marvel consists in the act of God's grace, where in infinite and consuming love He Himself provided the costly satisfaction (mercy seat) that we in ourselves were incapable of presenting (Rom. 5:8; Titus 3:4; 1 John 4:9–10). Something of this heart of God was captured by Elizabeth C. Clephane when she wrote,

> "And though the road be rough and steep,
> I go to the desert to find My sheep,
> I go to the desert to find My sheep."
> But none of the ransomed ever knew
> How deep were the waters crossed;
> Nor how dark was the night that the Lord passed through
> Ere He found His sheep that was lost.

The only adequate response to such love and grace is obedient faith. When we forsake all our own meritorious works and former loyalties and cast ourselves totally upon Jesus Christ as God's mercy seat in His own blood for our sin, we believe, in the biblical sense. At that point, the saving righteousness of God becomes effective in our lives (4:16–25).

But, Paul, why did Jesus have to die in order to reveal God's righteousness in the gospel? In verses 25–26 Paul attempts to answer this question. Jesus' propitiatory death first shows that God is really morally righteous. God showed restraint (forbearance; Gk. *anochē*, Rom. 2:4) in not visiting wrath upon our sins in the past ages before Christ came when "He passed over" (v. 25 NASB) our sins. Yet it was not due to moral indifference toward sin that He restrained Himself. Though the "sins committed beforehand" may be understood as sins in a person's life before one became a Christian,[12] most understand Paul to refer to the sins committed in *former* ages before the governmental act of God occurred in Jesus' death. In days past God did not exercise His full wrath on human beings for their sins; He was patient and merciful with them (Acts 14:16; 17:30). But in Jesus' death God manifested the truth that He was yet not any less wrathful against sin. The supreme penalty for our sins was borne by Jesus. This allows God to remain God—morally perfect—and yet forgive and receive sinners.

So, too, in the present, God's justice and holy hatred of sin are still maintained even when He, in grace through the gospel, takes sinners and puts them in right standing with Himself. Jesus' death vindicates the moral character of God (v. 26). Again (as in v. 24) Paul stresses the present tense of justification, "and the justifier [one who *is* justifying] of the one who has faith in Jesus" (NASB). He wants to emphasize not only that justification occurs now in this life, but also the idea of God's continual empowering of us to be *righteous*. Isaac Watts's familiar hymn captures well the sinner's response to such grace:

> When I survey the wondrous cross
> On which the Prince of glory died,
> My richest gain I count but loss,
> And pour contempt on all my pride.
>
> Were the whole realm of nature mine,
> That were a present far too small:
> Love so amazing, so divine,
> Demands my soul, my life, my all.

THE RESULTS OF GOD'S PLAN (3:27–31)

There are two results of this "faith alone" plan of justification. First, it excludes boasting (vv. 27–28). All boasting depends upon some supposed superiority earned through a system of meritorious works (ethical and religious)—that is, pride of accomplishment. The faith system, on the other hand, depends totally on the merciful act of God in Jesus Christ's death. Since God acting in *grace* has done everything, there can be no grounds for human meritorious accomplishment. If heaven were to be a place where we go because of our meritorious good works, we would turn it into hell by going around—as we surely would—boasting of all we did to get there.

Second, this plan of salvation by faith alone establishes the true unity of God as God over all people (vv. 29–30). The Jew would be the first to confess that God is One (*shema*, Deut. 6:4). How, then, Paul argues, could He be the one God of both Jews and Gentiles unless He had a plan of righting us with Himself that did not require all of us to be Jews (circumcised)? This plan is the faith plan that is equally valid for Jews (circumcised) and the Gentiles (uncircumcised).

But, Paul, doesn't what you have said about the faith plan (3:21–30) cancel out the Mosaic Law of God entirely? Paul answers emphatically, no (v. 31). In fact, what he has said rather serves to "uphold" (confirm, hold valid) the Mosaic Law. Although Paul could mean by the word *law* the whole Old Testament (3:19),[13] the more immediate context (faith versus meritorious works of law) favors a slightly different view. He probably refers to the charge that by his gospel of grace he is allegedly setting aside the moral commands in the Mosaic Law. Since antinomian (no obligation to keep the moral law) charges against Paul are later raised and dealt with in detail by the apostle (chaps. 6–8), it is likely that he here simply makes the flat statement that the righteousness of God revealed in the gospel fully agrees with the moral nature of God revealed in the commandments of the Old Testament.

These verses (vv. 27–31) bring to a close the most crucial and concentrated argument of the whole letter (1:18–3:31). Before proceeding, it might be well to summarize briefly the two main focal points.

First, Paul has described the human situation from the divine perspective. All of us, whether religious or irreligious, moral or immoral, have chosen to glorify ourselves rather than our Creator. Those without the knowledge of God in the Bible assert themselves in the form of rebellion against the natural order and their conscience and by so doing claim freedom from God, only to find that in the end they debase themselves and become inhuman. On the other hand, the religiously cultured with the knowledge of God in the Bible—or at least a sense of morality—assert their rebellion by, in pride, refusing to repent before God. By substituting the worship of their own self-righteousness, they have failed to keep the true spirit of the Bible, which is inward humble submission and obedience to the God revealed in the Scriptures. Both kinds of people are equally under God's judicial wrath.

Second, all hope is not lost, because God has Himself powerfully acted in history for the acquittal of the guilty. His holy wrath against our sin was meted out to Jesus Christ in His death on the cross when God made Him to become the new mercy seat through His blood. God shows thereby that He is fully just and able to put in the right all sinners who trust in Jesus Christ. To explain this good news, Paul has pressed into service the language of the law court (justify), the slave market (redemption), and the temple (mercy seat). We put our trust in God's act in Jesus Christ and experience full pardon, deliverance from sin, a new standing before God, and a new empowerment of the Holy Spirit to do God's will. In the remainder of the epistle, Paul will explain in more detail this new status before God as it relates to many different situations.

ABRAHAM AND JUSTIFICATION BY FAITH
4:1–25

Paul has established the principle that faith alone secures right standing before God, not works of human meritorious achievement (3:21–31). He has declared (3:27) that the faith system revealed in the gospel excludes all boasting based upon human meritorious achievement. God considers the faith of an individual, not circumcision, as the ground for justification. Chapter 4 expands further on these points and concludes Paul's major point on justification.

As far as the Jew was concerned, any discussion of the correct approach to God must consider Abraham, the father of Israel. Abraham is depicted in Jewish thought as having performed the whole law before it was given. He was viewed as the perfect example of all Jewish virtues.[14] Thus the case of Abraham was paramount. If he was not justified by meritorious works, then no one could be; if he was justified by faith, there can be no other justification for anyone. This chapter contains one of the most important discussions in the Bible concerning the relationship between faith and meritorious works. We will also want to note very carefully the helpful material Paul relates toward the end of chapter 4 stating the more exact nature of faith.

Paul shows that Abraham was justified by faith and not by works, as was also David (vv. 1–8). Since Abraham's circumcision postdated his justification before God, it could not have caused his acceptance before God (vv. 9–12). Furthermore, the promise given to Abraham, that in his seed all nations would be blessed, was given through the righteousness of faith and had nothing to do with the law (vv. 13–22). Finally, Paul argues that the same God who justified Abraham by faith likewise through faith justifies us in Jesus Christ, who died for our sins and rose again for our justification (vv. 23–25).

Abraham and Justification (4:1–8)

Paul begins with an objection to his whole view of justification. Paul, you say faith alone apart from meritorious deeds of the Mosaic Law justifies us before God, and therefore all boasting is excluded. What about our father, Abraham? Wouldn't virtuous Abraham, if he were in fact justified by works (as the rabbis teach), have something to boast about? Paul replies, Yes, he would, but in fact, before God, Abraham has no such grounds for boasting. Whatever you were taught about Abraham's boasting, forget it. The Scripture settles the issue when it says, "Abraham believed God, and it was credited to him as righteousness" (Rom. 4:3; Gen. 15:6).[15]

Current Jewish understanding of faith emphasized "faithfulness" and included the idea of meritorious work. Paul interprets the Genesis passage in a fresh light (vv. 4–8). First, he links together two pairs of opposites. "Works" and "obligation" are linked and set off in opposition to "faith" and "gift" (literally, grace). One who works gets paid, but one who does not work (and yet gets wages) must be "credited" (counted) as having gotten pay as a gift. Since Genesis says Abraham had righteousness "credited" to him (Rom. 4:11), it follows that he must have received righteousness as a "gift" (by grace) and not as a result of his meritorious works. As Abraham, so the one "who does not work but trusts God who justifies [pres. tense again] the wicked, his faith is credited as righteousness" (v. 5).

The reference to God justifying the "wicked" (impious) is

unique. At least two things clearly emerge: (1) justification (and righteousness) is clearly at its initial stage a forensic (courtroom) word that does not mean "to make ethically righteous" but "to acquit" or "to grant a status of right"; and (2) since it is the wicked (not the ethically righteous) who are justified, Paul is describing a unique divine act of grace without precedent in human affairs.[16] Yet God did this without condoning human sin.

Paul appeals further to Israel's great king and sweet psalmist, David (vv. 6–8). David is helpful to Paul's argument because although Abraham lived prior to the law, David was squarely under it. David, unlike Abraham, was a flagrant violator of God's law and yet was forgiven by God. Using the interpretive principle that when the same word occurs in two biblical passages, the first occurrence can be used to explain the later uses, Paul turns to Psalm 32:1–2 to show that David also teaches justification without meritorious works.[17] The "never count" (not credit) of sin mentioned by David is equivalent to "the credited [counted] . . . as righteousness" in Abraham's case. Both were acquitted without works because "credit" belongs only to the category of gift (grace or gift) and not merit (obligation). At each new turn in Paul's argument, it becomes clearer that justification is not God's just pronouncement on our human merit (Jewish view) or the imparting of goodness, but gracious forgiveness of sin and release from judgment.[18] Since justification for Paul includes both our being placed into or united to Christ (6:1–7) and the indwelling gift of the Holy Spirit (5:5), sanctification or nonmeritorious good works in the justified is inseparable from saving faith.

CIRCUMCISION AND JUSTIFICATION (4:9–12)

Paul, an objecter interjects, Abraham and David were circumcised before this blessing of forgiveness could come to them, weren't they? How then can the uncircumcised ever be justified before God? Isn't it necessary to be circumcised and keep the law? (Acts 15:1).

Paul's answer revolves around the question of chronology.

Abraham was in fact circumcised *after* he had been credited as righteous: "It was not after, but before [he was circumcised]!" (v. 10). He had been first acquitted by faith (Gen. 15) and then circumcised (Gen. 17) about fourteen years later! Paul sees a divine purpose in this order. Abraham was to be the "father of many nations" according to the divine promise to him at the time when he believed God and was justified (Gen. 15:5; Rom. 4:17, 18). If his fatherhood consisted only in the Jewish people (circumcised), how could God fulfill the fatherhood of many nations of the promise? (vv. 17–18). But if his fatherhood consisted mainly in a lineage of those who like Abraham had received the "righteousness that comes by faith" (v. 13), then the Gentiles (uncircumcised) could rightly be called the children of Abraham. He is first of all the father of the believing Gentiles and afterward the father of the circumcision (Jew), providing that they "walk in the footsteps [lit. Gk. *stoicheō*, "join the ranks"] of the faith" (v. 12). Faith is independent of circumcision.

Why, then, was Abraham circumcised at all if faith is enough? Paul explains that circumcision was a "sign" (outward token) or a "seal" (assurance, confirmation) of the "righteousness that he [already] had by faith while he was still uncircumcised" (v. 11). When God renewed the covenant agreement with Abraham some fourteen years after his faith was credited to him as righteousness (Gen. 15), He changed his name from Abram to Abraham ("father of many nations"). As a visible seal (confirmation) that Abraham's original act of faith was accepted by God, God gave him the sign of circumcision as an evidence that he was acquitted by faith. Abraham was then to transmit this sign to a covenant people (Israel), who were to receive it as Abraham did, that is, as a seal of righteousness credited by faith.[19] Circumcision originally had nothing to do with works of law. Correctly understood, the rite confirms the truth of justification by faith.

PROMISE AND JUSTIFICATION (4:13–22)

Paul already alluded to the promise to Abraham that he should be the father of many nations (vv. 11–12). He elaborates further in verses 13–22 on the relationship between the promise and the Law of Moses. *Promise, faith, grace,* and *heirs* are joined by Paul and put in antithesis to law (vv. 13–16). In the first place, the law did not come until 430 years after the promise (Rom. 4:13; Gal. 3:17). Second, the only principle that will ensure the literal fulfillment of the promise to Abraham of being a father to "many" nations (vv. 17–18) is faith. Since only the Jews were given the law, only one nation could participate in the blessing (forgiveness of sins, vv. 7, 9)—that is, if the fulfillment of the promise depended on the law observance. Anyway, law works wrath because of sin and would be incompatible with the promise of blessing (v. 15).[20]

What is promise? Promise has the same nature as grace. Paul's point here appears almost the same as in verses 4–5. Promise rests on complete trust in the one who has made the promise. It is not a legal contract where one stipulates pay for the labor. Where labor is contracted, we know we will receive our due; but where all rests on the promise of the benefactor (grace), we must believe to receive (as a gift) the promised benefit (v. 16). If law provides the basis of the inherited blessing, "faith" and "promise" have lost their meaning (v. 14).

What is faith? Verses 17–22 help us to understand further the essential nature of Abraham's faith. Since this faith is like gospel faith (vv. 23–24), it is quite important. In the first place, Abraham's faith arose as a result of God's word of promise to him: "I have made you a father of many nations" (v. 17). Authentic biblical faith only exists as response to divine revelation (10:17).

Second, his faith was directed toward God Himself. And Abraham's God was not unknown. He is a God "who gives life to the dead and calls things that are not as though they were" (v. 17). Abraham's God is a God who is the Source of all life and resurrection, the Creator. For Abraham to father a child, when he was impotent and Sarah his wife barren, required a God who could act and create life from the natural deadness of the womb. Abraham, at the time of the promise of the child Isaac, was about one hundred years old, and Sarah was about ninety (Gen. 17:17).

Furthermore, faith has a future aspect in that it also accepts as certain what God has promised before it is fulfilled: "Against all hope [in God's promise], Abraham in [human] hope believed" (v. 18). He simply in faith took the promise of God at His word. Abraham was "fully assured"(NASB)[21] and did not waver in unbelief at the promise of God (as those who denied Paul's doctrine of justification were doing), but he gave glory to God (vv. 20–21). He did what those in chapters 1 and 2 failed to do. Abraham acknowledged God as God, the Creator, as such altogether different from creation (holy), powerful where we are weak, living where we are dead.[22] No such trust in meritorious works of the Mosaic Law can give this kind of glory to God. Such faith God counted as righteousness to Abraham (v. 22). Such faith He will also count as righteousness to us.

ABRAHAM'S FAITH AND GOSPEL FAITH (4:23–25)

The same kind of faith that brought righteousness without meritorious works to Abraham's account also brings righteousness to us in the gospel of Jesus Christ. This trust finds its object in the same living God of Abraham. He is the God who raised up His own Son, not from a dead womb, but from the grave (v. 24). Although the faith that brings acquittal and right standing before God today is not identical in content to Abraham's (promise of Isaac's birth), gospel faith is the same in quality (nonmeritorious) and in its object (the living Creator God, who gives us promises and brings life out of death). We are asked to trust not a theological idea or generalization, but the living God who acts in history and in the death and resurrection of Jesus. Gospel faith, like Abraham's faith, involves trust in the God who acts in history.

To believe in the God who raised Jesus from the dead is also to believe in the divine explanation of that death, "He [Jesus] was delivered over to death for our sins and was raised to life for our justification" (v. 25).[23] Faith is not a blind leap to a God who is totally unknown. Faith trusts in the God of forgiving grace who is revealed fully in the death and resurrection of Jesus of Nazareth.

Paul has harmonized his teaching about justification with the Old Testament by explaining the account of Abraham and his faith. He has finished his main argument. Paul has talked about (1) the human situation of all persons under the wrath of God because of rebellion (1:18–3:20); (2) the present and future deliverance of the sinner from this wrath through the gracious and substitutionary death of Jesus (3:21–31); and finally (3) the appropriateness and indispensability of faith as the only way of securing this acquittal before God by his argument based on Abraham (chap. 4). This is truly good news.

At this point, Paul turns to consider the life and human situation of those who have by faith entered into this new status of acceptance before God (chaps. 5–8). Is the life of man altered in any way by his new relationship to God? Chapters 5 through 8 can profitably be viewed as Paul's effort to show that a new life actually exists, despite certain apparent problems to the contrary.

NOTES

1. "The Law and the Prophets" probably refers to the whole OT in a twofold division. Such a division is found in the Qumran *Manual of Discipline,* Zadokite fragments, and other Qumran literature.

2. Sam K. Williams, "The Righteousness of God in Romans," 274–76; also Richard N. Longenecker, *Paul, Apostle of Liberty,* 149–52. Moo disagrees, as does Schreiner. Although it is difficult to decide, we should perhaps retain the traditional translation of "faith in Jesus Christ" and let the redundancy stand as a further emphasis on faith.

3. The aorist tense of this verb has been unwisely limited by some interpreters to refer to participation in Adam's sin. However, the complexive (constative) aorist may simply view many acts as a whole (F. Blass and A. Debrunner, *A Greek Grammar of the New Testament and Other Early Christian Literature,* par. 332, 171). In this case the past tense is simply gathering the whole human race under one canopy of sinfulness. "Sinned" is the Greek word *hamartanō,* which literally means in classical Greek "to miss the mark" (of His glory? 3:23) but in biblical literature refers to rebellion against God or to transgression of His will.

4. Verbs ending in oō in Greek (if they are verbs of mental perception or connected to adjectives denoting moral qualities) denote not the making, but the counting or deeming, of the specific moral quality (C. K. Barrett, *The Epistle*

to the Romans, 75). This is usually called the forensic (courtroom) use.

5. As Paul's concept of righteousness was drawn from the OT word usage rather than the Greek, so must we see his concept of justification. In the Hebrew OT the equivalent word lying behind "justify" is *tsadak,* which primarily means to "cause to be righteous," that is, *show* to be righteous. It cannot mean to "treat as *if* righteous."

6. Further support for this idea is seen in the fact that the opposite of justification is not *unrighteousness* (1:18–19), which would make justification right living, but *condemnation* (Rom. 5:18; 8:34; see Barrett, 75 and TDNT). Justification, then, is that act of God whereby He acquits us (1 Cor. 4:4) of our moral guilt before Him (under wrath) and through grace puts us in a radically different relationship to Him and all His benefits. Perhaps the *Good News for Modern Man* (TEV) captures the thought when it translates: "they are all put right with him through Christ Jesus." Hence, justification means basically standing with God. It is neither ethical righteousness "imputed" (Rom. 4:24 KJV) nor imparted but is a status conferred on the ground of faith, not on the ground of merit (see Leon Morris, *The Apostolic Preaching of the Cross* [Grand Rapids: Eerdmans, 1956], chaps. 7 and 8, for a full discussion).

7. The present tense of the participle translated "being justified" stresses that justification is a *present experience* for all those who are needing the glory of God restored to their lives (v. 23). For the Jews in Paul's day, justification was always future, awaiting the balancing of the good works against the evil works of each person (TDNT). The teaching of Jesus (Luke 18:4), as well as Paul's, was radically different at this point. This viewpoint has recently been challenged in E. P. Sanders, *Paul and Palestinian Judaism,* 494, who argues that present righteousness is also a concept of Judaism. This is called the "new perspective" on Paul, which has been embraced, modified, and occasionally rejected by current conservative scholars of Paul.

8. Dietrich Bonhoeffer, *Cost of Discipleship* (New York: Macmillan, 1959), chap. 1.

9. G. Campbell Morgan, *Westminster Pulpit* (Westwood, N.J.: Revell, n.d.), 9:120–33. See more recently, Phillip Yancey, *What Ever Happened to Grace?* (Grand Rapids: Zondervan, 1998).

10. There are at least six different Greek words used for "redemption" in the NT (Morris, chap. 1). Paul does not say to whom the price was paid or exactly how Christ's death provided this tremendous effect. There can be little doubt, however, that Paul's thought included the idea of substitutionary death (Gal. 3:13–14).

11. The concept is fraught with problems both linguistically and theologi-

cally. *Theologically,* there are two views: the *firsts* as in the NASB, NIV (margin), and KJV, sees the term denoting a true sense of propitiation (satisfaction assuaging God's holy wrath against sin); and the *second,* as in the RSV, which regards the word as conveying only the thought of "expiation" (wipe out sin, removal of guilt). The two concepts are difficult to distinguish, but the former, more in agreement with Paul's argument, stresses specifically the wrath of God that is personally appeased by the sacrificial death of Christ (So C. E. B. Cranfield, *A Critical and Exegetical Commentary on the Epistle to the Romans,* 1:214–17). *Linguistically,* the word may be either a *noun* or an adjective. As a noun it could mean "mercy seat" (LXX uses the word 22 times for the golden lid of the ark where the blood was applied, Exod. 25:21; also Heb. 9:5) or "propitiation" (or "propitiatory victim" [Cranfield]); as an *adjective,* the thought would be "a means of propitiation." Morris argues cogently for the latter (p. 172); F. F. Bruce (*The Epistle of Paul to the Romans,* 105) for the former position. It is difficult to settle. However, a recent Cambridge doctoral dissertation argues that the word unquestionably refers to the "mercy seat" on the ark of the covenant (Daniel Bailey, "Jesus as the Mercy Seat: The Semantics and Theology of Paul's Use of *Hilasterion* in Romans 3:25." Unpublished doctoral dissertation, Cambridge University, 1999). This is the definitive work to date on the expression. Bailey translates the verse: "God has set out Jesus openly in his blood (=death) as the mercy seat (accessible) through faith" (p. 207). Jesus is the new mercy seat for the new people of God (Jews and Gentiles). It is here that God reveals Himself to us.

12. C. A. Anderson Scott, *Christianity According to St. Paul* (New York: Cambridge Univ., n.d.), 64ff.

13. Paul's discussion of the faith of Abraham and of David (chap. 4) would then be taken as a proof of this assertion (see H. P. Liddon, *An Explanatory Analysis of St. Paul's Epistle to the Romans,* 69–70; Barrett, *The Epistle to the Romans,* 84; Bruce, 109).

14. Jubilees 23:10: "Abraham was perfect in all his deeds with the Lord, and well-pleasing in righteousness all the days of his life." In Kiddushim 4:14: "We find that Abraham our father had performed the whole law before it was given" (cited by Cranfield, 1:227). Also 1 Macc. 2:51–52: "Remember the works of the fathers, which they did in their generations . . . . Was not Abraham found faithful when tested, and it was reckoned to him as righteousness?"

15. The Greek word *logizomai* means to count, reckon, estimate, consider, ponder, credit (William F. Arndt, F. Wilbur Gingrich, and Frederick Danker *Greek-English Lexicon of the New Testament* and *Other Early Christian Literature* [Chicago: Univ. of Chicago Press, 1979], s.v.). In the papyri it frequently means "to put to one's account" (James H. Moulton and George Milligan, *Vocabulary of the Greek New Testament* [Grand Rapids: Eerdmans, 1949], s.v.). The KJV in vv. 3–11 uses "count," "reckon," and "impute" all for the same verb. From v. 6 and v. 11 it is clear that what is

credited to us is righteousness (right status or relationship), not faith.

16. Jewish thought also taught that justification was a forensic act of God, but that it only occurred at the last judgment and would be a favorable verdict based on the outweighing of the good works versus bad works (Morris, 242). In Greek usage, "to justify the wicked" would mean to *condemn* or punish the wicked (TDNT). There may be an intended advance in thought between v. 7, where the plural is used ("they"), and v. 8, where the singular occurs ("the man"). If such is the case, the first line of the psalm quotation describes God's act of forgiveness that forms the basis of His judicial act of not taking our sin into account (i.e., justification). Thus God justifies the ungodly by first forgiving them, then creating a new reality. He also transforms and empowers them so that they can act and become what they already are.

17. This is a well-known rabbinical interpretive principle known technically as *gezerah shawah* (C. K. Barrett, ed., *New Testament Backgrounds*, 146).

18. Can this section of Paul be reconciled with James 2:14–26, where James seems to argue that justification is by faith and works? In the first place, James was probably written before Romans, so it could not be an attempt to refute Paul. Second, James's use of the words "justified," "works," and "faith" is not the equivalent of Paul's. In James, justification, as in Jewish thought, looks more at the *end* of one's life and whether the works done were in conjunction with real faith in Jesus Christ (see 2:1). Paul, on the other hand, views justification at the *beginning* of one's life in Christ and counts all works before that as unacceptable meritorious deeds. Works in James are like Paul's "fruit of the Spirit" (Gal. 5:22–23); while Paul calls for "faith working through love" (Gal. 5:6 NASB), James likewise describes a "faith without works [that] is useless" (James 2:20). The essential message is the same, but the context and emphasis are different and must be carefully considered.

19. A good illustration of this is the old twenty-dollar gold piece. The seal of the United States was imprinted on the coin as a sign that it was United States currency, but the value of the coin remained the same even if it was melted down and the seal obliterated. The same seal can be impressed on an iron slug, but the presence of the sign does not alter the intrinsic worthlessness of the slug. If the person who bears the sign of the circumcision (Jew) does not have the intrinsic righteousness of faith, the sign is worthless. On the other hand, if a person has the intrinsic righteousness of faith and yet lacks the sign (Gentile), he is still accepted before God.

20. This verse has perplexed many. It certainly anticipates what Paul will develop further in 5:13–14. At any rate, it seems parenthetical to his main thought, and the rest of the argument is quite clear.

21. Abraham's faith (and it was a biblical faith) was not based on doubt or

factual uncertainty about God. This is the error of the whole neo-Protestant view of justification by faith. Faith has content and rests upon sufficient historical evidence to place it above reasonable or psychological doubt. See an excellent discussion by C. F. H. Henry, "Justification by Ignorance: A Neo-Protestant Motif?" *Journal of the Evangelical Theological Society* 13 (Winter 1970): 3–14.

22. Barrett, *The Epistle to the Romans,* 98.

23. Paul uses identical words for the parallel work of Christ in His death and resurrection. The first "for" (our offenses) seems to carry retrospective force, i.e., "for our sins" Christ was put to death. The second instance, "for our justification," could also be retrospective. However, it seems preferable to understand the last expression as prospective, "in order that we might be justified" (Bruce, 119; Barrett, *The Epistle to the Romans,* 100; John Murray, *The Epistle to the Romans,* 154). In any event, no artificial separation of the effects of the death and resurrection of Christ should be entertained.

4

THE NEW SITUATION: FREEDOM
FROM THE WRATH OF GOD

5:1–21

Chapter 5 marks a turning point in Romans. Paul now assumes the reader has accepted his argument for justification by faith, and he proceeds to spell out the implications of this new relationship of grace in the lives of the justified ones. Paul shifts from argumentative to confessional style, from the second and third persons to the first, and from the indicative-declaratory tone to the subjunctive-hortatory. To accept God's free gift of righteousness also means at the same time to accept a new lordship over the life. Chapters 5 through 8 deal with the nature and effects of this radical new life in the world founded upon the "grace" in which we stand (5:2).

Because God has dealt decisively in Jesus Christ with the twin problems of death and sin (5:12–21), a life of rejoicing and righteousness is for the Christian not a mere fancy but a genuine reality (5:1–11). For example, Christians are empowered to struggle against sin (chap. 6); they are no longer under the Mosaic Law system without the Spirit that they could never fulfill (chap. 7); and they are set free from the dominion of sin and death in order to live a new life of righteousness and hope in the power of the Holy Spirit (chap. 8).

THE BENEFITS STEMMING FROM FREEDOM FROM THE WRATH OF GOD
5:1–11

Are there any benefits or fruits in the life that result from God's act of justifying us through faith? Paul relates that peace, joy, love, and hope mark the lives of those who have been justified before God (5:1–11). Finally, in a very difficult section at the end of chapter 5 (vv. 12–21), Paul portrays an analogy between Adam and Christ where the oppressive rule of sin, death, and the law is set over against the liberating dominion of righteousness, life, and grace.

Even though certain things are clear in this section and the next, it must be admitted that the precise flow of Paul's thought in this chapter is difficult. It is clear that positive blessings accrue to the justified, such as peace (v. 1), joy (exult NASB, vv. 2, 3, 11), love (vv. 5, 8), and hope (v. 2). On the other hand, it is not clear what lies in the back of Paul's mind to evoke this emphasis. Perhaps he is thinking of an objector who doubts that the faith method of justification is safe after all. Can we really be sure, Paul, that God justifies sinners simply by faith? Such an attitude lurking beneath the surface of a person's mind could destroy any permanent rejoicing over a new status before God. In the "much more" expressions (vv. 9, 10, 15, 17, 20), Paul, in using the common argument from the lesser to the greater, appears to be trying to offset any feelings of uncertainty that his teaching may have produced.

PEACE

The first consequence of having been justified by faith is "peace with God" (v. 1). This peace is not first of all a psychological tranquility or peaceful feeling. Rather, this peace must be the experience of the real status of a person who has been justified before God. It is the opposite of being under the wrath of God (1:18). Our relationship to God has been altered in justification from those who are rebels against the law of God to those who are fully acquitted, forgiven, and empowered to a new life of obedience to God's will. Peace depicts the conscious-ness of a new, deep, personal relationship with God.[1] Of course, the inner contemplation of this objective reality can and should produce a real attitude of composure and security. Consider, for example, the results of being under the wrath of God as they are manifested in life. We experience alienation from self and oth-ers, loneliness, and lack of purpose. Not to be any longer under the wrath of God should result in a positive consciousness of reconciliation with self and others and a meaningful reorienta-tion to God's whole created order (2 Cor. 5:17). Such a peace distinctly alters our life. The thought of this kind of peace leads Paul eventually into a discussion of reconciliation (vv. 10–11).

GRACE AND JOY

On the basis of this new reality of justification, Paul can now speak of "this grace in which we now stand" (v. 2). Being totally accepted by God through faith, the believer has continu-al peace with God—the cessation of hostility—and enjoys living constantly by God's grace. For Paul, grace encompasses not only the past free gift of forgiveness through the sacrificial death of Jesus (3:24), but also the whole present and future state of the believer. Such complete provision allows us to con-tinually "rejoice." The past and the present having been thus secured, the Christian looks forward to the full manifestation of God's grace in the future; he rejoices in the "hope of the glory of God" (v. 2). The hope of glory comes before us further in chap-ter 8. Note well the nature of the new life. At the same time, it is a life both present and coming, something at hand and a reality waiting for its future fulfillment.

Note here Paul's use of the interesting term "gained access" (v. 2). In Ephesians 3:12 the same Greek word *(prōsagogēn)* is translated to give the picture of a worshiper gaining access to the holy place of God by means of a sacrifice. In nonbiblical lit-erature the term can convey the thought of the admission of ambassadors to an audience with great kings (see 1 Pet. 3:18).[2] Our relation to Christ has gained for us this access to God's grace.

Following the Civil War, a dejected Confederate soldier was sitting outside the grounds of the White House. A young boy approached him and inquired why he was so sad. The soldier related how he had repeatedly tried to see President Lincoln to tell him he was unjustly deprived of certain lands in the South following the war. On each occasion, as he attempted to enter the White House, the guards crossed their bayoneted guns in front of the door and turned him away. The boy motioned to the soldier to follow him. When they approached the guarded entrance, the soldiers came to attention, stepped back, and opened the door for the boy. He proceeded to the library where the president was resting and introduced the soldier to his father. The boy was Tad Lincoln. The soldier had gained an "access" (audience) with the president through the president's son.[3] How much more should we rejoice in our access to the grace of the King of kings!

HOPE AND SUFFERING

Christian rejoicing, however, is not directed only to the glorious future. Paul says, "We also [even] rejoice in our sufferings" (afflictions) (v. 3). We rejoice in the future hope of the glory of God, but we also rejoice in present trials. Why should trials be the occasion for joy in the Christian's life? Because they turn us away from trust in ourselves to "perseverance." But why is perseverance so valuable? Because perseverance, or endurance, is the attitude or virtue that looks beyond the immediate affliction to find its ultimate meaning in God (James 1:2–4).

Trials, rather than destroying our faith, actually develop a "character" (v. 4).[4] In a humbling type of experience, distresses turn us away from self-trust to complete trust in God. Our persevering attitude in trials brings glory to Him and thus a tried, or proven, character to us (2 Cor. 11:30; 12:9). When we are brought to the place where we have nothing else but God, we suddenly realize He is all we need. When we thus look totally to God as a result of the trials, we are assured of His approval; and that approval strengthens our hope in the glory of God (vv.

4–5). Andrew Murray has captured the thought:

First, he brought me here, it is by His
    Will I am in this strait place; in
        that fact I will rejoice.
Next, He will keep me here in His love,
    And give me grace to behave as His child.
Then, He will make the trial a blessing,
    Teaching me the lessons He intends me to learn,
        and working in me the grace He means to bestow.
Last, in His good time He can bring me out again—
    how and when He knows.

I am here (1) by God's appointment, (2) in His keeping, (3) under His training, and (4) for His time. Thus, faith, rather than being insecure because of trials, actually uses suffering to strengthen our hope in God's future glory. It is by suffering that hope is tested and strengthened.

LOVE OF GOD

Further, this hope will not prove to be misdirected hope ("does not disappoint," v. 5). We know this because we already have the foretaste of its consummation—"God has poured out his love into our hearts by the Holy Spirit, whom he has given us" (v. 5). The pouring out of the Holy Spirit seems to vividly recall Pentecost (Acts 2). The love that has been poured out and continues to grip us (Gk. *ekcheō*, to pour out like a stream) is not our love for God but God's love for us (vv. 6–8). The validity of our hope is attested by the experience of the overwhelming of our hearts by God's love. We are made aware of this love by the presence and activity of the Holy Spirit, who was given to us at conversion and continues to fill us (see John 7:37–39). This is Paul's first clear reference to the Holy Spirit in the epistle. Because everything in the Christian life depends on the Holy Spirit, Paul will develop this truth more extensively in chapter 8. He cannot leave this theme of God's love until he has said something further.

In verses 6–8 Paul elaborates on the nature of God's love, which is best described by what it does. The description offers clear proof that God loves us, sinful as we are. God's love is demonstrated supremely in the cross: "Christ died for us" (v. 8). Paul is anxious to show us the unique nature of this love. God's love is totally unmotivated by any desirable qualities in the person loved. Paul calls us "powerless" (v. 6), "ungodly" (v. 6), "sinners" (v. 8), and even "enemies" (v. 10). Although some persons may evidence their love by giving their life for a just person (or cause), what is never heard of is people dying for their enemies, yet this is precisely what Christ has done.[5]

In verse 9 Paul returns to the original thought of the paragraph, the benefits of justification. Since justification by Christ's blood is now a present reality—"We have peace with God" (v. 1)—the future is more than secured.[6] The "wrath of God" certainly refers to the future "day of . . . wrath" and judgment of God (2:5). Although salvation awaits its final consummation in the future, the evidence of God's love and grace shown in our present acquittal should more than assure us of future deliverance from the judgment of God.

Since parallel expressions are used in verses 9 and 10 for "justification" and reconciliation, we may assume they are different metaphors describing the same reality. However, the basic idea in reconciliation seems to strike another dimension of justification than Paul has indicated previously and means "to reverse an unfavorable relationship between persons." Our relationship in sin before God constitutes us as "enemies" and requires the cessation of enmity and estrangement between us and God, or reconciliation: "For if, when we were God's enemies, we were reconciled to him through the death of his Son" (v. 10) refers to the past objective removal of the obstacle between God and us. The expression "much more, having been reconciled [justified], we shall be saved by His [resurrection] life" (NASB) refers to our acceptance of God's reconciliation and looks forward again with certainty, based on the evidence of the cessation of enmity, that we will through the life of Jesus be completely delivered from God's final wrath (Rom. 4:25; Heb. 7:24–25). Note that Paul always links our whole relationship to

God (past, present, future) with Jesus Christ.

Verse 11 simply repeats the thought of verse 10 and adds Paul's note of rejoicing in the fact that we who believe in Jesus now possess this reconciliation. So Charles Wesley captures the sense in his famous hymn:

My God is reconciled,
> His pardoning voice I hear;
He owns me for His child,
> I can no longer fear;
With confidence I now draw nigh,
> And "Father, Abba, Father" cry,
> And "Father, Abba, Father" cry. [7]

Probably this idea of reconciliation, more than any other Paul has used, stresses that in justification there is a reversed relationship to God. Relationship to God affects our whole life (Col. 1:20, 22; Eph. 2:16). For Christians, a whole changed life results from a faith response to God's love gift in Christ (2 Cor. 5:19–21). Can we do otherwise than rejoice with Paul in this whole new situation of reconciliation?

ADAM AND CHRIST
5:12–21

This passage (vv. 12–21) is generally recognized to be at the same time both the most profound and the most difficult in the whole book of Romans—if not the whole New Testament. Some see the section as an abrupt, unrelated, and generally unintelligible insertion into Paul's main argument. Others strongly insist it is the high point of the whole epistle, in the light of which the whole is best to be understood.[8] Some have also charged, perhaps justly, that it is precisely at this point in the book of Romans that evangelical theology, in failing to sustain interest, has weakened its position.[9]

The master thought of the whole passage revolves around the concept of two representative "headships" (Adam and Christ) and two consequent groups of humanity, where each person is linked solidly to each other and to their respective representatives. This explains Paul's constant use of the word "one," as in "one man" (v. 12), "one man's sin . . . One man, Jesus Christ" (vv. 16–17), and so on. The point to grasp is that Paul is viewing our condition of fallenness (under condemnation), as well as our condition of being saved (acquittal), not first of all as an individual matter but, in the one instance as well as in the other, as a matter of being *in* a mediator or representative (1 Cor. 15:22, 45–49).

I remember from the early 1970s an incident that drove this point home to me. A colleague and I were visiting the University of Leiden in the Netherlands. We were met at the Skipol airport by a professor from the university. I sat in the front seat and my colleague in the back. After we had made our way out of the airport and were traveling down the highway, the professor turned to me and said, "Why did you bomb Cambodia?" I was quite startled and after a brief pause I managed to say, "Er . . . ah . . . we didn't have anything to do with it. It was President Nixon's decision." This was during the Vietnam War and Nixon had widened the war by sending B52 bombers into Cambodia. The Dutch were infuriated morally, and they held any American as responsible for what had happened as what the representative American had done. Nixon had acted for us all because of his position as the representative of the American people.

Christ has a tremendous historical significance. When Adam departed from God, because he was the representative or mediator of the whole human race, his act was not something that concerned only him as an individual. In Adam's act of disobedience, sin and death became universal in the whole historical human order. On the other hand, through Christ, the new representative or mediator of humanity, in the same all-inclusive way and even more so, divine life has become universal in the historical human order. Death in the Bible is not simply the termination of all bodily functions. Physical death ensues because of our sinfulness and ultimately negates and condemns human life. It is death indeed because we die as we have lived—in a state of rebellion against our Creator and in alienation from others.

Life, on the other hand, is not the mere continuation of bodily functions. Instead, life follows from the gift of God's grace (righteousness, acquittal) through relationship with Jesus Christ. It is life indeed because of the blessedness in this human life of being freed from the slavery of sin and death (Heb. 2:15), and because it leads on to the goal of an eternal life in this same blessedness.

Our solidarity with other human beings is a reality we often overlook in the assertion of our individuality. John Donne's oft-quoted words eloquently express the truth of human oneness:

> No man is an island, entire of itself; every man is a piece of the continent, a part of the main; if a clod be washed away by the sea, Europe is the less, as well as if a promontory were, as well as if a manor of thy friend's or of thine own were; any man's death diminishes me, because I am involved in mankind, and therefore never send to know for whom the bell tolls; it tolls for thee.[10]

If we ask whether human nature can ever be changed, Paul might answer, no and yes. In Adam the race can never be changed. But a new humanity has come to birth: the old "Adam-solidarity" of sin and death has been broken up and replaced by the new "Christ-solidarity" of grace and life. However, at the present time these two humanities overlap in the individual life of a Christian. Those who were formerly in Adam, even though now in Christ, still bear the sentence of bodily death belonging to Adam's race. But those who are in Christ have assurance that they have received from God that justification which brings resurrection life in its train.

Underlying the whole passage (vv. 12–21) may be the question of how the one man, Jesus Christ, in His death and resurrection could provide such a universal and certain hope of salvation. The subject of the reconciliation of all people in verses 10–11 has perhaps stirred the question. Paul's answer lies, strangely, in appealing not to the deity of Christ, but to His perfect humanity. Jesus was our representative or mediator in *obedience* to God as Adam was our representative in *disobedience* to God. If the first human, Adam, could bring the whole race (in him) into sin and death by one act of disobedience, likewise (more so!) the Son of Man, the Last Adam, could bring the whole race (in Him) to acquittal and life by one act of righteousness (death on the cross).

In verses 12–14 Paul first emphasizes the representative role of Adam. It may be seen in the following diagram:

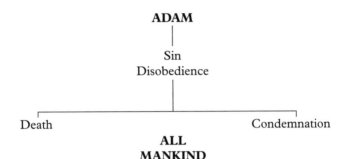

In passing, we may remark on the historicity of Adam, a debated subject in our day. If we insist on the necessity of more than the mere *idea* of a representative in Christ but the *actual,* historical figure of the human person, Jesus, as essential to the gospel, can we then eliminate the need for an actual, historical human person, Adam, in favor of the idea of a mere symbolical representative? Can the idea, rather than the actual historical reality, form the valid counterpart to the necessary reality in Christ's actual, historical significance? We believe it essential to Paul's argument that the first representative man, Adam, was as historically real as the last representative man, Christ.

Paul's expression stating the cause of universal death is: "because all sinned" (v. 12). Considerable discussion has developed over the years about the correct sense of this expression. Some argue that we all die because we all sin individually, as did Adam (Pelagian view).[11] But this explanation fails to account for why we all choose to sin and why infants still die who do not voluntarily sin. Others argue that Paul clearly intends that we see a definite connection between the sin and death of Adam and the sin and death of us all (vv. 13–15, 19). There are three main variations of this second view. The first, the more precise Augustinian, understands that we all sinned "in Adam" in the sense that we were seminally in Adam when he sinned, and thus in a sense we did what he did (cf. Heb. 7:4–10). The second more popular modification of Augustine's view takes the "because all sinned" to refer to our "solidarity" with Adam, and therefore the "all sinned" of verse 12 refers to the same events as the "one trespass" of verses 15–19—that is, the "Fall of Adam" (representative view). A third variation of Augustine sees the "all have sinned" (v. 12) to refer to everyone's actual personal sinning but as a result of their connection to Adam and his sin (contrast this with the Pelagian view above). In this third variation of Augustine, we all sin in our turn and die as a result, because we all inherit Adam's corruption. Although it is difficult to decide between variation two and variation three, we will follow the latter in the following exposition.[12]

Even in the absence of any specific divine commandments from the time of Adam to the time of Moses, universal sinfulness is evidenced, even though sin as violation of a revealed command (as in Adam and Eve's case) was not imputed to humans. But this is speculation. Paul says: "From the time of Adam to the time of Moses . . . those who did not sin by breaking a [divine] command, as did Adam . . ." (v. 14). There were no specific divine commands such as were given at Sinai. Sin was still universally and pervasively present among human beings and was death-inflicting (vv. 13–14). These verses most naturally support the view adopted above (v. 12), which understands that all human beings were corrupted in Adam's act of disobedience. Paul adds that Adam was a "type" of the One who was to come (i.e., Christ). Perhaps the word *analogy* would better suit Paul's use of the word "type," if understood as an historical counterpart. "In both cases the act of one man has far reaching consequences for all other men. It is not necessary that the ways in which the consequences follow from the acts should also be exactly parallel."[13] There really can be no adequate parallel to Christ, but Adam is the closest.

In verses 15–19 Paul sets forth in comparison and mostly by contrast the representative or mediator role of Christ to that of

Adam. Diagrammed, it might look like this:

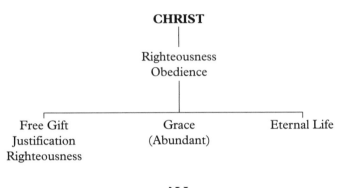

CHRIST

Righteousness
Obedience

Free Gift	Grace	Eternal Life
Justification	(Abundant)	
Righteousness		

**ALL
WHO RECEIVE
GRACE
(v. 17)**

Throughout, Paul goes out of his way to emphasize the fact that God's grace in Christ operates more inclusively and more intensively than Adam's sin and condemnation. He can only keep saying, "much more," "overflow," "abundant" in reference to Christ's work for us (vv. 15, 17, 20). Those who are touched by Adam's transgression are much more touched by the one man's act of righteousness.

Verse 17 is an important and beautiful verse. It refers to two governments, or systems (death and grace), under which all persons live: "Death reigned through that one man, . . . those who receive God's abundant provision of grace and of the gift of righteousness reign in life" (v. 17). Our chief problem is that we live under the oppressive dominion of both personal sin and a corporate system of sin. Both dominions produce in us the fear of death. But through the "abundant provision of grace and of the gift of righteousness" (v. 17), we can be released from captivity and enter into a whole new existence of acquittal and life in our new representative, Jesus Christ.

This life is available only to those who "receive" the gift (v. 17). In this way, Paul recalls all he has taught about the indispensability of faith (chap. 4). The entire passage (vv. 12–21) nei-

ther teaches universalism[14] nor strict individualism but repre-
sentationalism with individual responsibility. We got into the
mess not by individual decision alone but by relationship to our
old representative, Adam; we get out of the mess not by individual decision alone but by relationship to our new representative,
Christ. Note well how Paul teaches emphatically the necessity
of a faith response or "receiving" this grace in order for justification and life to come to us.

In verses 18–19 Paul continues the contrast between Adam
and Christ with the use of the words "all men" and "the many."
Again the problem of universalism arises. But Paul's thought is
that in Adam's trespass all of us actually came under condemnation, whereas in Christ's righteous act[15] all of us provisionally
come under acquittal, but only actually when we by faith
receive God's gift (2 Thess. 1:8–9). The "many" of verse 19
could refer to the "all" of verse 18, but the expression "the
many" refers to a group solidarity in a way that "all" does not
(Rom. 12:4; 1 Cor. 10:17). Probably this latter fact guards the
biblical doctrine of acquittal from the error of universalism
since only those who are in the "group" solidarity participate in
the results of the representative's act. Only those who by obedient faith are in "the many" of Christ's solidarity participate in
being constituted righteous before God (Mark 10:45).

But Paul, haven't you forgotten the most important historical event of all, the dispensation of the law? How does this
affect salvation-history? At this point his answer is simple and
to the point (later in chap. 7 a more elaborate answer is given):
"The law was added so that the trespass might increase" (v. 20).
Law "slipped in" (Gk. *parerchomai*) as an inferior part of God's
chief plan (i.e., the promise, Rom. 4; Gal. 3:19). Sin is revealed
in all its fullness as rebellion only in the presence of divine law.
Actually, law does not remedy the sin problem; it aggravates
and even increases it (Rom. 7:5–11). But the increase of sin
through the law cannot defeat God's grace because: "Where sin
increased, grace abounded all the more" (5:20). Finally, the
main threads of the section are summed up in verse 21 by con-
trasting the rule of sin through the tyranny of death with the
new rule of grace through righteousness (acquittal before God),

which leads to eternal life through (only through) the Lord Jesus Christ.

To summarize this section (vv. 12–21), we note that our ancestor, Adam, as the first *mediator or representative man*, plunged the whole human posterity into sin and death. From such a predicament the human race could not of itself escape. On the other hand, as a result of the appearance of the second and last *mediator or representative Man* and His unmitigated obedience to God, even to His death for others, there emerged a radically new humanity. He totally surrendered Himself to God, even to death, in order that that life which was peculiarly His as the obedient, Incarnate Son (i.e., eternal life) might spring forth to all His posterity.[16]

Our human condition in sin in the world can indeed be changed, but not by human action—only through divine intervention. Each element in this chapter converges upon the others to guarantee through God's grace the certainty of both the present love of God to us and our future security against any powers that would threaten to annul our eternal salvation. In the light of such certainty, anything less than continual rejoicing is a mockery of God's truth.

NOTES

1. Some Greek manuscripts at this point read: "let us have peace with God" (in the sense of "enjoy peace"). The change in one Greek letter in the word *(echomen* to *echōmen)* makes the verb "have" a hortatory subjunctive instead of an indicative. It is difficult to settle the matter. The context strongly favors the indicative over the subjunctive (see John Murray, *The Epistle to the Romans*, 158; Anders Nygren, *Commentary on Romans*, 193; C. K. Barrett, *The Epistle to the Romans*, 101), although some argue that the third verb (rejoice in sufferings) in verse 3 favors the subjunctive idea based on an observation of actual Christian experience, and thus all three verbs should follow the mss. that read the subjunctive. Cranfield agrees and adds that this peace, or reconciliation, with God is the theme of the whole section (*A Critical and Exegetical Commentary on the Epistle to the Romans*, 1:255). Richard N. Longenecker has argued in a recent article that this seeming little point can greatly affect the meaning of 5:1ff. and what goes before and after in the letter. He believes that in 1:16–4:25 Paul establishes what he has in common with the Jewish and Gentile Christians to whom he is writing. Whereas from 5:1–8:39 Paul is setting forth the distinctive nature of his preaching (i.e., "my gospel," 16:25) within the Gentile mission and this is his "spiritual gift" (1:11) to the Romans. If true, this

would shift the traditional view of the focus of Romans away from 1:16–4:25 (i.e., "justification by faith") to 5:1–8:39 where Paul sets forth his understanding of the gospel as including "peace" and "reconciliation" with God, that "deals with humanity's essential tension of 'death' and 'life' and that highlights the personal relationships of being 'in Christ' and 'in the Spirit.' This would make 1:16–4:25 essentially *parallel* to 5–8 where judicial and forensic categories of our salvation are complemented by language describing the same reality in more mystical and participatory terms. Chapter 8 then becomes the high point in Paul's gospel emphasis ("The Focus of Romans: The Central Role of 5:1–8:39 in the argument of the Letter," 49–69 in *Romans & The People of God*, Sven K. Soderlund & N. T. Wright, eds. Grand Rapids: Eerdmans, 1999.

2. TDNT, 1:132.

3. Abraham Lincoln, as cited by Donald G. Barnhouse, *God's River, Romans 5:1–11* (Grand Rapids: Eerdmans, 1958), 39.

4. The Greek is *dokimē*, which means an object or person who is tested and shown to be reliable, trustworthy, valuable (see 1 Cor. 3:13; 1 Pet. 1:6). In Phil. 2:22 the same word refers to the "approved" or "qualified" (for missionary service) person of Timothy.

5. The repetition in verse 7 seems redundant. There is no distinction here between a "good" person and a "righteous" person; both clauses express the same idea (Barrett, *The Epistle to the Romans*, 106; Murray, 167). See J. B. Lightfoot in Murray, 33, for the opposite view.

6. "Justified by his blood" (or at the cost of His blood) refers back to 3:25, where the emphasis is on the mercy seat nature of Christ's death. It is essential to the gospel to stress that Christ's life was poured out in death (blood) as the satisfaction for God's wrath against our rebellion. De-emphasizing the blood aspect of Christ's death tends to eliminate the wrath aspect of God's judgment upon us and the sacrificial nature of Christ's death and therefore the real significance of the gospel.

7. It is significant to note that Paul says we have *received* the reconciliation. There is a difference between the English word *reconcile* and the Greek term *(katallagē)*. In English, to speak of reconciliation as effected means that both parties (offended and offender) are mutually reunited. On the other hand, while the Greek word may also denote this same idea (see 1 Cor. 7:11), it may also convey the thought of a one-sided process where the obstacle to fellowship has been removed and the objective reconciliation offered to the offender. God is not Himself reconciled but removes the obstacle to fellowship (God's holy wrath against our rebellion) in the death of Jesus and now offers to sinful humans this reconciliation as a free gift through faith (2 Cor. 5:17–19). For this view see TDNT, 1:255ff. On the equally defensible view of dual reconciliation, see Leon Morris, *Apostolic*

Preaching of the Cross, 186ff. And see Wesley's hymn above.

8. Nygren, *Commentary on Romans,* 19.

9. Adolf Schlatter, cited in ibid.

10. John Donne, *Devotions upon Emergent Occasions* (Ann Arbor, Mich.: Univ. of Michigan, 1959), 108–9.

11. The "for that" of the KJV is *eph ho,* which means "because" (NASB, NIV). The Vulgate translation "in whom" *(in quo)* is a mistranslation but may reflect a true interpretation (F. F. Bruce, *The Epistle of Paul to the Romans,* 130). The "as" at the beginning of the section (v. 12) anticipates the completion of a comparison in a "so." The comparative "so" never seems to come. The sense, though, is clear from v. 19, where the "as" is repeated and followed with a "so" in a summary of the whole section.

12. Murray, *The Epistle to the Romans,* 186; Bruce, *Epistle of Paul,* 130; Nygren, *Commentary on Romans,* 214. See also Russell Shedd, *Man in Community* (Grand Rapids: Eerdmans, 1964), especially chap. 3; also Cranfield, *Critical and Exegetical Commentary,* 1:277.

13. Cranfield, *Critical and Exegetical Commentary,* 1:278–79.

14. Universalism is the teaching that ultimately all human creatures of God will be saved through the universal redemption of Christ. Rom. 5:18 and 1 Cor. 15:24–28 are especially appealed to for support of this teaching. Theological liberals, such as Nels Ferre, and some neo-orthodox theologians, such as Karl Barth, have in recent days advocated on different grounds the ultimate salvation of all human beings. See Bernard Ramm, *A Handbook of Contemporary Theology* (Grand Rapids: Eerdmans, 1966).

15. The Greek is *dikaiōma,* "righteous act" (TDNT). The same word occurs also in 5:18 as well as 2:26; 8:4. "Paul means not just Christ's atoning death but the obedience of his life as a whole" (Cranfield, *Critical and Exegetical Commentary,* 1:289); see also Phil. 2:6–11.

16. "Eternal life" is that distinctive *quality* of the life that was manifested in the human life of Jesus Christ (see 1 John 1:2). It is eternal in its *quality,* first of all, rather than its duration (though it does go on forever), since it is the incarnate life of Jesus Christ. This emphasis keeps us from separating eternal life from the present experience. Although it is future in one sense, it is also *now* in part in another sense (see John 5:24).

5

THE NEW SITUATION: FREEDOM FROM SIN'S CAPTIVITY

6:1–23

Paul's main argument and thesis of the letter is finished. He has advocated that all are under condemnation as rebels against God, but the Creator has intervened on behalf of all by providing acquittal and forgiveness for them through the new mercy seat, the substitutionary death of Jesus (1:18–3:31). Furthermore, he has stated that this acquittal before God initially comes to us individually irrespective of our moral virtues or lack of them. Acceptance before God comes solely by faith that trusts in the God who reveals Himself and who has acted for our salvation in Jesus' death and resurrection (4:1–25). Lastly, he has described the grounds whereby we may be continually rejoicing in assurance of our future salvation (5:1–11). Again, such certainty rests not on our moral accomplishments (law keeping), but solely on the grace of God (5:12–21). Paul even teaches that as sin increases, grace increases the more (5:20).

It is at this point that the apostle moves perilously close to the edge of an abyss—one step to the side and all that he has gained by what has preceded can be lost. For it would be easy to conclude, if we have understood Paul clearly, that, if the law is subordinate, and if grace is more manifested as sin increases, there is no reason for Christians to be morally good. Why not go on sinning that the supply of grace might be increased (v. 1)? Will not God be the more glorified because our continual sin will continually manifest His grace? This is the antinomian (complete moral freedom) error that misunderstands Christian freedom and unfortunately has been present in every era of Christianity, including today's. The grace of God in Jesus Christ is indeed freedom (Rom. 6:15–18; Gal. 4–5), but freedom *from* sin, not freedom *to* sin (1 Pet. 2:16).

A notable historical instance of the abuse of Paul's teaching can be seen in the Russian monk Rasputin, the evil genius of the Romanov family in its last years of power. Rasputin taught and exemplified the doctrine of salvation through repeated experiences of sin and repentance; he held that, as those who sin most require most forgiveness, a sinner who continues to sin with abandon enjoys each time he repents more of God's grace than any ordinary sinner.

In Paul's day, the form of the argument that abused the doctrine of justification took two twists. Paul devotes the lengthy section of chapters 6 through 8 to answering these two objections. The first is an ethical objection introduced by the question, "Shall we go on sinning so that grace may increase?" (6:1). This is answered in 6:2–14 by Paul's appeal to the reality in the believer's life of a radical inner change witnessed to in baptism and consisting in the fact of the believer's crucifixion and resurrection with Christ.

The second objection is more of a legal problem, introduced likewise by a question in 6:15: "Shall we sin because we are not under law but under grace?" Paul answers this distortion by first appealing to the true nature of Christian freedom, namely, captivity to righteousness (6:15–7:6); second, by showing the true function of the Mosaic Law (7:7–25); and third, by illuminating the nature of the life of freedom in the Spirit in chapter 8. These are the most important chapters in the entire New Testament for establishing that the Christian life is continual moral renewal and progressive holiness (sanctification).

Union with Christ in His Death and Resurrection
6:1–14

The charge (v. 1), it may be recalled, was to the effect that since more sin calls forth more grace (5:20), shall we not go on sinning to get more and more grace? Paul's first reaction is abhorrence—"By no means!" (v. 2).[1] Then he states that such a conclusion embodies an inherent contradiction: "We died to sin; how can we live in it any longer?"[2] At the outset, we can note that this fact of the Christian having died to sin is the fundamental premise of the whole argument in the chapter. The NIV unfortunately omits a special word here. We should read, "We who died . . ." The "who" of the verse is a specialized Greek form *(hoitines)* that gives this paraphrased sense: We who in our essential nature are Christians (acquitted in Christ), *we* have died. Death and life are not compatible. To be a Christian means to have died to sin. Therefore, it is a fundamental moral contradiction for a Christian to be still living in the sin to which he has died.[3]

But how did we die to sin? To answer this question, Paul uses three metaphors. He first appeals to the importance of our death to sin in the metaphor of Christian baptism. Certainly the truth of their death to sin was known to all the Christians at Rome: "Don't you know?" Yet how much of its real significance did they actually know? It may be difficult to know exactly where Paul depends upon common knowledge and where he goes beyond popular understanding to the fuller implication. But we may assume that they at least knew that to be "baptized into Christ Jesus" was equivalent to the fuller expression to be "baptized into the name of Jesus Christ" (see Matt. 28:19; Acts 2:38; 10:48; 19:5).

To be baptized into the name of Christ meant to be baptized (placed) into union with Jesus Christ. To be baptized into Moses was to come under the authority of Moses' leadership and to be a participant in all the privileges that that included (1 Cor. 10:2). To be baptized into the name of Paul meant to be baptized into the discipleship and dedication of Paul, an idea that Paul passionately rejected (1 Cor. 1:13, 15). Hence, baptism into Christ means baptism into union with Him, into dedication to Him, and into participation in all that Christ is and has done. Now if baptism means that Christians are united to Christ, it means, first of all, that we are united with Him in His death; that is, to use a second metaphor, we are co-crucified with Him (v. 6).

Furthermore, our union with Christ means that not only are we identified with Christ to the extent that we are "buried with Him through baptism into death" (v. 4), but in the same manner we are also united to Him in His resurrection (vv. 5, 8), so that now we might live (walk, conduct ourselves) in a new (resurrection) life (v. 4).[4] This new quality of resurrection life is later pointed out to be a kind of life that is lived in full obedience to the glory of God (v. 10).[5]

Paul proceeds in verse 5 to reinforce this fact that to be united with Christ means to participate both in His death and also in His resurrection life: "If we have been united with him [Gk. *symphutoi*, grown together] like this in his death [in the likeness of His death, NASB], we will certainly also be united with him in his resurrection [in the likeness of His resurrection, NASB]" (v. 5). The words "grown together" and "likeness" are very difficult to understand. This third metaphor, "grow together," may be understood in the sense of a tree graft. Again, the figure used stresses vital joining, or fusing.

But does "likeness of His death" refer to baptism or to the actual death of Christ? Probably neither. It signifies neither complete identity (that which is) nor mere similarity (that which is similar to), but a very close likeness (that which is precisely like). So it refers neither to water baptism nor to the death of Christ itself, but rather to the spiritual transformation that takes place at conversion when we become united with a death to sin precisely like Christ's. It is not required that we should die the actual physical death of Christ, but to die as Isaac did in the similitude and figure of his death; that is, to die to sin. Thus also the expression "We will certainly also be united with him in his resurrection" does not necessitate now an actual physical resurrection like Christ's but simply shows that the reality of our union with Him now in His resurrection life makes possible the distinctively new life of the Christian ("may live a new life" v. 4).[6] The form of the Christian life is both "cruciform" (shaped by the cross death of Jesus) and "resurrected" (shaped by the resurrection of Christ).

It seems that Paul has in mind in these verses *both* the inward reality of death to sin and the rite of water baptism. Water baptism, however, should be viewed in the context of the early church, where it was the means of expressing one's faith in Jesus Christ. As such, the reality and the rite are closely linked. However, it is also clear in Paul's teaching that it is a faith-response to the gospel that effects the reality of salvation, and not the rite itself (1 Cor. 1:17).[7]

More specifically, "our old self was crucified with Him" (v. 6). The old self refers to the whole unregenerate person as seen in Adam: human lifestyle under the rule of sin and death, judgment and condemnation (5:12–14). Under this figure, the radical and comprehensive nature of the changed life situation of the Christian is highlighted (Gal. 2:20; 2 Cor. 5:17). Such co-crucifixion took place for the purpose that "the body of sin might be done away with" (v. 6). The "body of sin" does not refer to the human body as such. It either refers to the individual human body in its old condition as a slave of sin[8] or, more broadly, it means the old race solidarity of sin and death that all share in Adam.[9] In either case, the emphasis lies in the distinctively new life into which we have been introduced through Jesus Christ.

This old condition was "done away with" (v. 6). The Greek verb for "done away with" is *katargeō,* meaning "to make completely inoperative" or "to put out of use." The very purpose, then, of being so united to Christ in His death is to bring about our freedom from the slavery of sin. Paul views this from the analogy of being slaves to the master of sin in our old condition, "anyone who died [with Christ] has been freed [Gk. *dikaioō,* "justified" or "acquitted"] from [the] sin [master]" (v. 7).[10]

Does this imply that Christians no longer can or do sin? Experience would answer an emphatic no. Paul also recognizes that bona fide Christians (justified ones) may in fact sin (1 Cor.

1:2, 9, 11; 3:1–4; 5:5; 6:11). What Paul is teaching is that the desirability and necessity of sin have been broken. Christians *may* sin, but the fact is that they no longer *must* sin, because this power of the sinful human life in Adam is annulled. God does not require perfect obedience to His commands (though there is no excuse for our sin), but He expects significant, substantial, and observable obedience to His revealed will (Schreiner).

But how can the broken power of sin over our lives be actually realized in our day-to-day experiences? Is the Christian life merely a negative activity of ceasing to do things we formerly practiced? Paul answers these questions by focusing attention on the positive side of our union with Christ. This is really the answer to the crucial question posed in verse 1 of why Christians should lead a moral life. In thinking of the death of Christ, our attention is immediately focused also on the historical counterpart of that death, the resurrection of Jesus.

In verses 8–10 the apostle describes the kind of death Jesus died and the kind of resurrection life He now lives. Jesus "died to sin once for all" (v. 10). Christ died once for all to the power of sin over His life. It is not that He Himself sinned, but in His total identification with us as sinners on the cross, He experienced the power of sin ruling over Him and bringing Him to death (2 Cor. 5:21; 1 Pet. 2:24). He died once in obedience to God, yet under sin's power in order that He might break the power of sin's enslavement over our lives (Rom. 8:3). Now Christ raised from the dead lives a life totally for God only (not subject again to death's power). He lives in complete obedience—He never lived otherwise—to God, yet without facing the prospects of sin and death ever again. So Christians who died this kind of death (once for all victory over the power of sin) also share with Christ in this new life (totally for God, of willing obedience to Him). If this is true, any suggestion that faith-righteousness apart from the Mosaic Law system leads us to continue living in sin and disobedience—the view apparently of some Jews and Jewish-Christians—is entirely contrary to the reality of our new relationship to Christ.

But this victory over sin in the life is not an automatic process. Paul states that we must continually (present tense) "count yourselves dead to sin [as an enslaving power] but alive to God in Christ Jesus" (v. 11). The practice of victory over enslaving sin comes not by trying harder or by self-abnegation, but by "counting." This is the same word used to describe God's "crediting" righteousness to Abraham by faith (4:3). "In Christ Jesus" we are newly related to God. This new relationship has put us in an entirely different position to the formerly enslaving sin. When a solicitation to do evil (to disobey God) confronts us, we are to count on the fact that we are now in Christ, part of a new humanity that is freed from the old captivity that led us to follow sin's dictates. Chrysostom (died A.D. 407) expressed the moral challenge in the memorable line: "If then you died in your baptism, stay dead!" Furthermore, we are alive with Christ's resurrection life to serve in obedience to God. Christ's victorious death to sin's power is also our victory; Christ's resurrection to continual life and obedience to God is also our new life.

But, one may sigh, after all, Paul, aren't we still human? Don't we live in a world full of lust and evil desires? Paul answers in verses 12–14 with exhortations based on the truth he has established in verses 1–11. The "evil desires" (Gk. *epithumiais*, desires, lust, greed) are the values and lures that lead us away from obedience to Christ (v. 12). They are the grave clothes that are carried over from the former life to the new. Specifically, they are the habits of sin learned in the old Adamic lifestyle. We must fight and rebel against sin's rule, because we are "as those who have been brought from death" (v. 13). For the Christian, life is a great paradox. We are dead to sin but still live with it; we are alive with Christ, yet still in the mortal body; we are fully righteous by God's justification, but still sinners needing to progress into full obedience to God in sanctification (v. 19). The Christian lives between two ages. We are called upon to live now in the old age as if the new age had already come. In reality, the believer through justification already participates in the future glory in Christ.

The key to this new life lies in: (1) "counting" (v. 11) and (2) "offer[ing]" (v. 13). To "offer" (Gk. *paristanō*) means to place at the disposal of another for service. As Christians, we are to stop offering our members (such as eye, hand, foot, mind, will) to sin as "instruments" against God for establishing unrighteousness. Rather, we are without delay to abandon our whole beings to God as alive in the resurrection life of Jesus and to offer our bodily members to God as weapons against evil for establishing righteousness (v. 13). Needless to say, the continual, moment-by-moment presentation of our bodily members to God can only be done after we have unreservedly presented our wills to Him. This distinction is reflected in the translation where the two different Greek tenses Paul uses for the two occurrences of the verb "offer" in verse 13 are handled differently.[11]

In verse 14, Paul states that sin will not lord it over us because we are "not under law, but under grace." What does it mean to be not under law but under grace? Although there are different views,[12] Paul probably does not have in mind the Christian's release from the moral nature of the Old Testament commandments (a view he is arguing against), but rather freedom from the Mosaic Law as a covenant system of both justification and striving after ethical goodness (sanctification). The old covenant law system causes sin to be strengthened and multiplied (5:20), because it offers nothing but condemnation to its violators (4:15; 7:10) due to the weakness of sinful human flesh (8:3). Hence, to be under the Mosaic Law covenant system is to be under enslavement to sin, because law aggravates sin and condemns the sinner, and yet in itself it has no power to deliver the transgressor. More of this later (7:1ff.).

Grace, on the other hand, stands for the whole delivering power and virtue of Christ's death and resurrection and our union with Him in that death and resurrection. Grace was manifested to remove us from the enslavement to sin by providing the power of the indwelling Holy Spirit and all that we need to serve God in obedient love. Do we see, then, how contradictory it is to ask whether we should live in sin that grace may abound?

BONDAGE TO RIGHTEOUSNESS
6:15–23

Although the moral problem of freedom from law is picked up more specifically in 7:1–6, Paul does begin in a general way to answer this obvious difficulty. He has just stated that we are free from the law and under grace (6:14). An objector might say, Well, if that's the case, Paul, can we not ignore the law and sin (violate law), since the law no longer is over us? Again Paul answers the question as before (v. 2), with an emphatic "by no means!" (v. 15). This response clearly shows that to be free from the Mosaic Law as a covenant system does not mean to be indifferent toward God's moral will. Freedom from the Mosaic Law is not freedom to sin. Without God's moral law, we lose the ability to recognize the seriousness of sin. Law without the Spirit may be powerless to prevent sin, but God's commands at least ensure that sin will be taken seriously. Since God's law reveals His will, the Christian can never be indifferent toward it. There is a sense in which Christians are not under law and another sense in which they are (Rom. 13:8–10; 1 Cor. 9:21). In our day of moral relativism and pluralism, it is especially important to listen carefully to Paul's teaching. More on this later (13:9–10).

In verses 16–23, Paul describes Christian freedom as bondage, or enslavement, to the will of God (righteousness). He employs the natural analogy ("human terms," v. 19) of the slave-master relationships to press home his point.[13] When we present ourselves willingly in obedience as someone's servant, we then become exclusively *that* master's servant and no one else's (v. 16). The slave-master analogy is quite appropriate, since no one could be the slave of two different masters at the same time. The nature of slavery precludes it. Jesus said, "No servant can serve two masters. . . . You cannot serve both God and Money" (Luke 16:13; see John 8:34). In a person's heart (religious center of human existence), only two options are available for his obedience. A person chooses as his master either sin or God. To choose to be free to follow one's own desires is actually to choose sin as master (Rom. 6:12). Sin leads ultimately to eternal death; obedience to God leads to eternal life (v. 23).

Paul is confident that the Romans have responded to that "form of teaching" (or pattern of teaching) preached in the gospel concerning obedience to God through Jesus Christ (v. 17). Note that the gospel came to them with definite content, because they became "committed" to it (Rom. 6:17 NASB; 1 Cor. 15:3).[14] We see from Paul's mention of this "form of teaching" that the gospel was not Paul's only; it was the common Christian message. The good news not only freed them from captivity to sin, but it also enslaved them to their new master, righteousness (v. 18). They were freed from sin to be servants of God and righteousness (ethical goodness, in this context).

Paul continues his exhortation to the effect that we should no longer put our bodily members at the disposal of impurity (serving one's passions, the old master), leading to more and more wickedness (moral indifference), but to offer those bodily members to the disposal of righteousness (the will of God, the new master) for "holiness" (v. 19). The term "holiness" (Gk. *hagiasmos,* better: "sanctifying") is part of a word group in the New Testament including the words "holy," "saint," "purify," "hallowed," and "holiness." It means, first of all, to be set apart wholly for the use, or service, of God. Secondly, it means to acquire, because of this relationship, certain moral qualities of the one to whom we are set apart (i.e., God). Sanctification proceeds from and is inseparably bound to justification, as fruit from the vine, and never justification from sanctification (i.e., the tree from the fruit). The process of sanctification is the work of the Holy Spirit, and Paul will develop this in chapter 8.

Finally, the passage stresses again the contrast between obedience to sin (as a master) in the former non-Christian life and obedience to God (as new master, vv. 20–23). The service done for sin and the service done for God each produces its own reward, or fruit, and also its own end (final) product. Sin's fruit consists in things of which the Christians are now ashamed and leads ultimately to (eternal) death (v. 21). God's fruit, on the other hand, consists in sanctification (ethical goodness) (Rom. 6:19; Gal. 5:22–23) and ultimately leads to eternal life (v. 22). To sum up, Paul states that the old sin master (life in Adam,

5:12–14) pays the ultimate wages of death.[15] Sin is a deceiver; it offers life and ends up paying death. As the "wages" are a continuous process, "death" may be thought of as not only the ultimate pay, but also as casting its shadow back into the present existence. On the other hand, the free gift of God (not wages) offers finally eternal life in Jesus Christ our Lord (v. 23), which also casts its shadow back into this life.

So the new rule of grace through justification by faith leads not to a life lived in sin but to a new life with Christ in the service of righteousness (God's will). The rule of sin under the Mosaic Law covenant system that enslaved us has now been broken and replaced by the rule of grace. But the Christian takes sin seriously because grace, rather than freeing us to be servants of our own sinful passions, has instead enslaved us to God and His righteousness, with the result of fruitful service and ethical sanctification.

The keynote, then, for the Christian life is single-minded obedience to God's will revealed in Jesus Christ our Lord. The controversial German theologian Dietrich Bonhoeffer has written some noncontroversial words about this costly grace:

> Cheap grace means the justification of sin without the justification of the sinner . . . who departs from sin and from whom sin departs. Cheap grace is not the kind of forgiveness of sin which frees us from the toils of sin. Cheap grace is grace without discipleship, grace without the cross, grace without Jesus Christ, living and incarnate. Costly grace is the grace of Christ Himself, now prevailing upon the disciple to leave all and follow Him. When he spoke of grace, Luther always implied as a corollary that it cost him his own life, the life which was for the first time subjected to the absolute obedience of Christ. Happy are they who, knowing that grace, can live in the world without being of it, who, by following Jesus Christ, are so assured of their heavenly citizenship that they are truly free to live their lives in this world.[16]

But what about this matter of the Mosaic Law (6:14)? How did we get from Mosaic Law covenant rule to righteousness rule? What about the Mosaic Law then? Isn't it a bad deal after all? Why was the Mosaic Law covenant given? We must hear Paul further in chapter 7 for these answers.

NOTES

1. See note 35 of chapter 2.

2. Cranfield distinguishes four different senses in which Christians die to sin, and corresponding to them, four different senses in which they are raised up: (1) died to sin in God's sight (*juridicial* sense, v. 2); (2) died to sin in their baptism (*baptismal* sense, v. 3), (3) die to sin daily by the mortification of their sinful natures (*moral* sense, v. 11); and (4) will die to sin finally and irreversibly when they actually die—and just as finally and irreversibly at Christ's coming, when they will be raised up to the resurrection life (*eschatological* sense, vv. 5b, 7) *A Critical and Exegetical Commentary on the Epistle to the Romans,* 1:299–300.

3. To "live" in sin suggests not occasional sin but to have sin as the moral atmosphere that our lives breathe (E. H. Gifford, "Romans," in *The Bible Commentary: New Testament,* 3:125).

4. The assumption of many to the effect that Paul has in mind by the use of the word "buried" the immersionist mode of baptism is strongly inferred but not necessarily warranted. There does not seem to be similar imagery in the uses of "united" (fused) (v. 5) or "crucified" (v. 6). Baptism itself signified full identification with Christ in His death to sin. One could see baptism as immersion if water baptism signified *only* death (under the water) and not also resurrection. Such may actually be the case. Infant baptism was not generally practiced in the New Testament church (Peter Stuhlmacher, *Romans,* 91).

5. From this point onward Paul drops the figure of baptism and speaks directly about our identification with Christ's death and resurrection. One of the major assumptions about baptism upon which these verses depend is that baptism is always linked closely with the conversion experience (faith in Christ), not as the efficacious element in justification, otherwise Paul would have dealt with it in chapters 3–5 (see Acts 10:48; 1 Cor. 1:18), but more as the seal or symbol of the righteousness given by faith (see Rom. 4:11). A true symbol is not the reality itself but points to something beyond itself as the actual reality. But there is a sense in which a symbol participates to some extent in the reality to which it points. Water baptism is the symbol that points to the already established reality of the codeath. While some argue for just Spirit baptism in this passage (W. H. Griffith-Thomas, *Commentary on St. Paul's Epistle to the Romans* [Grand Rapids: Eerdmans, 1946]), almost all commentators understand Paul to be referring only to water baptism. Probably *both* are in view. See the excellent discussion of this passage in James D. G. Dunn, *Baptism in the Holy Spirit* (Naperville, Ill.: Allenson, 1970), 139–51; also Moo, *Romans,* 362–63.

6. Gifford, "Romans," 127.

7. George R. Beasley-Murray, *Baptism in the New Testament* (London: Macmillan, 1962), 271–73.

8. Gifford, "Romans," 128.

9. F. F. Bruce, *The Epistle of Paul to the Romans*, 139.

10. Some see here (v. 7) a reference to a general maxim that we are no longer liable for supposed sins committed after our actual death (H. P. Liddon, *An Explanatory Analysis of St. Paul's Epistle to the Romans*, 111). Paul, however, speaks of our spiritual death to sin with Christ in baptism (Cranfield, 1:311).

11. There is a play on the Greek tenses in the two occurrences of "offer" in v. 13. In the first instance, the present tense is used with the negative. The sense is "stop offering." In the second instance, the Greek aorist tense is used with the effect of an immediate decisive, and final act: "offer yourself at once forever." It should also be noted that "righteousness" as Paul uses the term in this verse carries with it the idea of ethical goodness.

12. At least four prominent views can be identified: (1) not under the law's *authority;* (2) not under the law's *condemnation* of sinners, (3) not under the law's *justification* for obedience to it; and (4) not under the law's *contractual obligations* (see Richard N. Longenecker, *Paul, Apostle of Liberty,* 145–48). Good interpreters hold all four of the views (see Cranfield, *A Critical and Exegetical Commentary,* 1:319–20).

13. This is certainly Paul's point in verse 19 when he says, "I am speaking in human terms (NASB)," or in human illustration.

14. Actually the verb is passive in voice and second person plural. The NASB and NIV correctly render: "to which [pattern of doctrine] you were entrusted." They were delivered to the teachings of the Word of God, which created them in Christ and ruled their life. It is still true, however, that this body of truth was also delivered unto them (see 1 Cor. 11:23; 15:3; 2 Thess. 3:6).

15. The Greek *opsōniōn*, wage or pay, used especially for military service as a *bare* allowance (TDNT); see Luke 3:14; it was used also for slaves (James Hope Moulton and George Milligan, *The Vocabulary of the Greek Testament* [Grand Rapids: Eerdmans, 1959]).

16. Dietrich Bonhoeffer, *Cost of Discipleship*, 47.

6

THE NEW SITUATION: FREEDOM FROM THE MOSAIC LAW'S DOMINATION

7:1–25

This chapter continues to answer the objection that to be under the rule of grace and not law is to be indifferent toward sin. Paul has already answered this objection in one aspect by showing that the Christian is free from sin only to be a slave of God and righteousness (6:15–23). Previously, Paul has simply made assertions about the law: "Now we know that whatever the law says, it says to those who are under the law, so that every mouth may be silenced, and the whole world held accountable to God. Therefore no one will be declared righteous in his sight by observing the law; rather, through the law we become conscious of sin" (3:19–20); "Do we, then, nullify the law by this faith? Not at all! Rather, we uphold the law" (3:31); "Law brings wrath. And where there is no law there is no transgression" (4:15); "The law was added so that the trespass might increase" (5:20); "Shall we sin because we are not under law but under grace?" (6:15).

Paul's statements about the law seem to contradict one another. On the one hand, he obviously takes the law (that is, the Jewish law as contained in the Old Testament, especially the Mosaic) to be the definitive expression of God's will for the ordering of human life (2; 3:31). On the other hand, he maintains that the Mosaic Law does not enable us to escape the sinful and earth-oriented existence in which we find ourselves (3:20; 4:15; 5:13, 20).

Chapter 7 provides some clues in reconciling these apparent opposite polarities.

The history of the controversy over the function of the law in the Christian life is long and varied. Luther viewed the law as playing only a twofold negative role: (1) Its *civil* function is to restrain sin by threatening punishment, and (2) its *theological* function is to increase sin, especially in the conscience, and show us how corrupt we actually are. Calvin, on the other hand, attempted to synthesize gospel and law and saw its primary purpose for the Christian as *didactic,* or *instructional,* to help us to understand God's will and to excite us to obedience. Paul Althaus, a contemporary German theologian, has in recent days suggested another thesis. He understands the New Testament to teach that God's loving commands that express His desire for our fellowship have through the Fall become law, and as such are negative and prohibitive rules that condemn us. Yet through the gospel the same law is transformed once again into the loving commands of God. In this sense, he would concur with Calvin that the Christian is free from legalism but not from the commands.[1] Not to clarify this distinction between law and legalism can lead to two extremes: (1) modern forms of legalism or (2) pure license to sin in the name of "freedom."

In more recent times, the relationship of law or commands to Christian ethics has received renewed interest because of the popular teaching of the situation ethicists, who maintain that the only absolute moral norm for the Christian life is love. To the situationist, such as Joseph Fletcher, to be governed by the norm of divine commands is legalism. According to him, if I determine that love (as I understand it) is better fulfilled by setting aside one or all of the divine norms in any given situation, I am at liberty and must set them aside.[2] Since the apostles rejected moral lawlessness (1 John 3:4–6), the question of the Christian's relationship to the standard of God may be crucial in understanding who are authentically Christ's disciples today.

THE MARRIAGE ANALOGY
7:1–6

The question of why sin will not enslave us because we are under grace and free from the Mosaic Law (6:14) comes to the fore. It is for Paul the most important and yet the hardest point in his extended discussion. First, the general truth is stated that it is the nature of law (of any kind) to have power over us only as long as we live (v. 1). For example, the law of marriage (either Jewish or Roman) binds two people together as long as both are alive. But if the husband (or wife) dies, the law that binds the two in marriage is canceled, and in this case the widow is no longer under obligation to the law of marriage. She would be morally and legally considered an adulteress if, while her husband was alive, she was to join herself to another man; but, when her husband is dead, she is no longer bound by the law and may marry another (vv. 2–3).

Thus far, this is all Paul has said. His point is not to teach for or against divorce (and remarriage) in this context. He simply wants to illustrate the fact that in commonly accepted terms, death sets aside marriage law obligations.

But what does it mean? We should not attempt to press Paul's analogy into a full allegory (where every part has an analogous counterpart), or it will not be completely appropriate. In the application of the analogy that he gives in verse 4, the Christian corresponds to the woman in the illustration, and the law to the husband. As the law binding a woman to a man is set aside by the man's death, so the Mosaic Law covenant to which we formerly owed allegiance is set aside through our dying with Christ. A death having taken place allows a new marriage to ensue (i.e., to the risen Christ). Whereas we were formerly bound by the old covenant law (of Moses), now we have "also died to the law through the body of Christ,"[3] and we are free to be united to another Lord, "to him who was raised from the dead" (v. 4). The thought parallels chapter 6:5–8 and Galatians 2:19–20: "For through the law I died to the law so that I might live for God. I have been crucified with Christ and I no longer live, but Christ lives in me." Why was death to the law necessary? So that the "fruit" of the Spirit might spring forth (Rom. 7:4, 6).

Why was the law not able to bring life and fruit for God? Because before we were Christians when we were "controlled by the sinful nature" (Gk. *sarx,* "the flesh"[4]), the passions or impulses connected with sins were aroused in us through the law (v. 5). These passions used our bodily members to produce thoughts and acts characterized by death. It is the same idea that Paul developed in 6:20–22, with the added connection in this context between law and sin. Such was our condition—outside of Christ, grace, and the Spirit. "But now" (v. 6) that we are Christians, married to the resurrected Christ, we have been released (v. 2) from the Mosaic Law system that held us captive. "The new way of the Spirit" (v. 6) is a reference to the Holy Spirit (chap. 8), who effects the newness of life in service to God; while the "old way of the written code" refers to the legalistic approach to the written tables of the Law (2 Cor. 3:14), which were powerless to effect a righteous life before God because in the context of the whole law system they brought condemnation without the Spirit's enablement. But how or in what sense did the law of God hold us "bound"? (v. 6).

Paul with some of his Jewish contemporaries had believed that in the keeping of the law was found the only way to acceptance and peace with God (Deut. 4:1; 6:25; Rom. 7:10). As a legalist in pursuit of God's justification (righteousness), he attempted to keep the strict legal observances of the whole law (Phil. 3:6). Now Paul views the moral law as God's standard, but also in a negative fashion as arousing sin (5:20; 7:8) and leading a person to death and condemnation (7:9–10; 2 Cor. 3:7, 9). Why had his view of the Mosaic Law been so radically reversed? The only adequate answer lies in his confrontation with the risen Lord on the Damascus Road and his acceptance of Jesus as the Christ of God (Acts 9). The law had been fulfilled by Jesus.

But how did this change his view of the law? Something like this: Jesus was alive! This meant that God had accepted Him, and the curse of the cross was not Jesus' own but ours (Gal. 3:10–13). Paul had kept the law blamelessly, yet he had agreed in the justice of the crucifixion of the young Nazarene carpenter! He kept the law (he thought) and yet was still the "chief of sinners," because he persecuted those who believed on Jesus as the Messiah (1 Tim. 1:13, 15). The law then had not made him righteous before God, because he had misappropriated it as the occasion for sinful boasting in his own goodness. The law had worked just the opposite effect in Paul from what he had supposed. Instead of making him righteous before God, it really had condemned him. How then does sin pervert the right use of the law?

THE TRUE NATURE OF THE LAW
7:7–25

Actually Paul found in his experience that the law that promised to promote life instead provoked sin in him, and as sin increased death ruled. How so? When the law was originally given to Israel at Sinai (Exod. 20), it also offered the promise of life for those who did the law (Deut. 4:1). Yet in Paul's view, "if a law had been given that could impart life, then righteousness [acquittal and life] would certainly have come by the law [of Moses]" (Gal. 3:21). But something is wrong. The big problem is that all of us are transgressors of the law (Gal. 3:22). *Life*, under the old Mosaic covenant system of law, was only guaranteed to those who fulfilled perfectly the requirements of God's commands (Gal. 3:12; Lev. 18:5).

To break the law in one point was to be a transgressor of the whole law, and no transgressor of the law could receive life on the basis of lawkeeping (James 2:10). The effect of breaking one of the commandments of the law is not like the effect of breaking one of the bristles on a broom, where we can go on sweeping pretty well even with broken bristles. The effect of breaking a commandment is more like that of breaking a pane of tempered window glass; break it in one place and you shatter the whole glass. God does not grade on the curve! For breaking the Mosaic Law, the "curse" of the law fell on human life (Deut. 11:26–28; 27:26; 28:15–68).[5]

Paul interprets the curse of the law as ultimately involving condemnation and eternal death (Rom. 5:15, 18). Under such a law-principle of justification, our condition was hopeless. But God intervened through Christ, who, though He was born under the law, was not condemned by it because He fulfilled it (Matt. 5:17). Therefore, when Jesus died, He bore the curse of the law in His own body for us (Gal. 3:13). God took the condemnation that the law brought to us because of our violations and nailed it to Jesus on the cross (Col. 2:14; 2 Cor. 5:21; 1 Pet. 2:24). So in Christ's death we died to the slavery of the law's condemning finger, and we now serve God through the Spirit without any fear of condemnation for violating one of God's commands (8:1).

Wasn't the Mosaic Law, then, actually a bad thing ("sin," v. 7)? Paul's answer is emphatically no—"may it never be!" (NASB) "The Law is holy, and the commandment is holy and righteous and good" (v. 12 NASB). He must steer a close course between the twin perils of legalism and moral indifference to divine law. On the one hand, Paul affirms emphatically that there is nothing wrong with the law ("spiritual," v. 14), yet the law proves in experience to be powerless to rescue us from our sinful predicament. The problem is not the law; it is the sinful nature it has to work on that is the culprit. Even Rembrandt is powerless painting on tissue paper. Can we blame the anchor if the boat drifts when anchored in loose mud?

In verses 7–13 Paul seizes on the tenth commandment, against coveting, to illustrate how the holy command working on the sinful nature of man actually produces "every kind of covetous desire" (v. 8). Sin uses the good command as an "opportunity." The Greek *work (aphormē)* is often used in military and commercial contexts to denote the base of operations for an expedition or a war.[6] Sin launched an attack against us and viciously and deceptively used the commandment as a foothold for the advance.

When a harmless balloon filled with warm water is brought near a coiled rattlesnake, the snake strikes out at the heat and releases its poisonous venom into the balloon. Until the balloon is presented, the poisonous venom lays dormant in the glands of the snake, but the balloon provides the "occasion" for the release of the poison into plain view. Similarly the Mosaic Law without the Spirit, while good in itself, has the effect of drawing out the poison of our sin into deliberate acts of rebellion against God. In Bunyan's *Pilgrim's Progress,* the pilgrim, Christian, is taken by Interpreter into a large room (the heart) full of dust (sin). A man (law) comes to sweep with a broom, causing the dust to stir up so much that Christian is almost suffocated.[7]

Verses 7–12 describe Paul (and Jews coming under the Mosaic Law as well as all of us) either in his boyhood experience or in his experience as a Pharisee afflicted with guilt (also Israel when the law came at Mount Sinai). When a Jewish boy becomes old enough to assume his own responsibility for the commandments *(Bar Mitzvah),* he may discover also a new desire to enter into the prohibited world upon which God has placed what seems to him to be an unwarranted restraint.[8] Thus, in attempting to keep the commands of God without Christ's grace and the power of the Holy Spirit, he dies in the experience of disillusionment and disappointment. For instead of receiving life through the commands, he experiences death because he cannot find the power to perform the commandment and is thus separated from his Creator (vv. 9–10). But Paul hastens to emphasize that the fault lies not with the commandment, because it is a true expression of God's will, but with our sinful nature that takes the good command and through it brings death to us (vv. 11–12). Sin through the command is revealed in all its rebellious character (v. 13). Like an MRI diagnostic scan or an X-ray photograph, the law reveals the cancer of sin within us. Truly the law is "spiritual" in that it comes from the Spirit of God and is a true expression of His will (v. 14). God's law came that we might recognize our sin (3:20; 7:7).

We have deliberately avoided until this point the chief interpretive problem of this chapter, which has produced numerous divergent views. Here is the problem: When Paul uses the first person singular *I* (vv. 7–25) and the present tense (vv. 14–25), is he referring to his own experience as an unbeliever under the law (as believed by most of the church fathers) or to his experience as a Christian? Although the question of when this experience occurred is not really Paul's main point,[9] it has deeply bothered Christians from the earliest times to the present. In a lecture on Paul's description of himself as being "sold under sin," Dr. Alexander Whyte said,

> As often as my attentive bookseller sends me on approval another new commentary on Romans, I immediately turn to the seventh chapter. And if the commentator sets up a man of straw in the seventh chapter, I immediately shut the book. I at once send the book back and say, "No thank you. That is not the man for my hardearned money."[10]

It is also possible to take "I" in verses 7–13 to speak of Paul the unbeliever (and all unbelievers) and the "I" in verses 14–25 of Paul the Christian (and thus all Christians; Barrett, Murray, and Cranfield following Calvin). In a previous edition of this commentary I adopted this view, but I have now changed my mind! I believe the "I" throughout the whole passage (vv. 13–25) refers to both Paul and Israel. It is at the same time autobiographical for Paul but also paradigmatic of Israel's experience under the Mosaic Law without the Spirit (so Moo, Schreiner, and Thielman). See below for the exposition of this position.

If we dismiss the less likely position that Paul's "I" in verses 14–25 is merely a general reference to the human race or the Hegelian progress of history view of Stauffer, or to Adam,[11] there are traditionally three possible interpretations: (1) Paul (and all of us), the non-Christian Pharisee under the law (Greek fathers, Sanday and Headlam), (2) Paul (and all of us), the normal Christian (Augustine, Bruce, Murray), and (3) Paul (and all of us), the carnal Christian (W. H. Griffith-Thomas). Some have suggested that the reason there is no unanimity among commentators on this point of interpretation is that the passage relates an autobiographical experience, and depending on our own pre-Christian and Christian experience, we will lean toward interpreting Paul's experience in accord with our own.

Let us examine these traditional views more closely before a fourth more acceptable view to this commentator is explained. Those who favor view number one will cite the expressions in the passage that are felt to be incompatible with the Christian state: "I am unspiritual, sold as a slave to sin" (v. 14); "the evil I do not want to do—this I keep on doing" (v. 19); "making me a prisoner . . . wretched man I am!" (vv. 23–24). In favor of view number two are the expressions thought to be incompatible with a non-Christian experience: "I delight in God's law" (v. 22); "I myself in my mind am a slave to God's law" (v. 25); "the good I want to do" (v. 19). In favor of view number three is the fact that the person described seems to desire the good and hate the evil, but he lacks the power to overcome evil and ends in despair (vv. 18, 24). Since there is no reference to the Holy Spirit in chapter 7 (except possibly verse 6), it is obvious to those who argue for this third view that Paul describes himself as a Christian who is trying to live for God in the power of the flesh by law conformity. Thus, in the mind of those who feel the section describes the carnal Christian, Paul's main point is the inability of the law in itself (i.e., as a total *system*) to effect fruit unto God.

Although no view of the passage (vv. 7–25) is free from problems, there is a view that is gaining in popularity and that addresses the main difficulties in the previous views and seems to fit better the context of chapters 6–8. In this fourth view, the "I" of the section (vv. 7–25) is both an autobiographical reference to Paul's experience, and also at the same time a reference to Israel's experience under the Mosaic covenant. By extension it would refer to other Jews or Jewish-Christians than Paul and also to Gentiles who try to live under the Mosaic Law. Paul's burden is to show why the old Mosaic law-covenant without the Spirit was impotent to effect righteousness in the lives of those who lived under its demands (Moo, Thielman, Schreiner).

It is clear that there is a conflict, or battle, described in verses 15–25, which leads to total defeat and captivity to sin (vv. 14, 23). It is understandable that many Christians have found here something of their own continuing struggle and frequent defeat when battling temptation and sin in their lives. However, while not advocating that Christians attain sinless perfection or have no struggle with sin in their lives, the picture of Spirit-indwelt Christians ending up totally defeated and in captivity to sin— "making me a prisoner of the law of sin" (v. 23)—is unacceptable. Rather, what Paul is describing is his Jewish experience (and Israel's also) under the Mosaic Law, which demonstrates his view of the Mosaic law-covenant's inability to free us from the bondage of the rule of sin and death in our lives. This bondage can only be broken through the new covenant, which brings forgiveness in Christ's death, the new mercy seat, and the impartation of the Holy Spirit who enables us to keep the law (8:4).

Perhaps a few comments on words and meanings in verses 14–25 will help to draw this tedious discussion to a fruitful conclusion.

In verse 14, "unspiritual" (Gk. *sarkinos,* fleshy, weak) means sinful and transitory.[12] "Sold into bondage" (literally, under sin) refers to the captivity produced in us by sin working through the good law (see also v. 23). "I do not understand" (Gk. *ginōskō* of verse 15 reveals that Paul is perplexed by the strange way the Mosaic Law works on his sinful nature: He cannot practice what he desires (the law of God). Instead Paul (and Israel) ends up doing what he hates, which proves that he agrees in his conscience that the law is good even though he does not do it (v. 16).

The contrast between "I" and "sin living in me" in verse 17 should not be made the basis for any profound psychological theory. The statements should be understood as popular terms to describe Paul's inward conflict under the Mosaic law-covenant, and not a technical development of a particular theory of psychology.

In verse 18 the sense of the last clause is helped if we read: "but the power to perform the good is not." Verses 21–23 contain several references to "law." "In God's law" (v. 22) and "the law of my mind" (v. 23) are definite references to the Mosaic Law. "The principle" (v. 21 NASB) and "the law of sin" (v. 23) refer to a type of counterfeit law, or principle, operating in the sinful flesh that makes war on the true law of God and takes those under the Mosaic Law captive to do its evil bidding. In verse 23 the expression "making me a prisoner" refers to making military prisoners in the sense that sin, warring against God's will in my life, wins the victory and through law makes me a prisoner (see Luke 4:18; Eph. 4:8; 2 Cor. 10:5). For Americans, the prisoner of war experiences in Vietnam make this image more meaningful to our day.

"Wretched man" (v. 24) is Paul's wail of anguish; it is a very strong term of misery and distress. "This body of death" (v. 24) refers to the human body (good by creation) that through sin and the condemnation of the Mosaic Law has fallen under the dominion and condemnation of death. Paul's misery is due to a frustrated condition but not a divided self. He wants to serve God's commands in the Mosaic Law (vv. 15, 19, 21, 22, 25), but he finds his desire frustrated by the irrationality of his actual performance. He cries out for release from the sinful nature. As Tennyson, in *Morte d'Arthur*, cried, "O for a new man to arise within me and subdue the man that I am." But where can such release be found? Paul knows the answer because he writes as a Christian indwelt by the Holy Spirit: "Thanks be to God [release comes] through Jesus Christ our Lord" (v. 25). In another place Paul uses the exact same expression as a reference to the future bodily resurrection of the dead at Christ's return (1 Cor. 15:57). Those who believe verses 14–24 refer to Paul the Christian living the normal Christian life believe this proves their case that only at the resurrection will believers be delivered from this frustrated, defeated experience with sin. However, the reference can just as well be seen as *also* Paul's thanksgiving and anticipation of the realities he will present in 8:1–4 concerning the new covenant provision of the enabling presence of the Holy Spirit to give us victory. The present work of the Holy Spirit in the believer, which anticipates in a small measure the glorious future deliverance, enables him to partially rise above the weaknesses of the sinful flesh and live unto righteousness (chap. 8).

It may be argued that if Paul was indeed moving toward a conclusion in the chapter that would prepare his readers for an entirely new emphasis in chapter 8, he most certainly would have ended on the triumphant note of 25a. But he closes the discussion by giving what appears to be his (and Israel's) present experience: "I myself with my mind [inward man, spirit] am serving the law of God, but . . . with my flesh [I serve] the law of sin" (NASB). By ending thus, he emphasizes that the Mosaic Law (and all law) cannot deliver us from the rule of sin over our lives. It can only make things worse. Paul will argue for a totally different way to please God and to fulfill His law (commands) in the next section (8:1ff.). Here, as in Galatians 5:16–18, Paul will argue for a continuing struggle with sin in the believer's life, with the experience of a "substantial, significant, and observable victory over sin" yet without sinless perfection.[13]

NOTES

1. Paul Althaus, *The Divine Command*, trans. Franklin Sherman (Philadelphia: Fortress, 1966). A short but helpful Lutheran treatment of the law before and after conversion.

2. Joseph Fletcher, *Situation Ethics* (Philadelphia: Westminster, 1966). A popular treatment of this viewpoint.

3. Bo Reicke offers help in the difficult elements of the analogy when he suggests that instead of Paul having one idea in mind, two different motifs become blended in the argument: the law that has died to the Christian and the Christian who has died to the law. (JBL LXX [1951] 267. Cited by Richard N. Longenecker, *Paul, Apostle of Liberty* [Grand Rapids: Baker, 1976], 146).

4. Paul uses "in the flesh" (Gr. *sarx*) in at least two different senses, depending on the context. Christians are in the flesh in the sense of being in the mortal body (2 Cor. 4:11; 10:3; Gal. 2:20; Phil. 1:22, 24); yet they are no longer in the flesh in the sense of being dominated by sin, death, and law (Rom. 7:5; 8:9; Gal. 3:3; 5:24).

5. The law consisted also in a gracious provision for forgiveness of sins through the sacrificial ceremonies (Lev. 1–7). When an Israelite had sinned in violation of the law, his sin could be atoned for by the offering of a blood sacrifice. But God's purpose for the moral law remained the same until the coming of Christ (Gal. 3:21–22; Heb. 9:24–25; 10:1). The latter verse in Hebrews reminds us that the law did contain a "shadow" of good things to come in the gracious sacrificial system that pointed toward Christ.

6. W. F. Arndt, F. W. Gingrich, and F. Danker, *Greek-English Lexicon of the New Testament*, s.v. *"aphormē."* Käsemann reminds us that in Jewish tradition the tenth commandment was the core and summary of the law (*Commentary on Romans*, 194). Also Thomas Schreiner quoting J. A. Ziesler who adds further that the reference to the tenth commandment where inward desires are included in the same manner in which Jesus does (Matt. 5:21–48), *The Law*, 153. So also Frank Theilman, *Paul and the Law;* and

Moo, *Romans*, 438–39.

7. John Bunyan, *The Pilgrim's Progress*, new ed. (New York: Dutton, 1954), 31–32.

8. Paul's references to "coveting" (lust), "commandment," "life," "death," and "deceived" in these verses are strongly suggestive of the whole account of our first parents' original fall into sin recorded in Gen. 3. Cranfield downgrades the *Bar Mitzvah* explanation and argues that Paul is describing mankind's experience before the giving of the law (*A Critical and Exegetical Commentary on the Epistle to the Romans*, 1:351).

9. Paul's main point is to answer the charge that his teaching about not being under the Mosaic Law makes the law sin (v. 7).

10. Cited by F. F. Bruce, *The Epistle of Paul to the Romans*, 151.

11. TDNT, s.v. "ego."

12. Arndt, Gingrich, and Danker, *Greek-English Lexicon of the New Testament*, 743–44.

13. For a quite convincing attempt to argue for the view that in 14–25 it is Paul, the fleshly or carnal Christian see David Wenham, "The Christian Life: A Life of Tension?—A Consideration of the Nature of Christian Experience in Paul," chap. 6 in *Pauline Studies*, D. A. Hagner and M. J. Harris, eds. (Grand Rapids: Eerdmans, 1980). For a recent attempt to argue that 14–25 describes the normal Christian life in the Spirit see James I. Packer, "The 'Wretched Man' Revisited: Another Look at Romans 7:14–25," 70–81 in *Romans & The People of God*, Sven K. Soderlund and N. T. Wright, eds. (Grand Rapids: Eerdmans, 1999). Also for the view that Paul's experience under the law was not negative or guilt-ridden, see Krister Stendahl, "Paul and the Introspective Conscience of the West" in his *Paul Among Jews and Greeks* (Philadelphia: Fortress, 1980), 78–96.

7

THE NEW LIFE OF THE SPIRIT

8:1–39

The cry of Paul in 7:24, "What a wretched man I am! Who will rescue me from this body of death?" is now answered: "through [lit. "in"] Christ Jesus the law of the Spirit of life set me free from the law of sin and death" (v. 2). This new-life principle of the Spirit enables those who are acquitted *in Christ* (1) to live without "condemnation" (v. 1); (2) to fulfill the moral law (v. 4); (3) to rise above the operating principle of sin and death (v. 2); and (4) to enjoy life and peace (v. 6). In this chapter Paul describes many of the gifts and graces of the Holy Spirit, who now enables Christians to experience in part what they will have in full at Christ's return.

Romans chapter 8 has been called one of the greatest chapters in the Bible. If the Bible were a ring and Romans the jewel in the center, then chapter 8 would be the sparkling point of the jewel. Charles Erdman has splendidly captured the excitement of entering onto this holy ground:

> If the Epistle to the Romans rightly has been called "the cathedral of Christian faith," then surely the eighth chapter may be regarded as its most sacred shrine, or its high altar of worship, of praise, and of prayer. . . . Here, we stand in the full liberty of the children of God, and enjoy a prospect of that glory of God which some day we are to share.[1]

Truly spoken, for the chapter begins with "in Christ Jesus" (v. 1) and ends with "in Christ Jesus our Lord" (v. 39); it begins with *no condemnation* (v. 1) and ends with *no separation* (v. 39).

The undoubted emphasis in chapter 8 is upon the life indwelt by the Holy Spirit. Prior to this point in the letter there are only three references to the Holy Spirit, but in this chapter the Holy Spirit is mentioned some twenty-one times, more than in any other chapter in the whole Bible. This life in the Spirit is characterized as a life in which the establishment and fulfillment of God's will is evident (vv. 4, 12–14), a life that here and now bears the promise of resurrection and eternal life (vv. 6, 10–17), a life that is lived in hope (vv. 17–30), and a life that triumphantly experiences here and now the love of God in the midst of life's kaleidoscope of sufferings, joys, failures, injustices, losses, and successes (vv. 31–39).

Paul's long argument in vindication of the moral nature of the faith method of justification (6:1–7:25) now reaches its clearest and fullest statement in verses 1–11. Contrary to all the supposed objections, this method of justification was the only possible method by which sinful persons could be completely forgiven and released from their captivity to sin in order that "the righteous requirements of the law might be fully met in us" (v. 4).

Paul first summarizes the former arguments of the book. He relates how we have been simultaneously freed from the wrath of God and freed from the captivity of sin by being made part of a new way of life, which he describes as walking not "according to the sinful nature but according to the Spirit" (v. 4).[2] This new life in the Spirit (v. 2) becomes possible by the appearance in human flesh of the Son of God, who by His sinless life and sacrificial death doomed the rule of sin over human nature (v. 3). Jesus now gives birth to a new humanity, people who walk not according to the flesh but according to the rule of the indwelling Holy Spirit (vv. 4–14).

In this chapter, one should not overlook the recent monumental work of Gordon D. Fee, *God's Empowering Presence: The Holy Spirit in the Letters of Paul*, which includes extensive exegetical discussion of Romans 8.[3]

THE INDWELLING SPIRIT AND THE NEW MORAL LIFE
8:1–16

THE INCARNATION AND DEATH OF JESUS: THE DIVINE MEANS TO THE DEFEAT OF SIN IN HUMAN LIFE (8:1–4)

In verse 1 Paul states in summary and recapitulation, "Therefore, there is now no condemnation for those who are in Christ Jesus." The "therefore now" probably goes back to 7:6 where, followed by a lengthy explanation of the holiness of the law and the sinfulness of human nature (7:7–25), Paul has stated that we are now free from the Mosaic Law's dominion, which held us captive, and are able to serve God in the new life of the Spirit. There are also many parallels with the language of participation with Christ, as in 6:1–11.

To be "not under condemnation" (Gk. *katakrima*, 2:1[vb.], 5:16, 18) presents some difficulties for the modern reader. The statement seems to ground escape from "condemnation" not in Christ's work on the cross, but in the work of the Spirit in transforming sinners: "because [Gk. *gar,* "for"] through Christ Jesus the law of the Spirit of life set me free from the law of sin and death" (v. 2). This seems to suggest that what Paul is saying is that sanctification (the righteous life of the believer) is the ground of our "no condemnation" in the sight of God. To get out of this seemingly unacceptable theological conclusion—for Reformation Christians at least!—several alternatives have been advanced.[4] (1) Many take the "no condemnation" as a summation of Paul's argument in chapters 1–5 for justification (removal from judicial condemnation) by faith grounded in Christ's own righteous act in His substitutionary death on the cross (5:18; so Moo, Barrett). (2) Others believe that the "no condemnation" refers not to a judicial verdict but to the deliverance from the "penal servitude" of the law of sin and death (Bruce). This view lacks linguistic support. (3) Still others hold that "no condemnation" means justification as in view one above, but the grounds for this are seen to be not our holy lives but the justification effected toward us by Christ's death. In other words the "fruit" of justification is sanctification (Stott).

But exegetically the text is better understood to argue that here Paul is stating that the ground or reason why we are not condemned is that we are now "in Christ Jesus" (NASB, NRSV). Because of the indwelling power of the Spirit given to us when we were acquitted by faith in Christ's death (5:5) we are delivered from the power of sin over our lives so that personal moral transformation now stamps our lives as indicative of our family relation to God ("sons," "children" vv. 14–16). As Paul looks ahead to the final judgment, his expectation of deliverance is grounded at least in three acts of God: substitutionary atonement in Christ (3:21, 26), personal transformation by the Spirit (6:1–14), and the ongoing intercession of Christ (8:34). Popular Protestantism has necessarily stressed the first of these essentials. Unhappily, this has led to an inadvertent and relative neglect of the second and third.[5] Unfortunately, 8:1 has often been cited to justify this imbalance, when it really instead provides a much-needed corrective.

Finally, how does this interpretation relate to "works-righteousness," a vital concern of the reformers? Calvin could say, "We indeed, allow that good works are required for righteousness: we only take away from them the power of conferring righteousness" (*Commentaries on the Catholic Epistles*, 317). A similar sentiment is expressed in the Westminster Confession: "Faith, thus receiving and resting on Christ and his righteousness, is the alone instrument of justification; yet is it not alone in the person justified, but is ever accompanied with all the other saving graces, and is no dead faith, but worketh by love" (XI.2). Although we cannot be saved by good works, neither can we be saved *without* good works produced by the Holy Spirit in and through us.

Paul states again for us in verses 2–4 why there is no longer servitude to the sinful flesh. It is simply because Christians have been released from the former way of life "in the flesh" (NASB) by the invasion of a new principle (law) of life lived in obedience to the Spirit (v. 2). How did this new manner of life come to us? It was made available totally through God's own gracious, saving act in the coming and the death of His Son (vv. 3–4). Jesus entered into the world by fully identifying Himself with the sinful human flesh He came to redeem: "in the likeness of sinful man" (Gk. *sarx,* "flesh" v. 3). Yet it should be stressed first of all that "likeness" of sinful flesh means neither that Christ was sinful (see 2 Cor. 5:21; 1 Pet. 2:22), nor that He only appeared to be human, but that He came in real human flesh (He was fully human).

This real human flesh can be understood in two different senses. Some interpret the term "in the likeness of sinful flesh" (NASB) to refer to the fact that Jesus came in real human flesh that "looked like" every other person since Adam (sinful flesh) but His humanity was different than ours because Christ, unlike the rest of us, did not have a *sinful,* or fallen, human nature. Thus in this view Paul uses the term "likeness" of fallen human nature ("sinful flesh") to call attention to the difference between Jesus' human nature and ours with respect to sinfulness. Others understand Paul to use the word "likeness" here as he does often elsewhere to mean not "looks like" but in the sense of "form of" or "reality of" without any suggestions of mere resemblance (cf. 1:23; 6:5; Phil. 2:7). This last sense is better and would mean that "the Son of God assumed the selfsame fallen human nature that is ours, but that in this case that fallen nature was never the whole of Him—He never ceased to be the eternal Son of God."[6] Another way to get at this difference is to ask whether Jesus would have eventually died of old age or disease if he had not been killed or executed. The former view says no; the latter says yes. The early Fathers of the church argued that only what Christ assumed in the incarnation is redeemable. Christ's coming "for sin" means either that He came for a sin offering or that He came to deal with sin. The sin offering view is better supported (Schreiner, *Romans*).

Ultimately the purpose of His coming was to condemn "sin in sinful man" (v. 3). The law, by mere commanding, could not overcome the practice of sin in human nature. It could prescribe the will of God but provide no power for performing His will in face of our sinful flesh. Yet it was not the law's fault that sin prevailed and even increased under its rule. The failure lay in the "weakness" of the law to effect righteousness in us because sin ruined our flesh, making it powerless to respond (7:7–25).

But now God has done what the law wanted to do but could not do. He has condemned the rule of sin over human nature by creating a new humanity in Jesus Christ. By living a fully human life, totally in obedience to God, Jesus broke the rule that sin had held over human nature ever since Adam. He showed sin to be not natural to humanness but a usurper. By His own death, Christ provided the means where all who are related to Him can also enter into His same victory over the rule of sin (6:2–14).

Cranfield captures the essence of the amazing truth Paul is declaring in this verse:

> That Paul had in mind Christ's death . . . is scarcely to be doubted. But, if we recognize that Paul believed it was fallen human nature which the Son of God assumed, we shall probably be inclined to see here also a reference to the unintermittent warfare of His whole earthly life by which He forced our rebellious nature to render a perfect obedience to God. . . . For, on this view, Christ's life before His actual ministry and death was not just a standing where unfallen Adam had stood without yielding to the temptation to which Adam succumbed, but a matter of starting from where we start, subjected to all the evil pressures which we inherit, and using the altogether unpromising and unsuitable material of our corrupt nature to work out a perfect, sinless obedience.[7]

That same thought is now repeated in verse 4, where Paul says that Christ condemned sin in the flesh "in order that [purpose] the righteous requirements [Gk. is singular not plural][8] of the law might be fully met in us." The requirement of the law was that we should be holy before God. The whole law, Jesus said, is fulfilled in this, "Love the Lord your God . . . love your neighbor as yourself" (Luke 10:27; Rom. 13:9). Loving obedience both to God and to others was the holy aim in many of the law's commands.

However, in actual human experience, the law was not able to produce loving obedience because of the sin-controlled flesh. But now believers in Christ have this just goal of the law fulfilled in them because of the simple fact that in Christ they are no longer living unto themselves. Through union with Christ by faith, Christians have entered into a whole new way of life. They live according to the rule and resources of the Holy Spirit of God rather than the resources of the flesh. This change in relationship is captured well in the following:

> To run and work the law commands,
> Yet gives me neither feet nor hands;
> But better news the gospel brings:
> It bids me fly, and gives me wings.

(Author unknown)

The law of the Spirit of life in Christ Jesus (v. 2) is described in verse 4 as living not "according to the sinful nature but according to the Spirit." In verses 5–14 Paul shows what is involved in this new way of living in the Spirit.

But what then becomes of the Mosaic Law for the believer in Christ? Does verse 4 teach that Christians are enabled by the Holy Spirit to keep all the commands that they could not keep as non-Christians and thus to fulfill the law? No! Christians cannot keep the law *perfectly* either. This is why we need the continual intercessory work of Christ on our behalf (8:34). God does not demand perfect obedience but an obedience that is "significant, substantial, and observable" (Schreiner). The point is that the law demanded obedience to God motivated out of love for God. This demand is met through the gospel for those who by the grace of God have been put into a whole new relationship to God through Christ and the Spirit. This is what Paul is stressing. That the Christian will be sensitive to any revealed expression of God's will, including the Mosaic moral commands, is assumed by Paul, but Mosaic law-keeping is not the Christian's chief concern. Instead, we are to focus on the new life of the Spirit (see 7:6; 8:5–14), not on the old written code without the Spirit (see 13:8–10 for more on this point). "The law's requirement will be fulfilled by the determination of the direction, the [lifestyle] of our lives by the Spirit, by our being enabled again and again to decide for the Spirit and against the flesh, to turn our faces more and more toward the freedom which the Spirit of God has given us" (Cranfield). Our obedience to God's moral law (will) is absolutely essential to escape condemnation, but our obedience can only be the gracious gift of the Spirit's empowerment.

FOLLOWING THE PROMPTINGS OF THE SPIRIT (8:5–11)

Paul now turns to explain this life lived according to the Spirit (vv. 5–14). The Spirit comes to us as a gift (not merited in any way) when we become Christians. Through this gift God's love was poured out into the hearts of Christians (5:5). In 7:6 the Spirit is referred to as the agent of the new life. Jesus Christ is our justification and His character the goal of our sanctification; and it is the Holy Spirit who effects this moral transformation in us. The "Spirit of God" and "Spirit of Christ" appear to be identical terms (v. 9). Thus justification can never be separated from sanctification (Christlikeness). Both are inseparably linked to the grace-gift of God in Jesus Christ. Yet how does the Spirit in our experience effect sanctification?

First, the Holy Spirit produces in us a certain mind-set (vv. 5–8): "those who live in accordance with the Spirit have their minds set on [Gk. *phroneō*, are intent on following] what the Spirit desires" (v. 5). It may be helpful to note that certain terms Paul uses here denote either different states of existence (Christian or non-Christian) or different patterns of behavior. To "live according to the sinful nature [Gk. *sarx*, flesh]" is to be a non-Christian, under sin's power (vv. 8–9); on the other hand, to "live in accordance with the Spirit" or "Christ in you" is to be a Christian, under the Spirit's power. To "be controlled by the sinful nature" is equivalent to "live in accordance with the sinful nature," to live "in accordance with the Spirit," and "by the Spirit you put to death the misdeeds of the body." All of these terms mean to conduct our lives according to the standard, values, and resources of the life-giving Spirit within us (vv. 4–5, 13).[9] The presence of the Holy Spirit redirects our life toward God and creates in us new desires and values. To have the "mind controlled by" the things of the flesh or Spirit means to have one's thoughts, desires, and constant yearning directed toward either the life of the flesh (self) or the life of the Spirit (Christ). In this struggle we either take the side of the flesh or take the side of the Spirit.

The results follow (v. 6). To have one's mind directed only upon the things of self and this material world means cutting oneself off from the only Source of true human life and results in death now in this life (condemnation and evil) and eternal death to come.[10] On the other hand, to have one's mind directed upon God through the Spirit results in "life" (acquittal and sanctification) and "peace," the conscious enjoyment of reconciliation with God now in this life and at the final end when we stand before God.

Several years ago a pastor friend of mine moved to Houston, Texas. Some weeks after he arrived, he had occasion to ride the bus from his home to the downtown area. When he sat down, he discovered that the driver had accidentally given him ten cents too much change. As he considered what to do, there alternately appeared to his imagination little angelic figures sitting on his opposite shoulders and whispering instructions into his ears. One appeared and said, "You better give the dime back. It would be wrong to keep it. Christ wouldn't keep it." On the other shoulder a voice said, "Oh, forget it. It's just ten cents. Who would worry about this little amount? Anyway, the bus company already gets too much fare. With their millions every day they'll never miss it. Accept it as a gift from God and keep quiet." When his stop came up, he paused momentarily at the front door, and, handing the driver the dime he said, "Here. You accidentally gave me too much change." The driver replied, "Aren't you the new pastor in town? I have been thinking lately about going to church somewhere. I just wanted to see what you would do if I gave you ten cents too much change." When my friend stepped off the bus he literally grabbed the nearest light pole, held on, and said, "O dear God, I almost sold Your Son for ten cents!"

Paul further describes the mind directed toward the flesh (non-Christian) in its relationship to God (vv. 7–8). The flesh's interests are such that those who live to please themselves are in fact in a state of hostility against God. Such hostility is evident because the mind directed by the sinful flesh does not and cannot become obedient to the law (will) of God (7:14–25). It follows that such who live to please themselves cannot live to please God.

The opposite would be true of those who have been put by grace into the mind directed by the Spirit: Instead of disobedience to the law (will) of God, they respond with loving obedience; in place of walking apart from God, they walk with God.

In verses 9–11 Paul contrasts the state of the Christian ("controlled . . . by the Spirit") with the preceding description of those "controlled by the sinful nature" (vv. 7–8). In verse 9, "you, however," the "you" is emphatic: "but as for *you*." Paul clearly teaches in verse 9 that all Christians are "controlled . . . by the Spirit," which means that "the Spirit of God lives" in every Christian. In fact, he says, "if anyone does not have the Spirit of Christ, he does not belong to Christ" (as a justified one). To be "in Christ" or "in the Spirit" refers to our union with Christ; to have Christ in us (v. 10) or the Spirit in us (v. 4) refers to our ownership by Christ.

The Spirit "lives" (Gk. *oikeō*, to live in a house) in us in the sense of a person making his home in our lives. The figure of indwelling combines the thought that Christians are people whose lives are directed from a Source outside themselves with the idea that this life Source is also vitally related to them. Three times in verses 9–11 this indwelling of the Spirit is stressed. "Paul's thought is that through the indwelling of the Spirit Christ Himself is present to us, the indwelling of the Spirit being 'the manner of Christ's dwelling in us'" (Calvin as cited by Cranfield, *Romans,* 1:389).

What are the effects in our experience of this indwelling Spirit of God? Paul states that, even though the body is dead because of sin, the spirit "is alive because of righteousness" (v. 10). What he teaches is a modified dualism in Christian experience. At the present time a dual principle operates in Christians. On the one hand, they still possess a physical body condemned to death because of Adam's sin (5:15; 6:23). The seed of decay and death is now working in our bodies. Yet for Christians another reality is now at work. Life is also present due to the indwelling of the Spirit given to us through justification. The Spirit enables us to "live" in spite of the fact that the body has been stricken with a death wound (8:13).[11] Christians then, while still in the weak, sinful flesh, have been released from its power; while still in the body, which has received a mortal wound from sin, they have a new principle of life working in it through the righteousness of God in Christ. The Christian is totally dead on the one hand, yet fully alive on the other. Such a truth will spare us from either expecting absolute perfection in this life or giving in to complete pessimism concerning the present manifestation of Christ's love and righteousness in our lives. Moral transformation is a present reality in our lives because of the Spirit's work.

Furthermore, the presence of the same Spirit, who gives life now to believers living in decaying bodies, also is the guarantee that our bodies, destined to physical death, will be raised from death in the same manner that Jesus' body was raised (v. 11). The Father is the specific agent in resurrection as in the case of Christ (6:4), but as in Christ's case, the Holy Spirit also is an agent (1:4). Later in the chapter Paul will refer to this future hope of resurrection as the "redemption of our bodies" (v. 23). Again we are reminded that just as human nature was not made for sin but the usurper illegally took it over (v. 3), so also the mortal body was not made for death and will be in God's time, because of the Spirit of life, raised to immortal life (1 Cor. 15:51–53). This is no mere spiritual resurrection. What a glorious truth!

THE INDWELLING SPIRIT AND MORAL TRANSFORMATION INTO THE SONS OF GOD 8:12–16

But what about the life now in the body? Has the Spirit nothing to contribute? How does the "life" made possible because of our justification (v. 10) actually manifest itself in our death-bound lives? Paul has already said that the Christian as a Christian is one who lives not in accordance with the flesh (sinful nature) but in accordance with the Spirit (vv. 4–11). But does this mean that Christians now, because they are "in the Spirit," automatically follow God's will? The answer must be no, for in verses 12–16 Christians are specifically exhorted to "live according to the . . . Spirit." Remember in chapter 6 how Paul stated that because of their union with Christ in death and resurrection believers are "free from sin" and then he proceeded to exhort them to fight against sin and yield themselves as servants to righteousness? Delivered and yet not delivered. Here likewise we Christians have been shown to be ultimately free from death (vv. 11, 21) due to the Spirit who indwells, but we must in the present life fight the sin and death principle as it works itself out in our bodies.

To live in accordance with the sinful nature (the flesh) in separation from God leads to death both now and eternally. Since Christians have been removed from the servitude to the sinful flesh (self) and put into the service of the Spirit, who is the Spirit of life and immortality, they are obligated (morally) not to live their lives under the rule of the sinful flesh (v. 12). Rather, Christians are to "put to death the misdeeds of the body" that they might live (v. 13). Here is the principle for moving into the practice of holy living. It may be called spiritual neurosurgery. Phillips' translation reads: "cut the nerve of your instinctive actions by obeying the Spirit." "Put to death the misdeeds of the body" refers to our continual (present tense) activity as Christians whereby, through the enablement provided by the Spirit, we strike down in death those sinful practices of the body that are contrary to God's will.

More specifically, how this is done Paul does not say in this context. The "misdeeds [*praxeis*, habits, treacherous plots] of the body" are probably to be identified with "whatever belongs to your earthly nature" of Colossians 3:5, which are enumerated as: "sexual immorality, impurity, lust, evil desires and greed, which is idolatry" (see also Gal. 5:19–21; Eph. 4:22–5:14).

Although in this context the spiritual neurosurgery is primarily negative, it assumes that the process is a *renewal,* not simply a destruction. The dead leaves and branches of the sinful practices fall away only to make room for the "fruit of the Spirit" (Rom. 6:21–22; 7:4; Gal. 5:22–23). The weed-killer of the

Spirit is applied so that the grass of the graces of God might be free to grow. So in practice we do not seek mere patience or love or purity (this is a moralistic approach), but we seek the release of Christ's life, i.e., His patience, His love and purity, by following the promptings of the Spirit. The Christian life is an exchanged life. Such a process leads truly to "life" now as well as eternal and immortal life in the future.

Verse 14 is transitional. Paul concludes the thought of the previous verses by asserting that all who are thus "led by the Spirit of God [to be constantly putting to death the deeds of the body] are sons of God." In verses 16–17 the expression is "God's children." "The terms are synonymous here and should not be distinguished" (Schreiner, *Romans,* 423). The truth of the Spirit's leading suggests not general guidance as to what God would have us to do (vocation) but rather what we should be (character). All the children of God enjoy this leading; however, it is not optional. Because "leading" often implies the process whereby our desires lead us (2 Tim. 3:6 NASB), perhaps the thought of Paul is that the Holy Spirit imparts new desires and promptings into the redeemed life to which the Christian develops a sensitivity in responding both negatively (killing process) and positively (in the fruit-bearing process). "The daily, hourly putting to death the schemings and enterprises of the sinful flesh by means of the Spirit is a matter of being led, directed, impelled, controlled by the Spirit" (Cranfield, *Romans,* 1:395).

"Sons" of God includes being children of God but also involves in the Roman world of Paul's day the idea of a new mature stage in the child's development that related him to his father as a joint heir and master over all (Gal. 3:26; 4:6–7).

Alternately the Jewish background might be in Paul's mind, thus alluding to the Exodus of Israel from Egypt (slavery) and to God calling His redeemed people "sons" or "children" who were in turn "led" through the wilderness by God.

The Spirit, who now relates to us in a new way of life even though we are still in the old human sin nature (vv. 1–14), is also the "Spirit of sonship" (v. 15). Verses 15–16 continue the thought of the preceding verse by stressing assurance that as Christians we are actually related to God as "sons" and not as those under slavery. Fear comes from the absence of authentic hope and leads to enslavement by inferior earthly powers that promise deliverance. But Christians have been made true children of God (adopted)[12] and possess the assurance of genuine hope. The evidence of this family relation to God is the inward witness of the Holy Spirit. This witness of our filial relationship to God is seen most clearly in Christians' urgent praying where we cry, "Abba, Father." The expression, "Abba, Father" combines the untranslated Aramaic word *abba,* which means "father" in a very personal, intimate sense (Mark 14:36 with Matt. 26:42) with the Greek word for father, *pater.* Only Jesus uses this intimate form of prayer in the Gospels because of His unique sonship (Mark 14:36). When Christians cry out to God, the Spirit of sonship incites them to say as a child would to his father, "Abba," or "papa," or "daddy," or "dear father."[13]

Several years ago I visited Israel. Late one afternoon we stopped for the evening at a youth hostel in Tiberius, on the shore of the Sea of Galilee. I was standing on a veranda overlooking some small Jewish children playing below. Three or four of them had formed a group and were pointing at a small boy about two years old who was standing by himself, apart from the group. When the boy came to the conclusion that they were going to get him, he took off running as fast as his legs would take him, screaming, "Abba! Abba! Abba!" He wanted his daddy, and he wanted him right now!

Cranfield observes that

> the implication of this verse [16], understood in its context, is that it is in the believer's calling God "Father" that God's holy law is established and its "righteous requirement" (v. 4) fulfilled, and that the whole of Christian obedience is included in this calling God "Father." This verse, in fact, takes in principle everything that there is to say in the way of Christian ethics; for there is nothing more required of us than that we should do just this. . . . For to address the true God by the name of Father with full sincerity and seriousness will involve seeking wholeheartedly to be and think and say and do that which is pleasing to Him and to avoid everything which displeases Him.[14]

Furthermore, "the Spirit himself testifies with our spirit that we are God's children" (v. 16). This is an additional witness for our sonship borne directly to our spirit. This consciousness perhaps consists in the undefinable but real conviction through the promises of God that we now belong to God (1 John 5:6, 9–12). Note that the Holy Spirit is personal and that He is a distinct being separate from our own human spirit.[15]

THE INDWELLING SPIRIT AND AUTHENTIC HOPE IN SUFFERING
8:17–27

As children of God we are "co-heirs" of God. In fact, the only way we get in on the future inheritance is as "co-heirs with Christ" (v. 17).[16] Christ's inheritance is fabulous: "appointed heir of all things" (Heb. 1:2). Before Paul goes on to speak further of this future glory, which is like an inheritance that we receive solely because of our relationship to someone else, he first mentions a condition for sharing Christ's glory: "if indeed we share in his sufferings" (v. 17). Here we discover a further implication of our union with Christ (6:8). As Christ suffered before He entered glory (Heb. 2:9–10; 1 Pet. 1:11), so those who are identified with Him also suffer before they enter the future glory. "In this world you will have trouble. But take heart! I have overcome the world" (John 16:33). Yet this is a suffering "with Him." Christ is so united to His body, the church, that when the members suffer for the gospel and for righteousness' sake, He as the Head also suffers (Acts 9:4; Phil. 1:29; Col. 1:24; 1 Pet. 4:13). Why the suffering of the members of Christ's body must continue, Paul does not reveal (nor does any biblical writer). There is a mystery connected with suffering that God has not been pleased to explain to His creatures in the present. It is sufficient for faith to trust implicitly in the faithfulness of God Himself who will ultimately reveal that suffering was in some manner indispensable to the full manifestation of His glory.

In the meantime, Paul shows that there are good reasons for abiding faithful to God even in sufferings and persecutions (vv. 18–30). Each reason is related to a special ministry of the Holy

Spirit. First, the Spirit helps by creating a consciousness by His presence of the reality of the greatness of the future glory (vv. 18–25). Second, the Spirit definitely helps us to overcome our natural weaknesses (vv. 26–27). Third is the assurance that all things are working together for our good in the eternal purpose of God (vv. 28–30). Note the poetic quality displayed in this passage, particularly verses 19–22.

THE HOPE OF GLORY (8:18–25)

First, in verses 18–25 Paul looks for encouragement to the Christian hope of the greatness of the future glory: "Our present sufferings are not worth comparing with the glory that will be revealed in us" (v. 18). Just as real to us as our sufferings are now is the certainty of our sharing the future glory of Christ (2 Cor. 4:16–18). To what does the "glory" that lies in the future refer? First, it involves the release from decay and death of all of the children of God. Second, there follows the release of the whole creation from the captivity of corruption, sin, and death (Rom. 8:19, 21, 23). This freeing from decay not only affects our individual bodies (v. 23), but extends cosmically to the whole created order: "the creation itself will be liberated from its bondage to decay" (v. 21). Paul brings in the creation to show how great the effect will be of the future revealing of the children of God.[17] So great is this glory that the whole creation is anxiously longing[18] "on tiptoe" (PHILLIPS), eagerly awaiting the revelation in resurrection bodies of the children of God (vv. 19, 23). Why is creation so expectant? Because nature has been so subjected by God Himself to futility that it too might share the same hope of release from decay that will one day come to God's children (vv. 20–21). The hope of man does not lie in cryonics (freezing the dead) but in resurrection.

Paul speaks of the present creation as (1) subject to frustration, (2) not of its own choice, and (3) subjected in hope. "Frustration" (Gk. *mataiotēti*) means "to no purpose" or "against the norm, unexpected." It may be Paul's commentary on Ecclesiastes 1:2, "'Meaningless! Meaningless!,' says the Teacher. '. . . Everything is meaningless.'" From one point of view nature seems to be imbued with the seeds of futility, decay, and death ("bondage to decay," v. 21). Creation does not now fulfill its intended goal, which was to be our wonderful habitat. The forces of nature seem from time to time to work against themselves and us, and they do not achieve their intended ends. When drought, floods, hurricanes, or disease destroy vegetation and life, then beauty fades, vitality decays, and joy turns to weeping. This frustration produces what might be called a symphony of nature played in a minor key but with the expectation of a glorious finale. God has Himself subjected the created universe to a form of captivity resulting in this seeming lack of purpose in order to create "hope" in the glorious future release of creation along with the children of God (vv. 20–21).

However, the simplest and most straightforward interpretation would take "frustration" here ("futility" NASB) in its most basic sense as denoting the ineffectiveness of that which does not attain its goal. Paul's meaning then would be something like this: Creation was brought into being in order to glorify the Creator, God. But creation cannot reach its intended purpose without our willing participation, whereby creation is intelligently brought through our worship as an offering to the Creator. As Cranfield puts it:

> We may think of the whole magnificent theatre of the universe together with all its splendid properties and all the chorus of subhuman life, created to glorify God but unable to do so fully, so long as man the chief actor in the drama of God's praise fails to contribute his rational part (1:414).

In contrast, compare the amazing hymn of Francis of Assisi where "All creatures of our God and King" are exhorted to "Lift up your voice and with us sing, Alleluia! Alleluia! Thou burning sun with golden beam, Thou silver moon with softer gleam! . . . Thou rushing wind . . . Ye clouds. . . . Thou rising morn . . . Ye lights of evening. . . . flow'rs and fruits. . . . Dear mother earth. . . . Let all things their Creator bless, And worship Him in humbleness."

Paul does not say why God so subjected the universe; it may be tied up with human sin and the "curse" upon the ground (Gen. 3:17; 5:29). He who originally put the creation under our dominion has now put the creation under bondage to the effects of our sin and will make it a partaker of our blessing in the future (Matt. 19:28; Acts 3:21, "renewal of all things").

It is important in our day to note how Paul connects us with nature. The fate of nature is bound up with our fate. We cannot solve our ecological problems without at the same time attending to our own problem. Note carefully that we can only find a partial remedy to the problems of ecology (creation) until the ultimate problem of human existence in sinful flesh is remedied by the personal return of Jesus Christ and the creation of new bodies and a new environment (Rev. 20:6; 21:1–2). Hence freedom is the significant mark of glorification for both creation and the human body.

But the present experience is no mere bumpy hayride. "The whole creation has been groaning as in the pains of childbirth" (Rom. 8:22), and we also "groan inwardly as we wait eagerly for . . . the redemption of our bodies" (v. 23). Creation can do nothing but wait, groan (moan), and hope. Christians also do not escape this frustration in their spiritual conflicts. Life (out of death) and pain are the twin realities of authentic Christian existence. We too then must wait, groan, and hope, but Christians have something the creation lacks, namely, "the firstfruits of the Spirit." Firstfruits are the pledge or first installment of the whole harvest which is to come (Lev. 23:10; Rom. 11:16). The Spirit's present work in us is the pledge of all that God has promised to do in the future for us. The precise meaning of our present trials and apparently meaningless suffering is not clear, but because of the Spirit's encouragement we can wait to see the glorious outcome. Think of a caterpillar slowly advancing over the weaves of a tapestry. It can see only occasional changes in the color and sizes of the threads, but they would have no apparent meaning even if the caterpillar could understand. Yet when the caterpillar emerges from its chrysalis as a butterfly that can fly above the tapestry and see the beautiful design of the whole, the unexplainable pieces it has seen as it walked over the weavings will be instantly transformed.

Christians are not yet fully redeemed, even though they are fully accepted by God. They possess now a body destined for death (7:24; 8:10), but they also have received the indwelling Spirit who provides both enabling power to rise above the sinful Adamic natural life and a guarantee that our bodies will one day be freed through resurrection from death and decay (8:11; 2 Cor. 5:4). We are real children of God now and adopted (8:15), but we are not fully the children of God ("adoption," v. 23) until our physical bodies also have been released ("redeemed") from death and decay (including sickness) in the resurrection. The Spirit's presence and ministries in us are our encouraging guarantee or foretaste of the greater things to come (2 Cor. 1:22; 5:5; Gen. 24:53)!

In verses 24–25 Paul again poses a paradox. We were truly saved in the past moment when by faith Christ became our righteousness, but we were not fully saved because we were saved "in hope" of the future complete restoration. Our present salvation includes the hope of the future resurrection of our bodies (Phil. 3:21), but inasmuch as it is not yet realized ("seen") we must "wait for it patiently" (v. 25; 5:3–5). Faith is the means whereby we are given a salvation that includes hope. Therefore, faith and hope, though distinguishable, are inseparable in Christian experience. "Hope nourishes and sustains faith," remarked Calvin. Power for living in the present sufferings with Christ lies in the direction of this hope in our future glorification with Christ.[19] Truly the God of the future is greater than the God of the past (from our perspective). "Hope is the force behind every creative use of the imagination" (D. Gelpi). This future hope ought to affect our imaginations in the manner in which we confront the pain and darkness of the present. Focusing on the reality of God's future transforms the evaluation of our present experiences and decisions. Therefore, growth in hope is the key to growth in the love of God and in the love of others (Rom. 15:13).

THE SPIRIT'S HELP IN PRAYER (8:26–27)

Now the Spirit not only creates hope in us but also provides help for our infirmities (vv. 26–27). The tension between the suffering of the present time and the expectation of future glory certainly marks the Christian life on this earth and calls forth its groaning and longing. If the sufferings of Christ, which include all the forms of frustration and suffering under which we must live in the present age, weigh us down, so also does our "weakness" (v. 26). "In the same way the Spirit also helps our weakness" (v. 26 NASB) is Paul's description of the second help we receive in present sufferings. "In the same way" may refer to a comparison between the way the Spirit enables us in present suffering to experience the firstfruits of the certain and blessed future glory and thus wait patiently (vv. 18–25), and in the same way also the Spirit relieves our weaknesses by His help.[20] Our main weakness is spiritual, that is, our struggle to allow the new life of the Spirit to have freedom in us as we live in a body corroded with sin and in an environment scented with death. Our weakness may also lie in our uncertainty, confusion, and nagging unbelief in the face of suffering (vv.18–25, 33–39).[21]

The English word *helps* translates the Greek compound word *synantilambanō*. The root word means "to take hold" *(lambanō)*. The first prefix of the compound *(anti)* means "over against" or "face-to-face" while the second prefix *(syn)* means "together with." The great Greek scholar, A. T. Robertson, suggested the combined meaning to be: "The Holy Spirit lays hold of our weaknesses along with *(syn)* us and carries His part of the burden facing us *(anti)* as if two men were carrying a log, one at each end."[22] The word is found elsewhere in the New Testament only of Martha's plea to Jesus to tell Mary to get into the kitchen and *help* her (Luke 10:40; but see LXX Exod. 18:22; Num. 11:17; Ps. 89:21).

Probably the most comprehensive example of how the Spirit lends a hand to help us in our weakness is in the matter of prayer: "what we ought to pray for" (v. 26). Our problem is not ignorance of the *form* of prayer (how), but our weakness is an inability to articulate the *content* (what), that is, what we should ask for especially in sufferings that will meet our needs and at the same time fulfill God's will. The Spirit lends a hand by "interceding" for us to God (vv. 26–27). Christians have two divine intercessors before God. Christ intercedes for us in the court of heaven in respect to our sins (Rom. 8:34; Heb. 7:25; 1 John 2:1). On the other hand, the Spirit intercedes in the theater of our hearts here on earth in respect to our weakness. The Spirit pleads to God for our true needs "with groans that words cannot express" (v. 26). Creation is groaning (v. 22); Christians are groaning (v. 23); so also God the Holy Spirit groans. As God the Father "searches the hearts" (NASB) of His children—sobering but also comforting—He finds in their consciousness unspoken and inexpressible sighings.[23] Though inexpressible, they are not unintelligible to the understanding of the Father. Furthermore, these sighings of the Spirit in our hearts turn out to be spiritual desires in the will of God because in reality they are the expressions of the Spirit's intercession on behalf of our weaknesses (v. 27). In this manner, we can understand how God does "immeasurably more than all we ask or imagine" (Eph. 3:20).

When one of our preschoolers desires to write to Granny, my wife gives her a sheet of paper and a pencil, and she expresses her feelings in lines, circles, and zigzag marks. They are truly unintelligible signs. When Mother gets the paper back, she adds certain intelligible words to appropriate marks on the paper such as, "Hello, Granny" with an arrow to the first few scribblings, "We miss you" connected to other marks, and finally "Come visit us soon. I love you, Lynn." Mother truly has interceded for Lynn to Granny, even as the Spirit intercedes for us to the Father.

What are the practical implications of the Spirit's intercession? First, this truth helps us to recognize the distinction between the intention of our prayers and the actual specific requests we may voice to God. He is able to separate the two even when we cannot. A number of years ago my daughter, who was ten at the time, came and sat down next to me on the couch while I was reading the newspaper after dinner. She just sat there quietly. Sensing that this was not her normal behavior, I put down the paper and asked her if anything was wrong. "Oh, no," she said, "There's nothing wrong, Daddy." I asked her how things went at school. She said, "Fine." After a while I finally got her to admit that she had had a misunderstanding with one of her teachers during a study hall period. She was supposed to bring enough work to keep herself busy during the whole hour. But even though she had brought ample work, she had finished early and was quietly talking to a friend next to her. The teacher came up and severely reprimanded her for not doing her work. As a very sensitive girl, my daughter was crushed by this seeming injustice, and she wasn't able to function the rest of the day. Now she was in tears. After we had talked further about the matter, I asked her if she would like to pray together about the situation. She said, "Yes." I said, "How should we pray?" She said, "Pray that I won't ever see that teacher again!" Her real need was to be accepted and understood by her teacher. This was the intention of her request. But the best way she saw that intention's being fulfilled was not exactly what I had in mind. When I prayed I said, "Lord, help Lynn's teacher not to jump to false conclusions and to be more understanding, and help Lynn to be patient and forgiving." I interceded by interpreting Lynn's intention to God. In the same way, the Spirit intercedes for us.

Second, a further implication of the Spirit's intercession is that no believing prayer ever goes unanswered. There may be a revision of the ways that I propose. I must trust in the thousands of ways God has at His disposal. Nevertheless, I must enter into a dialogue with God and be ready, as were Jesus and Paul, to have my specific requests corrected by God's answer (study Matt. 26:38–44 and Rom. 15:30–32, and review the comments in this book on the latter passage). In this sense Luther could say, "It is not a bad, but a very good sign if the opposite of what we pray for appears to happen. Just as it is not a good sign if our prayers eventuate in the fulfillment of all we ask for. If everything were to go the way I want it, I would end up in that kind of false security which is really an instrument of the divine judgment."[24]

THE PLAN OF GOD 8:28–30

Finally, verses 28–30 gives us the third reason for patiently enduring suffering. It is the firm conviction that under the hand of the Sovereign Lord of all creation, "God causes all things to work together for good to those who love God, to those who are called according to His purpose" (v. 28 NASB). God has a plan. Everything in our lives contributes to the realization of that purpose. It is an all-comprehensive plan in that "all" things are included; not one detail of our lives is excluded. It is a cooperative plan in that all things are "working together" in concert; the individual ingredients, as in a kitchen recipe, have no virtue or ultimate significance in themselves apart from the providential combination into the divine pattern. The plan is beneficent in that the goal is "the good." It is also selective in that it applies only to those "who love God" who are in fact those "called" by God into His glorious purpose through the redemption effected through Jesus Christ.[25] Our good, C. S. Lewis pointed out, is to love God and fulfill His will for our lives.[26]

In verses 29–30 Paul focuses on the main events leading to God's eternal "purpose" for the Christian: ultimate glorification with Christ. He begins before time in the Father's foreknowledge and concludes beyond time in glorification; between these two, within time, come calling and justification. Please note two prominent features of this plan. First, God Himself is the designer and executioner of each link in the chain. *He* foreknows and *He* predestinates; *He* calls and *He* justifies and *He* glorifies. We, it seems, have no active part in the design or execution of the purpose. Our only part is our response of continual love to God (v. 28).

Secondly, all who begin and continue in this plan by continuing to love God also finish. Those "whom" He foreknew are those "whom" (NASB) He called; "whom" He called He also justified, and "whom" He justified He also glorified. God starts with one hundred sheep and arrives in glory with one hundred, not ninety-nine. When contemplating the suffering and setbacks of this present life, nothing can be more assuring than to know that the present is only a small segment between justification and glorification in a total plan that has had three stages already fulfilled. It fills us with a sense of humility and worth and dignity beyond all comprehension and a sense of God's ability to meet every challenge that would thwart His purpose in our lives.

"Those whom God foreknew" (Gk. *proginōskō*) presents a problem. Some following Augustine and Calvin believe that this word, when used of God, refers to more than mere knowledge beforehand (1 Pet. 1:2, 20). In this view, the word emphasizes the fact that salvation was initiated by God in His eternal loving choice whereby He chose us in Christ to be the objects of His loving purpose (see Amos 3:2; Eph. 1:4–6). Those who hold this view point out that as difficult as it may seem, foreknowledge always depends on God's election or choice of us and never on our election of God (2 Thess. 2:13–14). Others believe as did Theodoret of Cyr (d. 455) that these realities of predestination, calling, justification, and glorification ought not to be seen as *caused by* God's foreknowledge, but as known by Him because He is God (G. Bray, ed. *Romans*, 237). The crux issue is whether our salvation is caused by God's election of us or by our response to Him which He knew beforehand (see note 27).Those persons whom God chose to set His love upon are the very ones He also determined to "be conformed to the likeness of his Son" (v. 29). In this view, predestination (Gk. *proorizō*) is almost the equivalent of foreknowledge (v. 30; only "predestined" is repeated in the chain) but emphasizes the goal or end in view, while foreknowledge focuses on the persons involved (Acts 4:28; 1 Cor. 2:7; Eph. 1:5, 11). The goal of God's electing purpose is that Christ might be the eldest (firstborn) of many brothers and sisters in glory who bear His very image or likeness (1 Cor. 15:49; Phil. 3:21; Col. 1:18; Heb. 2:10; 1 John 3:2). Glorification involves receiving the full humanity of Jesus in a redeemed body adapted to full expression of the Spirit (1 Cor. 15:44).

Those who were predestined before time to this glory were called and justified by God in time (v. 30). Calling refers to God's gracious direct appeal to our hearts to respond in faith to His free offer of pardon and new life in the gospel of Christ (2 Thess. 2:14). It too is a word associated with God's election (Isa. 41:9; 1 Cor. 1:26–27); God calls (elects) us out of sin and death by the gospel of Christ. Calling is God's application in time of His election before time (Eph. 1:4–5). Our act of faith in the gospel of Christ secured our actual justification (acquittal and life), which has been Paul's burden throughout the letter. The final link that completes God's plan is our glorification with Christ (v. 30).

It should be noted well that all the relative pronouns ("whom" NASB) in these verses go back to the first substantive phrase in verse 28, "of those who love him." Paul puts this first in the Greek because he does not want anyone to miss it. But we must ask, are these called because they love God, or do they love God because they are called? Theologians have debated this issue for centuries.[27] The point that is important here in Romans is that Paul does not get caught up in this kind of theological speculation. All he says is that those who are foreknown, predestined, called, justified, and glorified are those whose earthly life since their conversion has been one great process of loving God.

Present distresses or reversals can never then be viewed as destructive forces against the Christian. Each fits into the present link in God's unfolding purpose. In some manner they are preparing us for the future revelation of His glory in the redeemed and in the whole creation. Reversals and distresses may pull us down. Yet on the other hand the contemplation of the reality of the future salvation (vv. 18–25), together with both the help of the Holy Spirit in our weakness (vv. 26–27) and the firm knowledge that all our experiences are working for our good in God's eternal plan (vv. 28–30) all combine to cause our spirits to rise in triumphant praise to God. It is He who has put us into an eternal relationship to Himself and freed us from all accusation (vv. 31–34) and all possibility of separation from His love in Christ Jesus (vv. 35–39).

THE INDWELLING SPIRIT AND THE TRIUMPHANT EXPERIENCE OF THE LOVE OF GOD 8:31–39

Verses 31–39 conclude with the highest rung in the ladder of comfort that, from verse 18 onward, writer, like reader, has been mounting. Paul wants to apply this knowledge of certainty and security to elicit from the believer a feeling of confident assurance.

QUESTION 1: "PERHAPS HUMAN THREATS WILL PROVE TOO MUCH FOR US?" (8:31–32)

God is for us (in forgiveness, in acceptance in Christ, and in the gift of the life-transforming Spirit). Who can legitimately accuse us before Him, for is He not the very One who, to show His love for us, sacrificed the greatest gift He could, His very own Son (vv. 31–32)? In the phrase, "He who did not spare his own Son," we can see an allusion to Abraham's offering up his only son, Isaac, whereby he showed his intense love for God (Gen. 22). In the present instance, God Himself is seen as expressing His supreme love for us in not even sparing His own Son from death. If God has already so proved His love to us (5:8), how can anything that happens to us be considered less than the evidence of the outworking of His good (v. 28)? "Along with him, graciously give us all things?" (v. 32b). Dwight L. Moody once illustrated this concept by remarking that if his friend, Mr. Tiffany, had offered him as a gift a large, beautiful diamond, he would not hesitate to ask Mr. Tiffany for some brown paper to wrap up the diamond.

QUESTION 2: "PERHAPS WE WILL FAIL BECAUSE OF SIN IN OUR LIVES?" (8:33–34)

Who can accuse us if God, who is the highest court of appeals, has already acquitted us (v. 33)? Who can condemn us to suffer the penalty and burden of a broken law if Christ Himself, our Judge (John 5:22), has died and risen and is now in heaven interceding to God for us (Luke 22:31–32; Rom. 8:34; Heb. 7:24–25)? Grace and grace alone has brought us into this certainty of acceptance with God.

QUESTION 3: "PERHAPS OVERLY DISTRESSING CIRCUMSTANCES WILL PROVE GOD DOESN'T CARE?" (8:35–39)

If no person can accuse us, who or what then can separate us from the eternal love of Christ for us? "Shall trouble or hardship or persecution or famine or nakedness or danger or sword?" (v. 35). Paul has already experienced all of these except the last and has found that his faith and hope were not destroyed but enlarged (5:3–5). As far as the "sword" (death) is concerned, Paul could refer to the Old Testament (Ps. 44:22) history of the persecution of God's people not as something marking God's disfavor but rather as (1) received for Him, "for your [God's] sake," (2) continually, "all day long," and (3) delivered unto death, "as sheep to be slaughtered" (v. 36).

Can any or all of these things in any amount ever detach us from the love of Christ? No! Paul answers, because in fact it is "*in* all these things" that God works out His plan for good (vv. 28, 37, italics added) and causes us to be "more than conquerors through him who loved us" (v. 37).[28] No earthly affliction or infliction can disturb this confidence in God's love for us. Cranfield emphasizes the grace involved: "It is not through any courage, endurance or determination of our own, but through Christ, and not even by our hold on Him but by His hold on us, that we are more than conquerors" (1:441). Oswald Chambers likewise describes this Christian attitude when he says, "Huge waves that would frighten an ordinary swimmer produce a tremendous thrill for the surfer who has ridden them. Let's apply that to our own circumstances. The things we try to avoid and fight against—tribulation, suffering, and persecution—are the very things that produce abundant joy in us. 'We are more than conquerors through Him' 'in all these things'; not in spite of them, but in the midst of them. A saint doesn't know the joy of the Lord in spite of tribulation, but because of it. Paul said, 'I am exceedingly joyful in all our tribulation' (2 Cor. 7:4)" *(My Utmost for His Highest).*

But further, Paul is also convinced that no factor of human existence (life or death), nor unseen spiritual power (angels, principalities), nor the expanse of space (height, depth), nor the course of time (present, to come), nor anything in the whole universe of God (any other created thing) can cut us off from this unbelievable consciousness of the love of God, the Father, manifested at the Cross and poured out in our hearts when we received the grace of God (vv. 38–39; 5:5).[29] Yet in all this glorious victory we are reminded to not forget the means or the focus of such triumph since it is "through him who loved us" (i.e., Jesus Christ) and "in Christ Jesus our Lord" (vv. 37, 39). An early fifth-century Christian witness well illustrates Paul's jubilation:

> When Chrysostom was brought before the Roman Emperor, the Emperor threatened him with banishment if he remained a Christian. Chrysostom replied, "Thou canst not banish me for this world is my father's house." "But I will slay thee," said the Emperor. "Nay, thou canst not," said the noble champion of the faith, "for my life is hid with Christ in God." "I will take away thy treasures." "Nay, but thou canst not for my treasure is in heaven and my heart is there." "But I will drive thee away from man and thou shalt have no friend left." "Nay thou canst not, for I have a friend in heaven from whom thou canst not separate me. I defy thee; for there is nothing that thou canst do to hurt me."[30]

There is more here in this chapter than any of us can fathom in a lifetime. The great challenge is to live our lives by the power of the indwelling Spirit and in an ever-deepening and widening experience of the unceasing and unconditional love of God for us in Jesus Christ.

This chapter is for me no mere academic exercise. Its truth has profoundly changed my life and captured my heart. I live on the fringes of its bank but yearn to move deeper and deeper into its strong currents. Isaac Watts captures something of the expected response in his popular hymn, "When I Survey the Wondrous Cross."

Were the whole realm of nature mine,
That were a present far too small:
Love so amazing, so divine,
Demands my soul, my life, my all.

NOTES

1. Charles Erdman, *The Epistle of Paul to the Romans* (Philadelphia: Westminster, 1925), 82.

2. The words "who walk not after the flesh, but after the Spirit," found in

the first verse in the KJV, are omitted by most modern versions because a number of early Greek manuscripts omit them. The same words appear at the end of verse 4, suggesting that a scribe may have accidentally repeated the phrase in verse 1. However, there is strong manuscript support for the KJV reading, and it fits admirably into the context if we understand Paul's thought at this point in the argument, i.e., sanctification by the life-giving Spirit (vv. 2–11).

3. Gordon D. Fee, *God's Empowering Presence: The Holy Spirit in the Letters of Paul* (Peabody, Ma.: Hendrickson, 1994).

4. I am indebted in this section to the perceptive article on this verse by Chuck Lowe, "'There Is No Condemnation' (Romans 8:1): But Why Not?" JETS 42/2 (June 1999), 231–50.

5. Loew, "No Condemnation," 249–50. Chrysostom says, "The grace of the Spirit put a stop to that war [7:23] by slaying sin and making the contest light for us, putting a victor's crown on our heads at the beginning and then drawing us into the struggle with enough help to win it" (Gerald Bray, ed. *Ancient Christian Commentary on Scripture, New Testament, VI, Romans* (Downers Grove, Ill.: InterVarsity Press, 1998), 200–201.

6. C. E. B. Cranfield, *A Critical and Exegetical Commentary on the Epistle to the Romans,* The International Critical Commentary, 2 vols. (Edinburgh: T. & T. Clark, 1975, 1979), 1:382; also Barrett, Moo, Dunn, and Schreiner, *Romans.* However, many of the church Fathers, in order to protect the sinlessness of Christ, rejected the connection of Christ's humanity with Adam's fallen human nature (Bray, *Romans,* 202–3).

7. Cranfield, 1:383; also Lowe, "There Is No Condemnation," 240–41. An alternate view is expressed by Moo and Schreiner *(Romans)* who argue that the "flesh" (NIV "sinful man") refers to Christ's own flesh. So the condemnation of sin refers to the death of Christ for the guilt of our sin and only indirectly to sin's power over our life, i.e., our sanctification. I believe that this view misunderstands the context of the whole of chapter 8, including vv. 1–3, which is the Spirit's work of sanctification.

8. This is the same word (Gk. *dikaioma*) discussed at 1:32; 2:26; 5:16, 18. The closest parallel is 2:26, where it means "righteous demand or requirement." Note that the verb "might be fulfilled" (NASB, NIV, "be fully met," Gk. *plērōthē)* is passive. For some (Moo, Fitzmyer) this means the believer is not involved. The reference is to the work of Christ on the cross; it is God's work. But again this forensic view of v. 4 is misplaced. Paul has in mind our obedience through the enablement of the Holy Spirit as vv. 5–11 emphasize (Schreiner, *Romans).* The exact expression in the Greek Bible occurs only here and in Num. 31:21 (*dikaioma tou theou,* "the [divine] just requirement of the [Mosaic] law").

9. It is also possible in another sense to "live in the world" (lit. "in the flesh," i.e., as a weak human being) but not "war as the world does" (lit. "after the flesh," i.e., drawing on the resources, standards, and values of sinful flesh). See 2 Cor. 10:2–3.

10. "The mind" *(phronēma)* set "on what that nature desires" is the noun form of the same verb used for "mind" in v. 5.

11. Most interpreters have understood the word "spirit" in verse 10 as a contrast to the "body" and refer it to the human "spirit" rather than the Holy Spirit (NASB, NIV, "the spirit is alive"). The objection to this latter view is simply that the Holy Spirit is the subject of the whole context and is immediately connected in verse 11 with life (see John Murray, *The Epistle to the Romans,* 2 vols. [Grand Rapids: Eerdmans, 1959], 1:294; C. K. Barrett, *The Epistle to the Romans* [New York: Harper & Row, 1957], 162; Anders Nygren, *Commentary on Romans* [Philadelphia: Fortress, 1949], 326; Cranfield, 1:390; also Schreiner, *Romans,* 415).

12. "Adoption" (v. 15 NASB) is the Greek *huiothesios,* "legally adopted son or child" (William Frederick Arndt, F. Wilbur Gingrich, and Frederick W. Danker, *Greek-English Lexicon,* s.v.), 2nd rev. ed. [Chicago: Univ. of Chicago, 1979]). It is a term used only by Paul and not found in the OT (LXX) or in classical writers, but the papyri manuscripts use it (James H. Moulton and George Milligan, *Vocabulary of the Greek New Testament* [Edinburgh: T. & T. Clark, 1901], 648; and G. Adolf Deissmann, *Bible Studies* [Edinburgh: T. &: T. Clark, 1901] 239). See Romans 9:4.

13. For some reason certain Aramaic words in the Christian tradition were left untranslated into Greek: e.g., "abba" (Mark 14:36; Rom. 8:15; Gal. 4:6); *"Eloi, Eloi, lama sabachthani"* (Matt. 27:46), *"maranatha"* (1 Cor. 16:22 NASB). Perhaps the precise shade of emotion in the original word or the traditional association was considered too precious to lose through translation. *Abba* was almost never used in prayer by the Jews but was common as a child's address to his own father (TDNT).

14. Cranfield, 1:393.

15. This point needs to be emphasized especially with the current postmodern emphasis of pluralism and the fact that in Eastern religions no distinction is made between God's spirit and the spirit present in all the world.

16. This right of equally shared inheritance even to adopted children is based not on Jewish law but Roman (E. H. Gifford, "Romans," in *The Bible Commentary: New Testament,* ed. F. C. Cook [New York: Scribner's, 1895], 3:154).

17. "The reference seems to be to the sum-total of sub-human nature both

animate and inanimate" (Cranfield, 1:411–12).

18. The Greek word for "wait eagerly" is *apokaradokia*, from *kara*, "head" and *dechomai*, "to stretch out," so "stretch out the head forward" in eager or anxious waiting (TDNT). Only Paul uses the word (Rom. 8:19; Phil. 1:20).

19. On the whole matter of glorification, one should not overlook the excellent book by Bernard Ramm, *Them He Glorified* (Grand Rapids: Eerdmans, 1963); on the creation and redemption relationship see John Gibbs, *Creation and Redemption: A Study in Pauline Theology* (Leiden: Brill, 1971).

20. It is possible to understand the "in the same way" as referring to our waiting eagerly; likewise the Spirit on God's part helps our weaknesses (Gifford, 3:157). A recent study argues that the correct connection goes way back to v. 16, the most recent verse that explicitly describes the work of the Spirit in and for the believer. In other words Paul is saying: "Just as the Spirit is at work within our hearts to confirm to us our adoption (v. 16), so *in the same way also* the Spirit is at work within our hearts to bear up our weakness" (Geoffrey Smith, "The Function of 'Likewise' *(hōsautōs)* in Romans 8:26," *Tyndale Bulletin* 49.1 (May 1998), 32, 37.

21. Smith, "The Function of Likewise," 37.

22. A. T. Robertson, *A Grammar of the Greek New Testament in the Light of Historical Research* (Nashville: Broadman, 1947), 593.

23. Ernst Käsemann and others (ancient and modern) believe Paul is here referring to "ecstatic cries" or speaking in tongues *(glossalalia)* (*Commentary on Romans*, trans. Geoffrey W. Bromiley [Grand Rapids: Eerdmans, 1978], 240–41). On the other hand, Cranfield, 1:421–24, argues that it is better to understand Paul's sense to be that these groanings are the Spirit's alone and are not expressed outwardly and are imperceptible to even the Christians themselves (so Moo and Schreiner, *Romans*, 445).

24. Cited by Donald Bloesch, *The Struggle of Prayer* (New York: Harper & Row, 1980), 29.

25. The NIV here follows a textual variant found in some ancient Greek manuscripts that reads, "God causes all things to work." Although it is possible that this is what Paul wrote (so NIV), the evidence and context strongly support the KJV rendering at this point: "All things work together for good" (John Murray, *The Epistle to the Romans*, 2 vols. [Grand Rapids: Eerdmans, 1959], 314); so also Moo and Schreiner, *Romans*.

26. C. S. Lewis, *The Problem of Pain* (London: Collins, 1940), 41; Cranfield comments likewise, "What he means ['for good'] is that they 'assist our

salvation' [Calvin]. . . . . All things which may happen to them, including such grievous things as are mentioned in v. 35, must serve to help them on their way to salvation, confirming their faith and drawing them closer to their Master, Jesus Christ" (1:428).

27. Three basic models of God's sovereignty and human salvation may be identified. (1) *Calvinistic.* God is viewed as having chosen before time certain individuals to participate in His salvation through Christ. In time He effectively draws them by grace through the Spirit to Himself and empowers them to believe the gospel. Augustine (4th cent.) and Calvin (16th cent.), among others, held this view. (2) *Arminian.* God is viewed as having foreknown (seen ahead) those individuals who would believe in Christ when they heard the gospel. On the basis of this foreseen response, God elects them to be His children and participate in the glory of Christ. All persons receive God's prevenient grace, which enables them to overcome the sinful bondage of the will if they decide to believe. Melanchton (16th cent.), J. Arminius (mid-16th, early 17th cent.), and John Wesley (18th cent.), among others, held this position. (3) *Corporate.* God is viewed as having chosen only Jesus Christ as an individual. All others who believe the gospel become part of the Elect One, Jesus Christ, and share in the corporate "election" in Him. Personal "election" in the NT is not for salvation but for service. Karl Barth (20th cent.), Alan Richardson (20th cent.), and Robert Shank (20th cent.), among others hold this view. See further for *Calvinist* view J. I. Packer, *Evangelism and the Sovereignty of God* (Downers Grove, Ill.: InterVarsity, 1957); for the *Arminian* view, William Greathouse and H. Ray Dunning, *An Introduction to Wesleyan Theology* (Kansas City, Mo.: Beacon Hill, 1982), 65–72; for *Corporate election* view see Robert Shank, *Elect in the Son: A Study of the Doctrine of Election* (Springfield, Mo.: Westcott, 1970). See further the notes in this book on chapters 9–11 of Romans.

28. "More than conquerors" is the Geneva Bible rendering (1557) of the Greek *hypernikaō*, which Paul has used to express the superlative *(hyper)* victory *(nikaō)* of the Christian over all of life's threatening evils. We "easily win the victory, or we come off as super victors" might also capture the force of Paul's word. The word occurs only rarely in pre-Christian literature (Arndt, Gingrich, Danker, s.v).

29. Paul seems to have the conscious experience of the love of God for him in mind. This is significant in that he says that *death* itself cannot separate him (and us) from the conscious experience of God's love, which would argue that Christian "soul sleep" at the time of death (until the resurrection) is less likely.

30. See Henry Hart Milman, *History of Christianity* (New York: Crowell, 1881), 4:144.

8

THE FAITHFULNESS OF GOD: THE CHALLENGE OF JEWISH UNBELIEF AND A WARNING TO GENTILE PRIDE

9:1–11:36

Some understand this lengthy section on Jewish unbelief in Christ to be parenthetical to the main thought of the letter. I will argue that chapters 9–11 form an essential link in the whole argument of God's righteousness and fulfill a necessary and climactic function to the whole doctrinal section. The problem Paul encounters at this point in his doctrine is twofold. First, if in the universal preaching of the gospel of Christ the priority of the message went "to the Jew first" (1:16 NASB), why then has the Jew so little share in this salvation? Hasn't the history of Jewish unbelief in Paul's gospel shown that it is basically incompatible with the Old Testament revelation?

Second, what has happened to the specific divine covenant promise of election and blessing given to Abraham and his seed? If the majority of the Jews are found to be rejected because they cannot accept this new faith that Paul preaches, how can God be seen as faithful and fulfill His Word of promise to Abraham? Or stated differently, doesn't the gospel as Paul preaches it nullify the whole Old Testament privilege of Israel as a people, which even the apostle himself has previously affirmed (3:1–2)? Further, chapter 8 has concluded with what seems to be the blessings promised to Israel in the OT (righteousness, reconciliation, sonship, the gift of the Spirit). What then has happened to the election of Israel, the covenant promises?

Paul's answer to this seeming discrepancy between his message of the gospel and Jewish unbelief lies in two broad directions. He shows, on the one hand, that the Jewish unbelief is not due to God's unfaithfulness but their own faithlessness. If they are rejected, it is because they have first rejected God (chaps. 9–10).

But this does not exhaust the answer. Paul also describes the outworking of a divine "mystery" in Israel's unbelief. Through Israel's unbelief, God's mercy and compassion will see unparalleled manifestation (chap. 11). More specifically, the promise to Abraham was not intended to be fulfilled to all Abraham's descendants but to a chosen seed or believing remnant both of Jewish and Gentile stock (9:6–10:21). Yet even though the integrity of God to His promises is fulfilled in the remnant, God also has in mind the eventual restoration of the whole people of Israel through their faith in Christ and through them a tremendous blessing for the entire world (chap. 11). Thus, the key word of these chapters is "mercy."

PAUL'S SORROW OVER ISRAEL'S UNBELIEF 9:1–5

PAUL'S SORROW (9:1–3)

Paul seems to move from the peak of joy in the previous chapter to the valley of sorrow in these opening verses. The great apostle to the Gentiles (11:13), who repeatedly has had to speak against certain Jewish views of justification by works of law held by some of his contemporaries, shows that he is not a feelingless renegade from his own people. Paul never renounced his Jewishness. He is continually and deeply grieved in his heart over the unbelief in Christ exhibited by his fellow Jews. Three times he appeals to the absolute sincerity of his feelings (v. 1). So intense was his sorrow over their failure to receive Jesus as Messiah that he wishes that he might even be "anathema" (accursed)[1] from Christ if it would mean their reconciliation to Christ (v. 3). Although this was not possible, his genuine love for those who were "my brothers, those of my own race" (not brothers in Christ) prompted this agonizing expression for their spiritual welfare. Do those who stand opposed to the gospel in our day (including Jewish neighbors) so break our hearts?

THE JEWISH PRIVILEGES (9:4–5)

Paul has already mentioned the "advantage" of the Jew in 3:1–2 (actually only one advantage was mentioned: the oracles of God). Now he elaborates eight privileges of being a Jew, against which his sorrow is intensified. To whom more is given more is expected and the deeper the sorrow when failure results. The advantage was eightfold: (1) the "adoption" was Israel's gracious calling to sonship with God as their Father in the Exodus (Exod. 4:22; Hos. 11:1); (2) the "glory" was God's visible manifestation whether in cloud and pillar of fire (Exod. 13:21–22) or in the sanctuary (Exod. 40:34–35); (3) the "covenants" were fivefold: Abrahamic (Gen. 15), Mosaic (Exod. 20), Palestinian (Deut. 29), Davidic (2 Sam. 7), and new (Jer. 31); (4) the "giving of the Law" (NASB) was at Sinai (Exod. 20); (5) the "temple service" (NASB) was the divine worship associated with the tabernacle; (6) the "promises" usually associated with the covenants included the main feature of blessings through the coming of the Messiah; (7) the "patriarchs" (Rom. 11:28); (8) the "Christ" or "Messiah" who came through the Jewish descent (v. 5).

The last part of verse 5 has been the subject of much debate because of the way it may be punctuated (the early Greek MSS have no punctuation). One punctuation makes the expression a final doxology to God the Father: "May God, who rules over all, be for ever praised" (see RSV, TEV, NEB). This punctuation is highly unlikely because an independent doxology to God at this point would be unusual, for Pauline doxologies regularly occur first in the sentence and are "an integral part of the preceding" statement.[2]

The other punctuation refers the "who" to Christ but differs on whether "God" should be referred to Christ, which precedes, or to "blessed," which follows: "who [Christ] is over all,

God blessed for ever" (KJV, NASB); or "Christ who is God over all, blessed for ever" (PHILLIPS, NIV). Either of the latter two renderings is preferable to the former because both refer Paul's doxology to the dual nature of Christ as being on the one hand Jewish flesh but on the other hand "over all" in His nature as Lord. Probably the NASB rendering is preferable here.[3]

THE PROMISE, GOD'S ELECTION, AND ISRAEL'S PAST HISTORY
9:6–29

Paul has sharpened the problem of Jewish unbelief in verses 1–5. If such privileges and promises were given to the Jews by God, how can they now be largely cut off from the blessings of the Messiah by unbelief? If God makes a promise, can't He keep it? What becomes of God's righteousness, which the gospel proclaims, if God's truthfulness and faithfulness have apparently failed in connection with God's Word to Israel? If God has reneged on His promises to Israel, how could Christians be certain that He would not change His mind toward them also? If the promises of God are revocable, then how can one have joyous confidence in God's eternal plan through Christ? Both the validity of the promises and, by implication, the character of God are at stake.

Paul gives four lines of argument to answer this challenge. The first concerns the nature of God's promises as being rooted in the free and righteous elective purpose of God in Israel's history (9:6–29). Paul will show from Israel's history that God's promise to Abraham was intended to be fulfilled only to those whom He sovereignly "called."

It is important at this point to get some background in first-century Jewish views of election. Problems that for years have entrenched theologians in chapters 9 and 10 might have been avoided if this material had been considered more seriously. Furthermore, by being preoccupied with these theological debates, many have also missed the real point of chapter 11.

The Jewish argument is well summarized by Berkeley Michelsen in his commentary on Romans in *The Wycliffe Bible Commentary*.[4] Paul's Jewish opponents would present this

view: "We have circumcision as a sign (Gen. 17:7–14) that we
are God's elect people. Members of God's elect people will not
perish. Therefore, we will not perish." Rabbinical evidence
shows that this was the attitude of many Jews in Paul's day.
Hermann L. Strack and Paul Billerbeck have prepared a *Commentary on the New Testament* in which they bring together
parallels from the Talmud and Midrashim that shed light on the
New Testament.[5] In volume 4, part 2, they have devoted an
entire excursus (#31) to the subject of *Sheol, gehenna* (place of
punishment) and the *heavenly garden of Eden* (paradise). The
following translations include names of tractates of the rabbinical writings from which their ideas about these places are
drawn.

> Rabbi Levi has said: In the future (on the other side—what the
> Greeks called the spirit world) Abraham sits at the entrance of
> Gehenna and he allows no circumcised ones from the Israelites to
> enter into it (i.e., Gehenna). (Midrash Rabba Genesis, 48
> [30a,49])[6]

In this same context the question is asked: How about those
who sin excessively? The answer is: They are returned to a state
of uncircumcision as they enter gehenna. The next translation
deals with the question of what happens after death to an
Israelite.

> When an Israelite goes into his eternal house (=grave), an angel is
> sitting over the heavenly garden of Eden, who takes each son of
> Israel who is circumcised for the purpose of bringing him into the
> heavenly garden of Eden (paradise). (Midrash Tanchum, Sade,
> waw, 145a, 35).[7]

Again the question is raised: How about those Israelites
who serve idols? As above, the answer is: They will be returned
to a state of uncircumcision in gehenna. Here is a translation
that looks at the Israelites as a group.

> All Israelites who are circumcised come into the heavenly garden
> of Eden (paradise). (Midrash Tanchuma, Sade, waw, 145a, 32).[8]

It is clear from these quotations that most Jews believed and taught that all circumcised Israelites who have died are in paradise and that there are no circumcised Israelites in gehenna. Note also that to be put in the category of the "uncircumcised" (Gentile) is to ensure the final end of gehenna (hell). Thus chapter 9 will center on the inclusion of the Gentiles into the people of God on the basis of faith. Paul's burden is to show the freedom of God's mercy.

In response to the claim that the Lord could not reject His elect people, Paul first of all replies by emphasizing God's freedom, righteousness, and sovereignty. God acts freely, acts in righteousness, and acts sovereignly because He is free, righteous, and sovereign in His own eternal being.

THE PROMISE AND ABRAHAM'S DESCENDANTS, ISAAC AND JACOB (9:6–13)

Has God failed to keep His Word to Israel? No, Paul asserts: "It is not as though God's word [the promises] had failed" (Gk. *ekpiptō,* "to be in vain," "to lose validity") and by implication God's own faithfulness (v. 6). The reason Paul asserts that the promises to Israel have not actually been empty is that the promise has always been linked to the purpose of God determined by election or calling (v. 11). From the very beginning onward in Israel's history, God has been selective in the application of the promise. He says, "Not all who are descended from Israel [physical lineage] are Israel [true spiritual seed]" (v. 6). The promise is valid only to those for whom it was intended.

Cranfield captures the thrust of Paul's point: "The fact that at the present time the majority of Jews stand outside the inner circle of election, which is the Israel within the Israel, is, since it conforms to the pattern of the working out of God's purpose from the beginning, no proof of the failure of that purpose" (2:471). All Jews are members of God's elect people (11:28). But not all are members of the Israel within the Israel, the election of grace (11:5–6), the company of those who are willing, obedient, grateful witnesses to that grace and truth. The terms used to distinguish the two forms of election in verses 6–8 can be set out accordingly:

Broader Israel Election	Specific Israel Election
"Descended from Israel" (6b)	"are Israel" (6b)
"his [Abraham's] descendants" (7a)	"Abraham's children" (7b)
"natural children" (8a)	"through Isaac . . . offspring" (7c)
	"God's children" (8a)
	"children of the promise" (8b),
	"Abraham's offspring" (8b)

Paul, in verses 6–13, uses two cases in the beginning of Israel's history to demonstrate that when God gave the promise of blessing to Abraham and his descendants, He did not have *all* the descendants of Abraham in mind. In the first place, God chose Isaac rather than Ishmael to continue the promise made to Abraham: "It is through Isaac that your offspring will be reckoned" (Rom. 9:7; Gen. 21:12); and the Word said, "Sarah will have a son" (Rom. 9:9; Gen. 18:10). In an argument parallel to that elaborated further in Galatians 3 and 4, Paul argues that the descendants of Ishmael through the bondwoman Hagar are of the flesh and not the heirs of the promise. His point is that God moved toward fulfilling the promise through selection as in the case of Abraham's children.

But we should be careful to note that this selection of Isaac over Ishmael to fulfill God's special purpose does not mean that Ishmael was excluded from God's mercy (see Gen. 16:10–14; 17:20; 21:13, 17–21). Certainly this point has a bearing today on Christian attitudes toward Arabs (descendants of Ishmael) vis-à-vis Jews.

But were not Abraham's children (Isaac and Ishmael) born of different mothers? God probably chose Isaac, it might be suggested, because he was born of Abraham's full wife, Sarah. To show that God's sovereign and free election has no reference to merit derived from the status or relationship of the mothers,

Paul shows the same principle operating in *one* mother, Rebekah, and the birth of her twins, Jacob and Esau. God's free election has nothing to do with the merits of special lineage or of an individual's own works. It all depends on God's sovereign will. God selected Jacob ("the older will serve the younger," Rom. 9:12) to continue the lineage through whom the promise was to be fulfilled even though such recognition was contrary to the Near Eastern custom of the right of inheritance going to the firstborn (vv. 10–12).

In verse 13 Paul appeals to a passage in the prophets to further support the practice of God's sovereign selection, "Jacob I loved, but Esau I hated" (Rom. 9:13; Mal. 1:2–3). Love and hate in this context do not have to do with God's personal emotional hatred or love but with the *choice* of the one over the other to continue the fulfillment of the promise.

Again a caution is in order. "It is important to stress that neither as they occur in Genesis nor as they are used by Paul do these words refer to the eternal destinies either of the two persons or of the individual members of the nations sprung from them; the reference is rather to the mutual relations of the two nations in history" (Cranfield, 2:479).

My children play a game involving various colored marbles. They inform me that I am to be interested only in marbles of a certain color, and I am not to try to take the others of different colors. In words similar to Malachi's they say, "Daddy, you *hate* blue [marbles], and you *love* red [marbles]." Thus I choose (love) the red marbles for my purposes and leave (hate) the blue ones alone for other purposes. God's purposes in salvation, however, are never carried out without respect to a human response of belief or unbelief. Paul will get to this point later (vv. 30–33), but first he must answer two objections to his concept of election.

GOD'S SOVEREIGNTY AND GOD'S JUSTICE (9:14–29)

The most natural objection to Paul's teaching on God's sovereign election (if correctly understood) is that it seems to make God unfair in that He chooses one and not the other (even before birth in Jacob's case) without any regard to their works. So an objector might say, "Is God unjust [unrighteous]?" (v. 14). Paul's answer is disappointing but instructive. He simply abhors the idea ("Not at all!") and shows that God does exercise His mercy in absolute freedom of choice. Paul assumes throughout that God is just and His actions of election are also consistent with His justice.

To support his view of God's justice in His merciful free choices, the apostle turns for further evidence to the words of God to Moses and Pharaoh (vv. 15–18). If anyone in Israel's history should have been chosen for his good works, it would be the great lawgiver, Moses, but it is to Moses that God says, "I will have mercy on whom I have mercy" (Rom. 9:15; Exod. 33:19). Not even Moses was shown God's mercy except on the basis of God's own choice to bless Moses (v. 15). All God's acts toward us are on the basis of His mercy; we deserve nothing, because we are in rebellion. If God comes to us in mercy, our status and blessing before God cannot be due to our willing or achieving. This is Paul's whole position on justification by faith (chaps. 1–8).

What about Pharaoh himself (Exod. 4:21)? It was precisely because Pharaoh hardened his heart that Israel was oppressed, and God could show His power in the Exodus and proclaim His name to all ages through the Passover celebration (Rom. 9:17). Upon whom He wills He shows mercy, and "he hardens whom he wants to harden" (v. 18). The hardening of Pharaoh's heart, which resulted from his unbelief (Exod. 4:21; 7:3; 9:12), was designed to show God's mercy. God's sovereignty even extends to the callusing of human hearts. But even this severe action was a means to the end of showing His mercy. Pharaoh first hardened his own heart following the first five plagues; then God hardened Pharaoh's heart in the last five plagues.[9] Pharaoh may also be a type of unbelieving Israel, who in spite of their unwillingness and disobedience become witnesses negatively to the saving power and truth of God.

In the diatribe fashion (see Rom. 2:1–4) Paul utters the actual words of another objection, "One of you will say to me: 'Then why does God still blame us? For who resists his will?'"

(v. 19). The objection is discerning and devastating. If God sovereignly hardens human hearts like Pharaoh's, how can He justly judge them as hardened sinners since no one can resist His sovereign will? It is the problem of human responsibility and God's justice. Again, Paul's answer is even more disappointing in one sense than the former but perhaps also more instructive. He does not answer the charge but simply says in the strongest way that our position as creatures does not qualify us to contradict the Creator (vv. 20–21). We must be silent! Just as potters may fashion their clay as they please (Jer. 18), so God has perfect liberty to make of humanity what He pleases. As the pottery cannot answer back challenging the design of the potter, so neither can we (Isa. 29:16).

But someone may object, "We are not pots and we *will* ask questions!" But Paul's reply rejects this kind of question because it presupposes *human* centrality and to try to answer it would tend to lower God to human reasoning and attempt to justify God theoretically. Rather, Paul affirms the centrality of God and will not lower God's actions to fit human reasoning. His response demands that first of all God be acknowledged as God (Rom. 1:21). Ultimately, as potters are responsible for the vessels they fashion, so God is, finally, responsible for what He does in history.

It is important to note that up to this point in the chapter there is really no concrete evidence to argue that Paul is talking about God's choosing some *individuals* for eternal salvation or for eternal condemnation. Rather, he has been arguing that God has perfect freedom to be merciful to whomever He wills and in a manner that He Himself chooses. The following verses (22–33) will reveal that God chooses to be merciful to all people, both Jews and Gentiles, upon the basis of their belief in the gospel of Jesus Christ. This is the election of grace (11:5–6).

Verses 21–24 expand the thought of potters having the absolute right to make vessels for whatever end they wish, either for aesthetic ends or for more common, menial ends ("noble purposes . . . common use"). Paul further draws upon the potter analogy but begins to narrow down the sense to his immediate concern. God makes "objects [instruments] of his wrath—prepared for destruction" (v. 22)[10] and "objects [instruments] of his mercy, whom he prepared in advance for glory" (v. 23).

Some argue that verse 24 makes plain that Paul has *persons* in mind: "Even us, whom he also called." Further, "calling" in the whole epistle refers to the individual call to salvation and justification (8:30). One cannot then, it is argued, regardless of the difficulty, weaken at least the latter part of the chapter's emphasis on individual election and calling (regardless of the earlier portions) to that of mere national or corporate election. Paul's very point, they say, is to the opposite effect; that is, God has by grace selected a group out of the nation to whom He will manifest His mercy (forgiveness), and He has fitted others to receive His wrath (deservedly because of their unbelief, vv. 30–33).[11]

Others argue that the references to "objects of his wrath" or "objects of his mercy" have corporate-groups (nations) in mind with individuals (like Pharaoh) as their representatives. They argue that this passage does not indicate (following Calvin) that God chooses some individuals for eternal salvation and chooses others for reprobation. "This saving grace in history operates by the method of the selection of instruments (or, to use the Pauline word, 'vessels') by means of which—whether by obedience ('vessels of mercy') or by disobedience ('vessels of wrath')—God's universal design is accomplished."[12]

But lest we charge God with arbitrary rigor, it should be noted that Paul's burden is to show that God's deliberate design in election was to show forth His mercy (v. 23). In order to do this, God exercised much long-suffering (patience) toward the vessels of wrath (Pharaoh and certain unbelieving Jews and Gentiles in Paul's day) by not immediately destroying them but giving them opportunity to repent before His final power and wrath is revealed (2:4–5).

Paul's main point seems to be that when unbelief and hardening arise, God has a purpose in that history (as well as for the individual). This purpose is first of all to reveal His wrath against rebellion and thereby proclaim to the world His power. Second, through unbelief God will cause His mercy to be brought upon those whom He calls. Ultimately, then, history is redemptive in its purpose. In glory and in wrath through election, God is working out His purpose in history of manifesting His righteousness.

In verses 25–29 Paul appeals to the Old Testament prophecies for the principles that substantiate his claim. He makes references to God's announcement to choose an elect company of both Jews and Gentiles to participate in His mercy. To show that God had in mind to "call" (to salvation) Gentiles, as a group, Paul quotes Hosea 2:23 and 1:10, which originally applied to rejected Jews as "not my people" and "not my loved one," to the effect that God would call to Himself those who were not His people (by application, Gentiles) and make them "sons of the living God" (vv. 25–26).

Furthermore, Paul quotes Isaiah to show that the Old Testament predicted that God would "call" not the *whole* nation of Israel through His promise, but only a remnant would be saved (Rom. 9:27–29; Isa. 1:9; 10:21–22; 11:11). Again, in Isaiah's day, God's wrath was poured out through the Assyrians on a disbelieving nation (Rom. 9:28), but God moved also in electing grace to preserve a remnant or seed (v. 29). So in all God's dealings with us, the promise of blessing (forgiveness) relates to the chosen seed who are of faith; and if unbelief prevails, it does not thereby nullify the Word of God.

ISRAEL'S FAILURE HER OWN FAULT 9:30–10:21

Paul has argued that Israel's unbelief cannot invalidate God's Word because God's promise is based on the principle of election. If God is totally free to show mercy upon whomever He wills, then our response to God's free choice is wholly accountable to God. His election is not unrelated to our belief. Even Augustine struggled with his belief that God gave us saving faith, but in some sense we had to consent or not consent to God's gift. Thus he says: "The will by which we believe is taken to be a gift of God. . . . But to consent to the calling of God or to dissent from it belongs to the will itself. . . . For the soul cannot receive and have these gifts . . . except by consenting. And so whatever it has and whatever it receives come from God, but to

receive and to have comes from the one receiving and having"
(*De Spiritu et littera,* XXXIV.60). Israel's stumbling was due to
her own misguided effort in attempting to find mercy before
God through law obedience rather than by faith. "Christ is the
end of the law so that there may be righteousness for everyone
who believes" (10:4).

Furthermore, this faith righteousness that Paul proclaims,
unlike the Mosaic Law, is easily available to all who will hear its
Word (10:5–13). Yet many Jews have heard this universally
preached Word of Christ, the Messiah, and have turned from it
in disobedience as the prophets foretold. They are therefore
fully responsible for God's rejection of them (10:14–21).

THE CAUSE OF THE JEWS' FAILURE (9:30–10:4)

Although certain Jews have not lacked enthusiasm for God
("pursued a law of righteousness," "zealous for God," 9:31;
10:2), their commendable sincerity has not helped them before
God because it was selfishly misguided. The Jewish moralist, in
attempting to attain acceptance before God by keeping the law,
has, in fact, not attained this acceptance (righteousness) as did
the believing Gentile. Why? Because, as Paul has already argued
through the first part of the letter (chaps. 1–8), all are sinners
and cannot approach God on the basis of good works. We can
come to Him only in humble acceptance by faith of God's provision in Christ (vv. 30–32).[13] This "stumbling stone" (i.e., Christ
and faith righteousness; 1 Pet. 2:6–8) was prepared by God and
foretold by Isaiah, the prophet (Rom. 9:33; Isa. 8:14; 28:16). If
the image of running is still in Paul's mind, then the picture of a
runner tripping over a hurdle and losing the race vividly captures his point (vv. 32–33).

The misinformed zeal for God held by certain of his Jewish
people intensifies the tragedy of their rejection (Phil. 3:6). It is
Paul's earnest desire that they may realize their error and turn to
Christ for deliverance from their sin (10:1–2). Charles Erdman
commented that there would be no lack of converts to the
Christian faith if all who profess to follow Christ felt for the
spiritual welfare of their fellow countrymen this deep concern

expressed by Paul for his own people.[14]

For Jewish (or Gentile) legalists the error begins with their failure to judge themselves correctly in view of their own moral and spiritual shortcomings. Supposing themselves to be all right or as good as others, they develop a spirit of proud self-seeking, which is the root of sin. They end up by boasting in their own moral achievements (v. 3; 3:27). In seeking to establish before God their own righteousness, moralists overlook God's way of righteousness, which comes as a grace-gift through faith in Jesus Christ. It is an ironic tragedy—zeal for God, but rejection by God. These statements of Paul should forever settle the thesis that sincerity in place of truth suffices before God. Sincerity indeed may be indicative of a right attitude toward God, but not necessarily, as the present case reveals. Nor can ignorance be pleaded as an excuse before God because no one is totally ignorant of God's truth, and we are morally responsible for what we ought to know (1:19–20).

To all who have faith, Christ is an "end" (Gk. *telos,* goal, termination) of the Mosaic Law covenant to obtain justification (v. 4). When one submits to Christ as God's means for justification, it puts an end to the attempted (but futile) seeking for justification through the moralistic approach to the Mosaic Law (v. 3).[15]

THE RIGHTEOUSNESS OF FAITH: IS IT TOO DIFFICULT? (10:5–13)

In these nine verses the righteousness that comes through the Mosaic Law (v. 5) is contrasted with the righteousness based on faith (vv. 6–13). The latter is not only available (vv. 5–8), and universal in its appeal (vv. 11–13), but rests upon the historical fact of Jesus' death and resurrection (vv. 9–10).

What about obedience to the law? Was not the keeping of the law the prerequisite for having life (Lev. 18:5; Luke 10:28)? If God gave the law and commanded total obedience to it, can it be maintained that obedience to it would have no relevance? Paul seems to argue in verse 5 that Moses taught that the achievement of righteousness before God on the basis of obedience to the law was at least a theoretical possibility.[16] However,

Paul argued earlier in the letter that the law came in to increase the trespass (5:20). It may not be impossible to reconcile these two opposites if we remember that when we attempt to keep all the law without the Spirit we discover that we are powerless to do it and thus judged sinful by the same law through which we sought acceptance and life (Deut. 27:26).

Some Jews' (and all Gentile moralists') real mistake, according to Paul, is not that they do not take the law seriously but that they fail to take it seriously enough. Moralists count on two illusions. They believe, on the one hand, that on the ledger of life certain good works in the credit column will in the long run cancel out many of the debit marks in the other columns and ultimately put them in the black before God. On the other hand, they also hold to the false belief that whatever does not balance up will be overlooked by God's indulgence. But God does not keep any such credit books of good versus bad, because He has an entirely different way of balancing out the debit column. Righteousness comes only through faith in the Lord Jesus Christ.

In verses 6–8 Paul combines references to the Old Testament law (Deut. 30:11–14) with statements about the gospel. It is clear that the words "do not say in your heart" (Rom. 10:6) are aimed at the attitude of unbelief in the gospel. What is not so clear is Paul's use of the phrases "who will ascend into heaven?" and "who will descend into the deep?" which are borrowed from the Deuteronomy passage. Does Paul mean that the words that were originally applied to the law in the Old Testament have equal significance when applied to faith in Christ? Moses' warning in Deuteronomy is against the taunt of unbelief expressed when a person claims that the revelation of the law is too difficult (impossible) to fulfill because it is inaccessible (in heaven or beyond the sea). Likewise, Paul sees the danger of unbelief in the gospel as evidenced when we demand before we will trust Christ to have firsthand empirical proof of the Incarnation ("bring Christ down") and the resurrection ("bring Christ up from the dead").

But faith operates on the basis of the *Word* of divine witness proclaimed in the message of Christ, and therefore salvation-faith is immediately possible when one hears the gospel message. How important this truth is that connects the truthfulness of the historical facts of Jesus' death and resurrection with the preached Word of the gospel witness. This means that when I believe the gospel message by faith I do not need to actually witness or be able to infallibly verify those historical events to have their certainty and efficacy immediately applied to my life. This does not eliminate historical investigation of Jesus' life but keeps such exploration as secondary and nonsalvific.

Verses 9–10 describe the twofold content of this faith righteousness: namely, (1) "If you confess with your mouth, 'Jesus is Lord'" (the Divine King from heaven); and (2) "believe in your heart that God raised him from the dead." The kind of faith that grants forgiveness and acceptance before God consists basically in two articles. Along with acceptance of Jesus as Lord goes the second, God raised Him from the dead. The resurrection is a crucial historical event because it marks out Jesus, the Lord from heaven, as absolutely distinct from any other lord. He is the One in whom alone the Father has accomplished His redeeming work for the world (Heb. 1:3).

No special point should be made in verse 10 over the dual use of "heart . . . justified" with "mouth . . . saved." The biblical idea of the heart refers to the religious center or volitional core of our life and should not be limited to only the affections or emotions. What the heart believes will be uttered by the lips. As Paul says elsewhere, "No one can say, 'Jesus is Lord,' except by the Holy Spirit" (1 Cor. 12:3; Matt. 12:34). To "confess" means to declare, avow, profess, proclaim. It seems evident that the "confession" is to be made out loud before others, with the mouth, not by some other action.

Along with an affirmation from Isa. 28:16 to the effect that one who trusts in the Lord will not be "dismayed" (or "disillusioned," TDNT), Paul strikes the note of the universality of this faith salvation in verses 11–13. Everyone (Jew and Gentile) who calls upon the name of the Lord shall be saved (Joel 2:32). The Old Testament foretold of this universal salvation available to all who evidence their faith in the Lord. Calling upon His name is an act of worship.[17] But why, then, haven't some Jews believed? Why have they apparently been rejected in favor of the Gentiles? Paul now turns to this problem.

THE FAILURE OF FAITH: PERHAPS THEY DIDN'T HEAR? (10:14–21)

Perhaps ignorance of the gospel is the problem? In verses 14–15 Paul constructs a five-link chain to emphasize that ignorance is not the cause of the Jews' failure. We will only call (for salvation) upon one in whom we believe. Faith must have a proclaimed conscious object, which requires a message and a messenger. Finally, a genuine messenger or an apostle who is commissioned by the Lord Himself must be "sent" (Gk. *apostalōsin*) (v. 15). This last link is confirmed by a reference to the Old Testament where God approvingly mentions the ministry of *sent ones* (apostles) to Israel for salvation purposes (Isa. 52:7).

Paul abruptly breaks the chain at this point and raises the issue of Israel's partial unbelief, "Not all the Israelites accepted the good news" (v. 16). The hearing of the message was only beneficial when it was received by faith (Heb. 4:1–2). "Those along the path" writes Luke, "are the ones who hear, and then the devil comes and takes away the word from their hearts, so that they may not believe and be saved" (Luke 8:12). Even Isaiah confirms the truth Paul is stating by predicting that the message (report) concerning the Messiah would fail to be accepted (Isa. 53:1).

In verse 17 Paul summarizes ("consequently") his main point by affirming the connection between the message proclaimed by Christ's apostles and faith that calls upon the name of the Lord for salvation. Saving faith, then, arises in response to the message (Word preaching) about Christ (His lordship and resurrection, v. 9).[18] Faith has a perpetual relationship to the Word and cannot be separated from it any more than can the rays from the sun whence they proceed.

In verses 18–21 Paul speaks more pointedly to why part of Israel failed to respond to Jesus, the Messiah (Christ). Perhaps they, in fact, did not have opportunity to hear the gospel of Christ? Paul answers quite emphatically to the contrary, "Of course they did." The language of Psalm 19:4, which Paul uses to describe the universal saturation of the world with the gospel message, has raised an important question (v. 18).

Does the revelation of God in nature, to which the psalm refers, carry with it the gospel message? In this case Paul would be saying that the Jews heard the gospel in the witness of nature (so Calvin). While this sense is possible, the context argues for a different meaning. Just as the revelation of God in nature is universal (Ps. 19:4), and makes no distinctions between Jew and Gentile, so the historical revelation of God in the gospel of Jesus has gone forth with universality to all places and to all peoples. Israel indeed had heard the proclaimed message in the first century at least. They could not plead ignorance of Christ. The faithful obedience of our first-century brethren in spreading the message of Christ to their known world regardless of the cost certainly should inspire us. Schreiner gives a further sense to the words by arguing that if even the Gentiles have heard this message of Christ's salvation, then Israel should have perceived that this was the "the fulfillment of the OT prophecies that God's kingdom would encompass the whole world—then the age of fulfillment has dawned and Israel has certainly heard the good news that Isaiah (52:7) foretold would be proclaimed" (*Romans*, 572).

Finally, the apostle discusses a further reason offered to explain why Israel failed to embrace Christ by asking, "Did Israel not understand?" (v. 19). Perhaps the gospel preachers spoke unintelligibly and Israel misunderstood their message? Again the answer implied is no, for both the Law (Moses, v. 19) and then the prophets (Isaiah, vv. 20–21) declared that God was going to work significantly among the Gentiles ("not a nation;" "nation that has no understanding") and as a result Israel would be "envious" and "angry" (v. 19). Such strong emotional response could not but be the result of first of all a clear understanding of the universal character of the gospel message, which puts Jew and Gentile on equal footing.

Furthermore, the Gentiles' response was immediate and grateful, from a people who were not even associated with the Lord (v. 20; Isa. 65:1). Yet, to Israel, God through the prophet declared (Isa. 65:2) that He had unceasingly stretched forth His hands in unwearied love only to have his pleading met with rebuffs (see also Matt. 23:37–39). Surely there is a great mystery surrounding why anyone rebels against the love of the Creator.

It seems clear from this chapter that the failure of some of Israel to respond to Christ's Word lies neither in their lack of knowledge nor in their failure to grasp the meaning of the message. Their rejection goes back to their own choice of unbelief and disobedience. It is not because God has withdrawn His love and promises to them.

ISRAEL'S FAILURE NEITHER TOTAL NOR FINAL 11:1–36

Since some in Israel rejected the gospel of Christ, does this mean that they have been entirely rejected by God? Is the national election of Israel over? Has the plan of God in calling this people been frustrated by their obstinacy? Who will now do what God intended Israel to do? Paul's answer is twofold and definite. First, God has not rejected Israel as a people. Paul is exhibit number one that God still has a purpose for the Israelite people as a whole. Paul represents not merely the fact that a Jew can become a believer in Jesus as the Messiah and remain an Israelite. Rather, Paul as an *Israelite* has become a witness to the Gentiles. In him, then, there is a strong argument for Israel's future hope as a people (see below). Second, God is not through with this people as a whole nation, but He has planned a glorious revival among them sometime in the future (11:11–29). These two aspects of the Jews' present and future are both introduced by a separate question in verses 1 and 11.

JEWS' FAILURE NOT TOTAL (11:1–10)

Paul asks, with all that he has just said in mind (10:18–21), "Did God reject his people?" (v. 1). The form of the question in the Greek expects a negative answer, so he answers immediately with the strong negative, "By no means!" (see 3:4). The principal reason for his confidence in God's favor toward the Jewish people as a whole is that he himself comes from pure Jewish ancestry and yet believes in Jesus as the Messiah. Very often the point is made simply that the existence of Messianic Jewish believers in the world proves that God has not rejected the total Israelite community.[19] Cranfield asserts that

> the most probable explanation is that what Paul has in mind is not just the fact that he, a Jew, is a Christian, nor yet that he who has been so fierce an opponent of the gospel is a Christian, but the fact that he, a Jew (and one who has particularly ferociously opposed the gospel) is God's chosen apostle to the Gentiles. Were God intending only to save a mere handful of Israel, had He really cast off the people of Israel as a whole, would He have chosen an Israelite to be the apostle to the Gentiles and the chief bearer of the gospel message? In his person the missionary vocation of Israel is at last being fulfilled, and Israel is actively associated with the work of the risen Christ. This is a more cogent evidence of God's not having cast off His people than is the simple fact that one particular Jew has come to believe.[20]

"God did not reject his people, whom he foreknew" (v. 2a) reflects the language of Psalm 94:14 (cf. 1 Sam. 12:22). God remains ever faithful to His covenant promises to Abraham (Gen. 22:17-18). We should not (contra Calvin) understand "his people" *(laos)* in verse 2a to be a reference to the elect believing remnant but to refer to the general election of Israel as a whole as it does in verse 1. The fact that God "foreknew" them in the sense of deliberately joining them to Himself in covenant love excludes the possibility of Him casting them off (see 11:28-29).

Paul turns in verses 2b-5 to one of the many cases in the Old Testament where the nation in large measure had turned away from God's will, yet there were still those who followed Him. It forms a parallel to the problem of unbelief in Paul's own day. Elijah's circumstances in the revolt against God incited by Jezebel forced him to conclude that he alone of the whole nation was still a true follower of the Lord (1 Kings 19:10-14). Yet God's Word came to him and revealed that there were some seven thousand others whom God had "kept" for Himself who were still obedient to Him (v. 4 NASB). Paul identifies himself with Elijah in his aloneness and also in the mild but encouraging rebuke of the Lord, who reminded the prophet that there was a chosen remnant out of Israel that constituted the true Israel through whom God's covenant purposes would continue (cf. 9:6–8, 27).

"So too [as in Elijah's day], at the present time there is a remnant [of Jewish believers in Jesus] chosen by grace" (v. 5). Since the remnant can only exist by God's choice, it must be by grace and not on the basis of our meritorious law works. Paul digresses briefly in verse 6 to emphasize his main argument that appeared earlier in the letter (3:27–4:25). God deals with us only on the basis of His grace (hence, faith) and not our meritorious works. Grace and meritorious works are mutually exclusive principles in winning acceptance before God. If God's election is the basis of the remnant's existence, then it must be based on God's grace, which precedes all human works; otherwise grace ceases to be grace, and works cease to be works. In other words, if we confuse such opposites as grace and meritorious works, words lose their meaning (Eph. 2:8–9; Rom. 9:11). "It was God, by His own decision and for the accomplishment of His own purpose, who made the remnant to stand firm; and for this very reason its existence was full of promise for the rest of the nation" (Cranfield, 2:547).

But what of the "rest" of the nation of Israel who were not the remnant? Paul says they were "hardened" (v. 7) in accordance with the Old Testament predictions in Moses' writing (Rom. 11:8; Deut. 29:4), and in David's statements (Rom. 11:9–10; Ps. 69:22). Hardening is a divine judgment arising out of unbelief (see Rom. 9:17–18; 11:20; Matt. 13:14–15; Heb. 3:12–13). Unbelief brings blindness, insensitivity, bondage ("their backs be bent forever," Rom. 11:10), and social discord ("table become a snare," v. 9). One cannot refuse the divine grace without at the same time positively opposing God (Mark 9:40). Such opposition brings God's active judgment in the present life much in the same manner as the threefold reference to divine judgment ("God gave them over") in chapter 1. But this is not the last word God has for "the rest" (see vv. 23, 26, 31).

The expression in verse 7 to the effect that Israel did not

obtain what it sought for can mean nothing less than that the majority of the people did not obtain righteousness or justification before God (9:30; 10:3). The elect remnant obtained the justification by faith, but the rest did not.

ISRAEL'S FAILURE NOT FINAL (11:11–32)

If the majority of the Jewish nation stumbled over the gospel, even though a remnant believed, does this mean that God is through with the people as a whole or as a nation? Paul's question in verse 11 is very important: "Did they stumble so as to fall beyond recovery?" That some Jews have "stumbled" into unbelief and disobedience the apostle has already clearly stated (9:32). But what does he mean by the phrase, "so as to fall"?

Some understand the "fall" to refer to Israel's final rejection as a religious community in the sense that God has purposed ("so as") that as a whole they should never recover. The negative reply, "Not at all!" would then deny that this was true. Furthermore, the latter part of the chapter (vv. 12, 25–27) would also support this idea that God is not finished with the nation as a spiritual community when it refers to the future salvation of "all Israel."[21]

The chief problem with this view is that it does not do justice to the rest of verse 11: "Because of their transgression [stumbling], salvation has come to the Gentiles to make Israel envious." In this use of the words, "because of their transgression" (Gk. *paraptoma*, trespass, sin, 5:15), the reference is clearly to their stumbling into sin and unbelief.

Another sense, then, for the word "fall" is preferred. Paul's real question is whether the Jews' stumbling into the sin of unbelief was purposed by God so that they might lose their covenant relationship involving not only a future redemptive purpose but also a present purpose. Paul answers in strong abhorrence to the effect that they have not fallen down completely, and he proceeds to state two present divine purposes in Israel's temporary stumbling: (1) that the gospel of salvation might go to the Gentiles and (2) that as a result of Gentile blessings the Jews might be stirred to jealousy and desire to come to Christ (vv. 11, 14). Both purposes are merciful in their design. This much, then, is clear. The exclusion of the majority of Israelites is temporary and, while it lasts, serves a particular gracious divine purpose in the present.

In the first instance, the immediate result of the partial Jewish rejection of Christ was the historical turning of the apostles to the Gentiles (Acts 13:46; 18:6; 28:28). Thus even in her disobedience, Israel still fulfills her calling as a link between the Messiah and the nations. Second, as a result of the conversion of the Gentiles, the Jews will be stirred to jealousy over the working of God among those who were formerly not His people. Paul's own ministry to the Gentiles can be viewed as ultimately a means of reaching at least some of his fellow Israelites with Christ's gospel by making them jealous (vv. 13–14).

In verses 12 and 15 Paul contrasts and compares the present effects of the Gentile conversion with the future effects of Israel's repentance:

	ISRAEL	GENTILES
PRESENT	"transgression" (v. 11) "loss" (v. 12) "rejection" (v. 15)	"riches for the world" (v. 12) "riches for the Gentiles" (v. 12) "reconciliation of the world" (v. 15)
FUTURE	"how much greater riches" (v. 12) "their acceptance . . . life from the dead" (v. 15)	"the full number of the Gentiles" (v. 25)

Paul sees a glorious future for the people of Israel as a whole and through them a tremendous blessing for the whole world. This latter truth is highlighted in verse 15 by the difficult expression "life from the dead." The phrase probably does not describe the resurrection from the dead (most commentators since Origen including now Cranfield, Moo, Schreiner, and Dunn) or the revival of the nation of Israel. Rather, it should be understood as a figure to describe some future glorious vivified condition of the whole world that occurs as a result of Israel's conversion since it parallels the expression "reconciliation of the world" (see comments at v. 25).[22] Whatever tremendous thing Paul has in mind, it can only be described with the dramatic figure as the difference between death and life (v. 15).

To develop his argument further that the nation of Israel will still enjoy a future restoration as the people of God, Paul selects two analogies in verse 16. The "first piece" (NASB) or "firstfruit" of the dough was a small portion of the newly kneaded lump that was set aside and, after having been baked into a loaf, offered to the Lord (Num. 15:19–21).[23] The consecrated offering of a part of the dough to the Lord was to sanctify, or set apart for God's purpose (make "holy"), the whole mass of dough. But who are the firstfruits of Israel? Some refer them to the Jewish believing remnant of whom Paul has been speaking in the context (v. 5). In this view, the few Messianic believers, like Paul himself, would be the pledge that the whole nation would eventually be saved.[24]

Most commentators, however, prefer to understand the firstfruit to mean the ancient forefathers (patriarchs) of Israel (v. 28). Because the first members of the Israelite people were holy, that is, the patriarchs such as Abraham, who were truly consecrated to God, the people which came from these godly forefathers of the covenant form a whole with these patriarchs. Even though temporary unbelief and rejection has overtaken some in the nation, the covenant people will yet appear in the future in their real character and purpose as God's people. The temporary and partial unbelief of even a number of generations of Israelites, Paul would argue, cannot annul the continuing holy purpose of God destined for this people as a whole.

In the second metaphor of the "root" and "branches" of a tree, Paul further stresses the same point (v. 16). The tree bears the same character as the root. If the root (Abraham, Isaac, etc.) is holy (belonging to God), so are the branches (the whole nation springing from the root). It is in the character of Israel as a covenant people, whose origins are good (i.e., the patriarchs), that Paul sees the hope for their future restoration as a whole nation. Just as the believing wife or husband sanctifies (makes holy) the whole covenant marriage union of a believer and unbeliever, so that the children are not considered illegitimate or rejected by God (1 Cor. 7:14), so the believing forefathers of the Jewish people sanctify the whole covenant posterity in the sense that they are destined to fulfill God's purpose as a covenant nation.

Verses 17–24 continue the figure of the tree with its root and branches. In this section Paul is concerned to ward off some dangerous misconceptions about his teachings that might arise in the minds of the Gentile Christians to whom he is writing. Because the Israelite people are likened by Paul to branches from a holy root (v. 18), it might be argued that their present unbelief and rejection cancels out God's covenant with the patriarchs and denies any future for the Jews as the people of God. Paul, haven't they blown it by their response to Christ? Didn't they get what they deserved because of their unbelief? Hasn't God now taken us Gentiles to be His new people in place of the ancient Jews? This raises the important question concerning what kind of attitude Christians should have toward nonbelieving Israelites. A number of important facts must be considered, and each seriously, if we are to develop a correct attitude toward these ancient people of God and toward ourselves as Gentile Christians.

Paul first stresses the humble position of Gentile Christians. Extending the imagery of the tree (v. 16), Paul states that even though a portion (historically) of the Jewish people have stumbled into unbelief, their trespass has only resulted in the breaking away of some of the branches and not in the uprooting of the whole tree, for the root is holy. Christians should not, then, feel that God is finished with the Jewish people as a whole. They are, despite their temporary rejection, still God's covenant people.

There is a common misconception among Christians today. Some have disregarded as visionary all predictions of a future national resurgence of Israel as a spiritual entity, and they appropriate the promises made specifically to the nation of Israel in the Old Testament exclusively to themselves in some spiritual sense as the distinctively new people of God, the new Israel. This belief still persists even though the present political state of Israel (since 1948) is forcing for some Christians serious reconsiderations. Instead Paul sees one continuous covenant people of God under the figure of the "olive tree." The root, or stock, from which believing Jews and Gentiles all receive their spiritual strength and nourishment, is found in the patriarchs who bear the original promises of salvation in Christ (Gal. 3:16). The branches are either individual believers or generations of believers who derive their life from the continuous covenant family of God to which they belong.

The branches are of two kinds: (1) The original branches are the Israelite people, some of which have been "broken off" because of their unbelief in God's promise (v. 20), and (2) the "wild olive" branches are Gentile believers that are grafted into the covenant family of God. Paul's use of "wild" olive tree (v. 17) and the reference to grafting "contrary to nature" (v. 24)[25] further stress the humble position of Gentile Christians who were not originally even part of the tree.

Paul warns the Gentiles as a group not to gloat over the fallen branches (unbelieving Jews). There are two reasons for this: (1) Gentile believers are enjoying the blessings of God because they have been made part of the covenant promises given to the patriarchs of Israel and not the other way around: "You do not support the root, but the root supports you" (v. 18); and (2) the Gentiles stand in relationship to God because of faith. If they begin to exhibit pride in their position, God will remove them from the tree in the same manner He removed those proud, unbelieving Israelites (vv. 19–22). Faith (absence of pride, 3:27–28) alone provides our only hope, peace, and security. Our proper attitude toward God is always reverent "fear" (v. 20 NASB).

These lessons are greatly needed today. What could be more unscriptural than for Christians to despise or discriminate against unbelieving Jews? Not only have Christians inherited the blessings that were brought into the world by Jews, but did not even Jesus say, "Salvation is from the Jews" (John 4:22)?

Furthermore, Gentile Christians must not be skeptical about the problem of continuing Jewish unbelief, since it is much more natural for God to put the Jew back into his own inheritance than it is for God to save the Gentiles (vv. 23–24). It must be remembered that Paul is talking about groups of people or generations and not individuals as such.

Paul now turns more directly to the prediction of the future Israelite revival in verses 25–27. He still wishes to further warn Gentile Christians against congratulating themselves for being wiser than the Israelites, wiser, since they responded to the gospel whereas many of the latter rejected it. It should never be forgotten by Christians that Israel both as an ethnic and as a spiritual entity has a glorious future in the outworking of God's purpose in history. Since there are several important terms in these verses and each has its own problems, it may be well to discuss them briefly.

1. The *mystery*. "Mystery" is Paul's characteristic way of referring either to a past secret purpose of God that has now been uncovered and made known to us (Rom. 16:25; Col. 1:26–27; 2 Thess. 2:7), or to a future purpose that is made known now for the instruction and attitude of the believer (1 Cor. 15:51). The mystery is this: A partial (not total) hardening (not blinding) has occurred in the present among some Jewish people because of their unbelief (v. 7) and will continue until the fullness of the Gentiles is brought about, and then all Israel will be saved. Paul here speaks of the Israelite people as a whole or group and not every last individual in the group. He says in effect that the people's hardness to the word of the gospel of Christ is "partial" (NASB) not total (because of the believing remnant); temporary, not permanent ("until"). What is also new revelation here is that the conversion of all Israel will take place after and not before the harvesting of the Gentiles into the kingdom.

2. The *full number of the Gentiles* (Gk. *pleroma*, "fullness"). What does "full number" (v. 25) mean? A number of views are possible. First, in verse 12 Paul refers to the "fullness" (Greek is same in both) of Israel as the opposite of their diminishing (only a remnant is now saved). So the fullness of the Gentiles could mean their "full number" in comparison to the small number who up to Paul's time were converted (so Cranfield).

The fullness might be reached whenever in any generation the final person filling up the total number of elect individuals is converted. But the word never has this meaning elsewhere in Paul or the NT or the Greek OT (LXX).

Second, in the light of what the same word ("fullness") means in verse 12—no longer a redeemed remnant but a converted mass—it seems better to understand "full number of the Gentiles" to indicate some sort of sweeping revival in the future resulting in the conversion of most of the Gentiles just prior to the great harvest of the Israelites.[26]

Third, others attempt to relate the fullness of the Gentiles to the fulfillment of the "times of the Gentiles" spoken of by our Lord in Luke 21:24. The sense would be "a partial hardening has happened to Israel until the fullness of the times of the Gentiles has come." Israel's acceptance is preceded by the moment in which God put an end to Israel's oppression by the Gentile nations.[27] But "Gentiles" in Romans 9–11 almost always means Gentile Christians (9:24, 30; 11:12–13), and "times of the Gentiles" has an oppressive, unfavorable connotation; "full number of the Gentiles" like the "fullness" of Israel (v. 12) has the sense of a favorable divine blessing.

Fourth, one further modification of the first view deserves mention. The fullness of the Gentiles might have reference to geographical fullness, that is, it would refer to the full complement of the Gentiles, or the Gentile nations as a whole.[28] This note of universality of the evangelization of the Gentile nations is sounded by Christ in the Olivet discourse when He says, "And this gospel of the kingdom will be preached in the whole world as a testimony to all nations, and then the end will come" (Matt. 24:14). Again, the reference, as in the first view, would be to some great evangelization effort of Christianity reaching all the Gentiles that will precede the conversion of Israel and in some way be related to that later event. It need not mean that every Gentile would be converted, but enough would be to refer to the whole ethnic group or entity. The main objection to this modification, as we understand it, is that "fullness" refers more definitely to conversion than to mere evangelization.

It seems preferable to us to adopt the second view while

admitting there are still unresolved ambiguities.

3. *And so*. It may appear that this little "and so" (v. 26) is not important, and to isolate it smacks of pedantry. But if we make the text read "then" or "after this," we will not totally distort the sense of Paul, but we may miss the deeper thought. The use of "and so" stresses some *logical* (but may include temporal) connection between the fullness of the Gentiles and the salvation of all Israel. The "and so" might refer to the manner of Israel's deliverance, that is, that Israel will be saved by means of the coming Redeemer, described in the following words: "The deliverer will come from Zion" (v. 26). But probably it is better to see the term as referring back to the whole mystery explained in verse 25: the strange detour by which Israel's partial unbelief continues until God brings in the fullness of the Gentiles.[29] Whether the Gentile fullness will provoke Israel to emulation or some other means will be used is not clear.[30]

4. *All Israel to be saved*. Finally, what is meant by "all Israel" (v. 26)? Some understand Paul to be referring to *spiritual* Israel composed of both believing Jews and believing Gentiles (Gal. 6:16). This interpretation was held by a number of early and later church fathers (Theodorus; Augustine, in some texts; Luther, Calvin, and most of the Reformers).[31]

However, the context and exegetical factors strongly favor an alternate view.

Paul's entire usage of the word *Israel* in this section of the book (chaps. 9–11), especially in chapter 11, and even the preceding verse, make it virtually certain that he is denoting the ethnic Israelites, which could not include Gentiles. This more limited use becomes clear by also noting the subject of the following phrase: "their fullness" (v. 12); "if they do not persist in unbelief, they will be grafted in" (v. 23); "their disobedience . . . they too have now become disobedient . . . they too may now receive mercy" (vv. 30–31); and, "all [in] disobedience so that he may have mercy on them all" (v. 32).

"All" Israel, then, must refer to the forgiveness of the whole Jewish people or nation, the whole ethnic group in contrast to the saved remnant of Israelites in Paul's day and ours. It is the whole people, rather than a small part, that will be converted to the Messiah (so teach Origen, Chrysostom, Ambrose, Augustine in *City of God,* and Jerome).[32] In other words, the "partial" hardness will be removed.

In verses 26 and 27 Paul appeals to the Old Testament to support his position that the whole of the Jewish people will one day be saved. He quotes from Isaiah 59:20–21 and 27:9, which refer to the day when the Messiah (the Deliverer) will remove all ungodliness from Jacob (Israel) and forgive the whole people their sins. This fact supports Paul's contention that God will one day restore the whole people in the blessings of the new covenant. It is not certain whether the reference in Isaiah to the Messiah's coming refers to His first coming and the still-future implication to Israel of that coming, or whether Paul had in mind the second coming of Christ. Either will do justice to the context.

Further, the existing fact of Israel's present partial unbelief does not militate against Paul's view of the full salvation of the whole people in the future because Israel has a unique paradoxical relationship to God: They are at the same time both "enemies" and "beloved" of God (vv. 28–29 NASB).

Israel—the gospel—enemies of God—for your sake

from the standpoint of—the election—Israel—beloved of God—for the sake of the fathers

On the one hand, they are enemies of God because they have rejected the gospel message, which is of divine origin. But on the other hand, they are beloved of God because of His covenant-electing purposes for the people. The latter phrase in each instance shows the eternal purpose in God's actions. "On your account" explains why the majority of Jews are under God's wrath: It is because in God's providence the Gentiles were to be extended the call to salvation. "On account of the patriarchs" (Abraham, Isaac, Jacob) explains why Israel will yet be blessed and received as a people. God's covenant promises to the patriarchs concerning their national blessing through salvation in the Messiah have not been abrogated despite the unbelief of many of the Israelites. In verse 29, Paul emphatically states, "God's gifts and his call are irrevocable," that is, God's covenant promises are irrevocable because of His own faithfulness (3:3). Two false conclusions might be drawn from this. One would be to argue that God has two covenants and hence two different ways for people to be saved: one covenant for Israel (i.e., the Mosaic Law covenant) and another covenant for Gentiles (i.e., the new covenant through Christ). This popular two covenant view is certainly not Paul's view (3:30; 4:11–12, 16). Both Israelites and Gentiles need to be evangelized, called to repentance and faith in Jesus, God's Messiah. This in no way overlooks the fact that individual Jews are either in or out of right relationship to God on the basis of their faith, nor does it mean that they are not accountable in judgment before God.

In verses 30–31 Paul reiterates the truth he has already stated several times. The salvation of the Gentiles was occasioned by the unbelief of Israel (v. 30). But Israel's salvation will be occasioned not by the Gentiles' return to unbelief but by means of the great mercy shown to these non-Jews (v. 31).

Finally, in verse 32, Paul concludes by drawing our attention to the relationship between human disobedience and God's mercy. It is only in the context of disobedience that mercy can operate. Both Israel as a group and Gentiles as a group are consigned to disobedience, but God's purpose is to show mercy. Paul is not teaching that all individually will be saved but that God's mercy is extended to all people without discrimination (Gal. 3:22).

PAUL'S PRAISE (11:33–36)

Paul has been granted a small window into God's great plan for man. He stands back in awe and wonder. He worships Him by exclaiming, "Oh, the depth of the riches of the wisdom and knowledge of God! How unsearchable his judgments, and his paths beyond tracing out!" (v. 33). God's ways and thoughts are unfathomable to created intelligence. His exhaustless grace and goodness (riches), His providence (wisdom), and His understanding (knowledge) elude all attempts to trace out their causes or their directions because God is Himself the inscrutable origin of these characteristics (v. 34, from Isa. 40:13). Only poetry can do justice to this idea:

Your way was in the sea,
And Your paths in the mighty waters,
And Your footprints may not be known.
(Ps. 77:19 NASB)

This is the reason for worship and the occasion for faith. This is ever God's way with us: to reveal enough of Himself and His plans that we may glimpse the wisdom and movement of His ways and stand in awe, but only enough to reserve the mystery of His being just beyond the veil of our deepest gaze.

Furthermore, no one stands in relationship to God as a benefactor or innovator. God always acts in grace and love toward us; therefore, neither we nor our predecessors can ever build up a store of merit: "Who has ever given to God, that God should repay him?" (v. 35, from Job 41:11).

Paul closes with a burst of praise to the sovereign God: "For from him [source] and through him [agent] and to him [goal] are all things" (v. 36). He is the center of all the created, historical, and personal order. God is the Alpha and the Omega (the A and the Z), the beginning and the end, the first and the last (Rev. 4:11). If in this one case of His dealings with Israel, we can catch a glimpse of the vindication of His mysterious providence, in other cases we can wait for the explanation of His wisdom and the final evidence of His love and mercy. Surely, then, to *Him* alone belongs the glory forever and ever. So be it!

This is the expression of a faith that trusts when it cannot understand, that loves when it cannot explain, that reasons correctly that nothing but good can ultimately come from God to those who accept His grace and love Him through the Lord Jesus Christ.

ADDITIONAL NOTE ON CHRISTIANITY AND CONTEMPORARY JEWS AND ISRAEL

This is not the place for an extended discussion of Jewish-Christian relations or of the modern state of Israel in its prophetic, political, and religious aspects. But it seems hardly appropriate to write a modern commentary on these chapters and not say something about the relationship of Christians to Jews and to the political state of Israel.

CONCERNING EVANGELICALS AND JEWS

What attitudes are appropriate for Christians to have toward Jews who do not believe in Christ as Messiah and Lord in the light of Paul's teaching? In the first place, Christians should shun any form or even the subtle suggestion of anti-Semitism (a discriminatory view of a person or group simply because they are "Jewish"). Further, we ought to strongly condemn and actively oppose anti-Semitic actions on the part of others, as well as repent ourselves of any past or present associations that Christians may have had with this kind of deplorable activity. Jews, of course, for the most part know only the "convert or be killed" history of Christian witness. Kenneth Kantzer rightly states, "As evangelicals demonstrate in tangible ways their abhorrence of anti-semitic actions, they will declare a crucial truth to the Gentile world at large: *to attack Jews is to attack evangelicals, and such attacks will be resisted by evangelicals as attacks against themselves.*"[33]

Theologically we must repudiate the age-old myth that the Jewish people were responsible for the death of Jesus. A few (not all) Jewish leaders together with the Roman-Italian governor, Pontius Pilate, were involved in the historic death of Jesus. From a New Testament theological perspective, these few people acted as representatives of the unbelieving world in carrying out God's eternal purpose in the redeeming death of Jesus (Acts 4:28). Our sins were ultimately responsible for Christ's death (2 Cor. 5:21). In fact, it may be possible to see in the suffering of Jesus the Jew some mysterious link with the suffering of worldwide Jewry throughout the ages and vice versa.

Nor should what is basically an in-house family debate between Jews of the first century be taken out of that historical context and thereby falsely make the New Testament into an anti-Semitic writing. We must be very careful hermeneutically not to make references to "Jews" in the first century refer to all Jews of all times. Again as Kantzer points out, "Christians are not sensitive to this problem, but they would be if their grandfather, two uncles, and six cousins had died in the furnace of Buchenwald."[34]

Finally, should Christians seek to evangelize Jews? Because Paul emphatically makes no distinction between Jew and Gentile in terms of their *need* of the gospel (Rom. 1–3), there can be no question that believers in Christ have the responsibility to bear witness to Christ and the gospel to Jews as well as to Gentiles. Perhaps the manner of that witness will be different to Jews. Since they are already God's elect people, we do not seek to convert them to another religion but to witness to the fulfillment of their own faith in Jesus the Sin-Bearer. One of the least offensive ways for Christians to bear their witness to Christ today to Jews is through dialogue encounters and by provoking the Jews to jealousy as Christians demonstrate by their lives of integrity, justice, and love the presence of God working among them.[35]

Whether Jews should be singled out as a *group* to be evangelized is very problematic. Although Paul holds out hope that individual Jews such as himself will come to faith in Jesus, does he not indirectly admit the failure of the mission to the Jews as a whole (10:21; 11:15) and the continuance of this failure until the future divine coup d'état to save Israel (11:26–27)? In any event, we would not be too far from Paul's position in Romans 11 to suggest that "the God of Abraham now revealed in Christ, the God of grace in whom both Jews and Christians share an immemorial faith, encompasses them in a unity which their present non-negotiable differences over the significance of Jesus as the Messiah must not be allowed to destroy, even though they will not be resolved before the end of history."[36]

PEOPLE AND COUNTRY

We have seen by careful exegesis that Paul clearly teaches a revival among the Jewish people when they are restored as a people to the blessings of God in the olive tree. The question is whether this future restoration must also involve the ancient land of Canaan, or Palestine.[37]

There is no doubt that in the Old Testament God's promise

to Israel as a people is connected explicitly to one particular land area, Canaan (Gen. 12:1; 13:12; 17:7–8; Deut. 30:1–10). Dispersion and separation from the land is the repeated mark of God's judgment for Israel's disobedience, and the restoration of the land is the mark of God's grace to the nation (Deut. 28:64–66; 30:1–10; Isa. 62:4; Ezek. 36:8–12, 28, 33–36; Amos 9:11–15; Zech. 10:9–10). The latter two passages especially emphasize how closely the salvation of Israel as a people is connected to the land of Palestine.

Some believe that in the New Testament words of Jesus there seems to be further continuity with this same Old Testament thought. Jerusalem's destruction in A.D. 70 is not to be the last stroke in the connection of land and people, for Jesus predicts, "Jerusalem will be trampled on by the Gentiles until the times of the Gentiles are fulfilled" (Luke 21:24). This last of the great prophetic discourses seems from this viewpoint to reiterate that no matter how insurmountable the difficulties, land and people will one day be reunited, and Israel will fulfill its destiny in Palestine. In this view, Scripture is not clear as to whether this return precedes their national repentance or follows it.

Other evangelicals believe that the question of land is either ambiguous or reinterpreted in the New Testament without denying the future reconciliation of the Jewish people as a whole (see fn. 37). What is clear is that there is coming a time within this age in which God's faithfulness will triumph over Israel's unbelief and Israel will realize her destiny as a people (perhaps in Palestine) as the great evidence of God's saving activity in the world.

THE POLITICAL STATE OF ISRAEL

What should be the attitude of Christians toward the Jewish State of Israel established in 1948? To begin with, regardless of our prophetic assessment of the significance of a Jewish return to Palestine, some things need to be clearly said. Christians cannot support any anti-Israel rhetoric or acts that have roots in anti-Semitism. There are friends of Israel and there are enemies of Israel. It is difficult to see how any Christian could justify being an enemy of Israel. Certainly Israel has a right to live and thrive in its native homeland.

Among the friends of Israel there are two types. One is uncritically supportive of the Israeli state and its policies. Many evangelical Zionists fall into this category. The other friend, I think the better one, is critically supportive of Israel. Though giving no support to Israel's enemies, these latter friends seek a just resolution to the festering problem of Palestinian Arab rights in the land. It is important to emphasize, however, that what Israel's critical friends seek is not to judge Israel by a different standard than other nations but to call both Israel and the other nations to account before a higher standard, the standard of God's justice revealed in the Bible and insofar as international law supports this standard.

There are two peoples in Palestine, the Jew and the Palestinian Arab, both involved in a struggle for existence and dignity. Christians cannot side in every case one against the other but must maintain the legitimate rights of both belligerents if they are to be a reconciling presence in the conflict and not mere partisan political pawns.[38]

As to the eschatological dimension, the chief question for the Christian concerning the present state of Israel is whether this has any connection with the predictions of Israel's national repentance and possible reunion with the land of Palestine. It is a difficult and complex question, but one that is notably significant. When the Christian considers the way in which the State of Israel came into being, he may wonder if God could have had any direct hand in it.[39] If God is not directly involved in the formation of the present State of Israel, it would be difficult for Christians to maintain any special divine significance in it over any other recent nationalism. Yet God has in Israel's past history overruled their questionable activities to accomplish in them His own purposes. Take the Jacob and the Joseph narratives as an example.

However, since I as a Christian have no direct way of knowing which of these alternatives is actually the case, my prophetic position as a Christian toward the present State of Israel is somewhat ambivalent. Theologically, if I decide that God is preparing or actually beginning the process of Israel's restoration, I may be drawn in my sympathies to them and desire to support their welfare and their rights in the land. Yet, I must hold them accountable to the same higher standard of God's justice to which I hold my own or another country. I must be ready as a loving but critical friend to condemn acts or policies of injustices toward Palestinians as I would any other government.

The same attitude should hold true for the person who believes that the present state of Israel is not God's doing but merely human political aspiration. We must support the welfare and rights of Palestinians in the land. Yet one cannot lightly dismiss or overlook acts of injustice done by Arabs or their leaders to their own people or to Israelis. In the present conflict, the Christian must not identify totally with either the Arab or the Israeli political position. Both peoples have historic rights to the land. Christians must also remember that some 10 percent of Palestinians identify themselves with the Christian faith. This should not be our only motivation for our support as critical friends of the Palestinians, but it should not be overlooked. Instead, one must be the reconciling ingredient between the two parties.

THE MILLENNIAL KINGDOM

Although there are numerous worthy Christian views on the question of a future divine earthly kingdom of peace established in history, it seems quite appropriate to think of this kingdom in association with the restoration of Israel as a people. The Old Testament views this kingdom of peace as occurring within history following the return of Christ to the earth (Isa. 2:2–4; 4:2–6; 9:6–7; Zech. 14:8–11). Whether the New Testament can support this historic premillennial expectation is greatly debated among Christians. Students are invited to consult my more lengthy discussion of this problem in two other publications.[40]

PROSPECTS OF WORLD REVIVAL

It has been argued exegetically for the interpretation of Paul's thought that favors the view that there will be an extensive expansion of Gentile Christianity (the "fullness of the Gentiles") just prior to and in connection with the repentance of Israel. Are there signs that this era may be close, now that the new millennium has arrived? Of course, any answer to this question must be speculative. However, there are several interesting developments to note. Several decades ago, a noteworthy revival of large scope was observed among American youth that appears to have had implications in the worldwide community and has created a significant "Jews for Jesus" movement within its wake. Furthermore, as subjective as it may seem, numerous leaders in the evangelical church feel we are on the brink and may be into a great worldwide revival.[41]

Finally, one is greatly impressed that in Israel today the Bible is the center of cultural focus. Young people must memorize in Hebrew the entire historical books (Genesis through Chronicles) plus the prophets (Isaiah through Zechariah) before they can enroll in high school. Although largely of historical and moral emphasis, this preparation of Jewish minds and hearts might in the future play a significant role in the nation's turning to the God who raised Jesus the Messiah from the dead. There is also a significant openness in Israel today toward discussing the relationship between Jews and Christians.

Thus Paul has dealt decisively with the major objection to his doctrine of God's faithfulness raised by Jewish unbelief: Israel has stumbled due to its own unfaithfulness, not God's, and furthermore God is working out in the Israelite people's unbelief a divine mystery that will magnify His mercy in an unparalleled manner (chaps. 9–11).

Paul's main argument of the book is now completed (1:18–11:36). There yet remain several areas of more immediate concern pertaining to the outworking of this new life in Christ as it touches the real world of the Roman Christians.

NOTES

1. The Greek word *anathema* corresponds to the OT *herem*, "devoted to destruction," and often is translated "accursed" (see Josh. 6:17; 7:1; 1 Cor. 12:3; 16:22; Gal. 1:8–9). Like Moses of old (Exod. 32:31–32), Paul wished to lose his own salvation for the salvation of his fellow Jews.

2. C. E. B. Cranfield, *A Critical and Exegetical Commentary on the Epistle to the Romans*, The International Critical Commentary, 2 vols. (Edinburgh: T. & T. Clark, 1975, 1979), 2:467. For arguments favoring the "God" doxology view, see Ernst Käsemann, *Commentary on Romans*, trans. Geoffrey W. Bromiley (Grand Rapids: Eerdmans, 1978), 260–61.

3. See John Murray, *The Epistle to the Romans*, 2 vols. (Grand Rapids: Eerdmans, 1959), vol. 2, Appendix A, for an excellent discussion of the problem. Murray adopts the traditional KJV rendering as superior to others. So also Bruce Metzger, "The Punctuation of Rom. 9:5," in *Christ and Spirit in the New Testament: Studies in Honour of C. F. D. Moule*, ed. Barnabas Lindars and Stephen S. Smalley (Cambridge: Cambridge Univ., 1974), 95–112; also Cranfield, 2:464–70; and Schreiner, *Romans*, 489.

4. Berkeley Michelsen, "Romans," in *The Wycliffe Bible Commentary*, ed. Charles F. Pfeiffer and Everett F. Harrison (Chicago: Moody, 1962), 1209–10.

5. Hermann L. Strack and Paul Billerbeck, *Kommentar zum Neue Testamentum aus Talmud und Midrach*, 4 vols. (Munich: Beck, 1922–28).

6. Ibid., 4.2.1066.

7. Ibid.

8. Ibid., 4.2.1067.

9. Carl F. Keil and Franz Delitzsch, *Commentaries on the Old Testament*, 13 vols. (Grand Rapids: Eerdmans, 1949), 1:453–57.

10. The Greek verb is *katartizō*, which means "to suit," "to fit," "to establish," "to foreordain" (TDNT). The verb interestingly is passive in voice, which may suggest Paul is softening the active role of God in thus making such a vessel (although ultimately God is responsible). In verse 23 the vessels of mercy are directly prepared (active voice) by God for glory.

11. See especially John Piper, *The Justification of God: An Exegetical and Theological Study of Romans 9:1–23* (Grand Rapids: Baker, 1983); Moo and Schreiner also follow suit.

12. A. Richardson, *An Introduction to the Theology of the New Testament* (New York: Harper & Row, 1958), 281. See also Robert Shank, *Elect in the Son: A Study of the Doctrine of Election* (Springfield, Mo.: Westcott, 1970), 113–45; also L. Morris, *Romans*; Clark Pinnock, ed., *The Grace of God, The Will of Man: A Case for Arminianism* (Grand Rapids: Zondervan,

1990); W. W. Klein, *A Corporate View of Election* (Grand Rapids: Zonder-van, 1990).

13. The use of "law" of righteousness in verse 31 may be similar to the use of law in 3:27; 7:21, 23; 8:2 and means principle or rule or order. Or it may refer to the Mosaic Law, which when legitimately pursued by faith was designed to lead them to righteousness.

14. Charles Erdman, *The Epistle of Paul to the Romans* (Philadelphia: Westminster, 1925), 101.

15. The sense of this verse is greatly debated. How or in what way is Christ the "end of the law" for righteousness? There are three principle views: (1) termination (Käsemann, Moo), (2) goal (Cranfield), and (3) fulfillment (R. Banks). View 1 may mean either termination for justification (Murray) or termination as a way of expressing obedience and piety before God ("end . . . so that there may be righteousness"). View 2 means that Christ is the true intent of the law, the real meaning and substance of the law. View 3 means that Christ fulfills the law in the sense that He has brought the law to completion and transcends it (Matt. 5:17). So Robert Banks, *Jesus and the Law in the Synoptic Tradition* (Cambridge: Cambridge Univ., 1975), 245, n. 4. Although it is not possible to be certain here, it is suggested that "end" of law here should not be viewed as teaching either that the law was fulfilled in Christ or that the *aim* of the law was to be a pedagogue until Christ (Gal. 3:24), both of which are true. Rather, Christ is the end or *termination* of the law both in the sense of 7:6 as well as in the sense that the believer no longer seeks for justification in the law. Of course, this latter view has also two possible senses of "justification in the law." The first would view it in a sal-vation history sense. It was proper to find justification in the Mosaic Law covenant by faith as did David (4:6–8). Now, however, this justification is directly through faith in Christ. A good case can be made for this view if we stress the "for everyone" of the verse. Gentiles who could not be justified by the Mosaic Law covenant through faith can now be justified in Christ apart from the Mosaic Law. Thus the gospel of Christ universalizes salvation to all. Second, the expression could mean that for those who use the law covenant wrongly to justify themselves by works righteousness (v. 3) Christ is the end of that type of self-seeking use of the law (so Schreiner, *Romans*, 547–48).

16. Cranfield argues (following Barth) that it is more probable that Paul is here applying the words of Lev. 18:5, not to the impossible, hopeless task of keeping the law in order to have life, but to the achievement of the one Man, Jesus Christ, who alone has done the righteousness in the law perfect-ly and thus won eternal life for Himself and for all who believe in Him (2:522). Though attractive, this view does not have much to support it.

17. Murray, *Epistle to the Romans*, 2:58. Cranfield points out that "the fact that Paul can think of prayer to the exalted Christ without the least repug-

nance is, in the light of the first and second commandments of the Deca-
logue, the decisive clarification of the significance which he attached to the
title *kyrios* ["Lord"] as applied to Christ (e.g., in this verse and in v. 9)"
(2:532).

18. The Greek here would permit the thought either of the Word about
Christ (obj. gen.) in the sense of the apostles' preaching, or the Word originated by Christ in the sense that the substance is His Word (subj. gen.). In
either case the authority of the Word is emphasized. It is the very Word of
Christ (John 3:34; 5:47; Eph. 5:26; 1 Pet. 1:25).

19. "Messianic believer" is a term used to describe a person of Jewish cultural and religious heritage who has come to believe in Jesus as the Messiah
(the Divine King of Israel). There is a more modern trend developing in
America and especially in the state of Israel, for Jewish Christians to drop
the name Christian and refer to themselves simply as "Messianic Jews." A
reliable source (Dr. Louis Goldberg) indicates to me that there are some 57
Messianic Jewish congregations in Israel today and 200 in the U.S. The term
"Christian," we should remember, was not used of the followers of Jesus
until many years after His death and resurrection and at first only by pagans
in derision of the way believers in Christ belong to and follow the Lord
Jesus Christ (Acts 11:26; 26:28). See David A. Rausch, "The Emergence of
Messianic Judaism in Recent American History," *Christian Scholar's Review*
12 (1983): 37–52.

20. Cranfield, *Critical and Exegetical Commentary,* 2:544.

21. There is now a growing scholarly consensus following Karl Barth
(*Church Dogmatics, II,* ed. G. W. Bromiley and T. F. Torrance [Edinburgh:
T. & T. Clark, 1936]; 2:195–305) that rejects the former popular position
that saw the church as the new Israel replacing the old Israel as the elect
people of God. Cranfield typifies this new understanding when he says, "I
confess with shame to having also myself used in print on more than one
occasion this language of the replacement of Israel by the church" (2:448, n.
2). Others who likewise repudiate this replacement language are: Hans
Kung, *The Church* (New York: Sheed & Ward, 1968), 132–50; Hendrik
Berkhof, "Israel as a Theological Problem in the Christian Church," *Journal
of Ecumenical Studies* 1 (1969): 329–47; Herman Ridderbos, *Paul* (Grand
Rapids: Eerdmans 1975), 354–61; Bruce Corley, "The Jews, The Future,
and God (Romans 9–11)," *Southwestern Journal of Theology* 19 (1976),
42–56; W. D. Davies, "Paul and the People of Israel," *New Testament Studies*
24 (1977), 4–39.

22. Murray, *Epistle to the Romans,* 2:83–84.

23. The Greek *aparchē* (firstfruit) occurs a number of times in the NT: Rom.
8:23; 16:5; 1 Cor. 15:20, 23; 16:15; James 1:18; Rev. 14:4.

24. C. K. Barrett, *The Epistle to the Romans* (New York: Harper & Row, 1957), 216; F. J. Leenhardt, *Romans* (London: ET of CNT, 1961), 286; and Cranfield, 2:564.

25. Though the normal process of grafting involves placing a good, strong shoot on a weaker stem to transfer the strength of the better tree to the poorer, Paul's phrase "contrary to nature" recognizes this and shows that he was familiar with the normal horticultural process but wished to use this analogy to press home his point. See W. D. Davies, "Romans 11:13–24. A Suggestion," in *Paganisme, Judaïsme, Christianisme*, ed. E. de Boccard (Paris, 1978), 131–44, where he suggests that the wild olive figure at one and the same time both puts down the Gentiles (the wild olive had no useful fruit) and compliments his own Jewish people (the cultivated olive). He also shows that the olive was a symbol of Athens.

26. Murray, *Epistle to the Romans*, 2:94f.

27. Hendrik Berkhof, *Christ the Meaning of History* (Atlanta: John Knox, 1966), 144.

28. Erdman, *Epistle of Paul*, 127.

29. Berkhof, *Christ the Meaning of History*, 146.

30. Corley, "The Jews," 53–54 identifies three possible views of the "and so": (1) modal (logical)—"in this manner"; (2) correlative view—"so . . . as," i.e., "in the following manner . . . just as it is written"; and (3) temporal view—"then . . ." (this latter is Corley's view as well as Käsemann's, *Romans*, 313).

31. H. P. Liddon, *An Explanatory Analysis of St. Paul's Epistle to the Romans* (Grand Rapids: Zondervan, 1961), 217.

32. Ibid.; this view is also held by Murray; F. F. Bruce, *The Epistle of Paul to the Romans* (Grand Rapids: Eerdmans, 1963); Erdman. For a strong case arguing the same view, see Peter Richardson, *Israel in the Apostolic Church*, Society for New Testament Studies Monographs, no. 10 (Cambridge: Cambridge Univ., 1969), 126–47. He denies that Gal. 6:16 refers to Gentiles; see also W. D. Davies, "Paul and the People of Israel," NTS 24 (1977): 4–39. Contra to E. Palmer and H. Ridderbos who hold that the term refers to all the elect Israelites predestined to salvation.

33. Kenneth Kantzer, "Concerning Evangelicals and Jews," *Christianity Today*, 24 April 1981, 13. See also the evangelical-Jewish dialogue books: M. Tanenbaum, M. Wilson, and J. Rudin, eds., *Evangelicals and Jews in Conversation on Scripture, Theology and History* (Grand Rapids: Baker, 1978); M. Tanenbaum and M. Wilson, eds. *Evangelicals and Jews in an Age*

of Pluralism (Grand Rapids: Baker, 1984). Valuable, too, are the less conservative but provocative A. Roy Eckardt, *Elder and Younger Brothers* (New York: Scribner's, 1967) and *Your People, My People: The Meeting of Jews and Christians* (New York: Quadrangle, 1974); and the Jewish author Yechiel Eckstein, *What Christians Should Know About Jews* (Waco, Tex.: Word, 1984).

34. Kantzer, "Evangelicals and Jews," 14.

35. So states Eckstein, *Christians*, 292.

36. W. D. Davies, "Paul and the People of Israel," *New Testament Studies* 24 (1977): 34.

37. I am here in part following the excellent summary of Berkhof, *Christ the Meaning of History*, 147ff. I do not think this author can by any standards be labeled "dispensationalist." For a differing evangelical view, see Derek Prince, *The Last Word on the Middle East* (Lincoln, Va.: Chosen, 1982) and W. S. LaSor, *Israel: A Biblical View* (Grand Rapids: Eerdmans, 1976). See also Gary Burge, *Who Are God's People in the Middle-east? What Christians Are Not Being Told About Israel and the Palestinians* (Grand Rapids: Zondervan, 1992).

38. See the excellent position on this advanced by Markus Barth, "Israel and the Palestinians," in *Jesus the Jew*, trans. Frederick Prussner (reprint; Atlanta: John Knox, 1978), 43–96; also Fred J. Khouri, *The Arab-Israeli Dilemma*, 2d ed. (New York: Syracuse Univ., 1976). See G. Burge (fn. 37).

39. George Giacumakis Jr., "The Israeli-Arab Conflict in the Middle East," in *Protest and Politics*, ed. R. G. Clouse, R. D. Linder, and R. V. Pierard (Greenwood, S.C.: Attic, 1968), 227–50; also "Christian Attitudes Toward Israel," in *The Cross and the Flag*, ed. Clouse, Linder, and Pierard (Carol Stream, Ill.: Creation House, 1972), 203–15.

40. Alan F. Johnson, *Revelation*, The Expositor's Bible Commentary, Frank E. Gaebelein, ed., vol. 12 (Grand Rapids: Zondervan, 1981), 577–86, published as a monograph, 1997; also *What Christians Believe, A Biblical and Historical Summary* (Grand Rapids: Zondervan, 1989), 441–43; 458–460.

41. Bill Bright, *Come Help Change the World* (Old Tappan, N. J.: Revell, 1970); Rufus Jones, "Will the Church Miss It?" *Bulletin of the Conservative Baptist Missions* (Fall 1971); Robert E. Coleman, "The Coming World Revival?" *Christianity Today* 15, no. 21 (16 July 1971): 10–12; "The New Christians," *Christianity Today* 15: 20–23; "The New Rebel Cry: Jesus Is Coming!" *Time*, 21 June 1971, 56–63; "Jews for Jesus," *Time*, 12 June 1972, 66–67.

9

THE CHRISTIAN WAY

12:1–15:13

As in most of his other letters, Paul first sets forth the theological truths of Christian faith and then follows out these truths into several more concrete or specific areas or cases of actual Christian living in the world. In earlier chapters, the apostle has already struck the note of moral transformation of the entire life through the Spirit. Such new life is inseparably wed to God's action of forgiveness (chaps. 6–8).

It should be carefully noted that Paul, unlike many Christian teachers and preachers today, bases his call to Christian character upon the theological truths he has before spoken about; he roots the expression of Christlikeness to the truths they believe. We will not find in Paul the often repeated but erroneous sharp distinction between "doctrine" and "life." Exhortations to live a certain type of ethical life that do not grow out of and find their basis in the gospel truths and the redemptive-transformative message are mere moralisms, impotent in the end to effect the real transformation of the moral life. To make any significant difference, then, between Paul's doctrinal sections and the practical sections manifests a failure to grasp this relationship. Furthermore, it should also be noted that the sections of doctrinal teaching embody ethical teaching, and the sections of ethical teaching before us implicitly or explicitly teach doctrine. Doctrine is ethical; ethics is doctrinal.

But now the question could be put to Paul: Just what, precisely, is the relationship between all this theology and doctrine and my actual Christian experience and conduct?

More specifically, Christian ethics is the outworking of Christian redemption and Spirit transformation, or what is called *sanctification* (from "to make holy"), which, it must be repeated, is absolutely necessary for receiving eternal life at the final judgment (2:7; 6:22). Our conduct springs from union with Christ (6:1–4). Jesus Himself constitutes for us both the form and, through the Spirit, the actualizing or transforming power of the Christian lifestyle. Our motivation for this life of discipleship lies in the desire to be obedient to Christ, which is an essential element in faith and salvation (1:5), as well as an expression of our deep gratitude to God, who has shown to us by grace His forgiving and justifying mercy.

In the following chapters, Paul sketches the specific relevance of the obedience of faith in Jesus Christ to the more general but actual situations of life. Three major themes are touched upon: (1) the relations of Christians to one another (12:3–13); (2) the relations of Christians to non-Christian society, including the state (12:14–13:14); and finally (3) a special problem in the relationship of believers to one another, arising from their differences in cultural and religious backgrounds (14:1–15:6). Although the somewhat loose connection in thoughts through the chapters emphasizes the spontaneity of the Christian ethic as it confronts the complicated spectrum of ethical situations, there is nevertheless an underlying regularity in the application of the principle of life in the new being in Christ, which is to walk in love.

THE LIVING SACRIFICE
12:1–2

Paul begins with the foundation of all Christian living. In these two verses we find the secret that unlocks the unlimited possibilities of genuine Christian life in the world. Calling the

Christians in Rome "brothers" (a family term, which most certainly includes men and women) the apostle appeals to them to make the supreme offering of complete dedication to God.

Paul bases his appeal "in view of God's mercy" (v. 1). The best clue to the meaning of this statement is found in the "therefore," which indicates that Paul grounds his present appeal on what he has previously said in his letter. God's mercy means God's merciful activity toward sinners through Christ, which Paul has been expounding in the previous sections of the book and especially in chapters 9–11 (see 11:32). A Christian, then, is one who has experienced the mercy of God.

But what are Christians to do? They are admonished, "Present your bodies a living and holy sacrifice" (NASB). The language draws upon the sacrificial ritual of the Old Testament offerings: "present" (offer on the altar), "sacrifice," "holy," "acceptable to God" (NASB). Straining for some adequate image of the proper response of the believer to God's mercies, Paul, as previously (3:21), thinks of the sacrifices and especially the burnt offering (Lev. 1:3–17). When an Israelite wanted to express his devotion to the Lord, he selected an appropriate animal or bird and brought it to the tabernacle to present it to the Lord. He laid his hands on the head of the animal, signifying substitutionary identification, and killed it, whereupon the priest burned the entire carcass upon the sacrificial altar. The offering was "holy" to the Lord in that it was wholly His (the priest did not get any part). This act of worship and service was an "acceptable" odor to the Lord (cf. Eph. 5:2).

George MacDonald has poetically captured the nature of the presentation of ourselves to God in the following story: "The Old Man of the Earth stooped over the floor of the cave, raised a huge stone, and left it leaning. It disclosed a great hole that went plumb-down. 'That is the way,' he said. 'But there are no stairs. You must throw yourself in. . . . There is no other way'" (from *The Golden Key and Other Stories*).

By "body" Paul does not mean simply our personalities or selves but our physical bodies with all their functions (6:6, 12; 8:10–11, 23).[1] We are to serve God in these temporal earthen bodies, not in some imagined other-worldly vision or fancy. By

stressing the sacrifice of the body, Paul may have been counter-
ing certain latent Greek philosophical ideas that taught the dep-
recation of the body and our eventual liberation from its captivity. Perhaps some thought that because the "body is dead
because of sin" (8:10), it could not be acceptable to God for service.

"Spiritual act of worship" is more difficult. The word "act
of worship" (Gk. *latreia*) is a single word and means to serve
God by sacrifice. Because the whole service of the priests in the
Old Testament was viewed as a service before God, the same
term has both the connotation of service to God and worship of
God. Under the new covenant, in this age, every believer is a
priest and can serve God by the sacrificial offering of his body
in an act of worship to Him (1 Pet. 2:9).

This service-worship is further described as "spiritual" (Gk.
logikē). Although the Greek word Paul uses is related to the
Greek word for "reason" or "rational" (Eng., *logical*), the
meaning may come closer to the thought of something that is
true or has inner reality in contrast to the merely external, material form. Worship in both Judaism and pagan ritual tended
toward the outward, more material form.[2]

Christians, in contrast to those external ritual religions, are
to present their physical bodies as an act of true, inner, Spirit-
directed service to God (John 4:23–24; Rom. 12:1; Phil. 3:3).
"It implies that any cultic worship which is not accompanied by
obedience in the ordinary affairs of life must be regarded as
false worship, unacceptable to God."[3]

The complete abandonment of our bodies to God's service
constitutes the indispensable foundation or core of Christian
living. Such a commitment should be made as a decisive, accomplished event, as the Greek tense of "present" suggests. All
future decisions and actions will constantly be made in the context of and in keeping with this initial dedicatory step. Perhaps
the best analogy is marriage. From the first act of each spouse
giving himself or herself totally to the other there follows a
whole life lived together in the context of that original pledge.

We are simply kidding ourselves if we are trying to do Christian things and yet have never pledged ourselves fully to Jesus

Christ. God's grace is free, but it is not cheap, for God gave us the most costly gift He could give, the suffering unto death for our sins of His own beloved Son. The discovery of this gift is like finding an incomparable pearl or a million-dollar treasure in our backyard (Matt. 13:44–46). What lesser response to this love and mercy of God would be enough? As Isaac Watts wrote,

> But drops of grief can ne'er repay
> The debt of love I owe;
> Here, Lord, I give myself away,
> 'Tis all that I can do.

As the late Sam Shoemaker stated, to be a Christian means "to give as much of myself as I can to as much of Jesus Christ as I know." There is the initial offering and the progressive, repeated offerings in the context of this first dedication.

In verse 2 Paul describes the general nature of the growth process that is the natural and inseparable outworking of our supreme act of divine service related in verse 1. The "world" means this world that will "pass away" (1 John 2:17) and probably should be rendered as "age" (Gk. *aiōn*). The term *age* in biblical teaching views the present world as under the control of various alien powers such as sin, death, the flesh, and lust (Gal. 1:4). Its chief characteristic is lust or greed and selfishness (1 John 2:15–16). The world, or present age, has much more to do with attitudes and values than things; it is much more related to selfishness than certain kinds of activities. This age will pass away (1 Cor. 7:31); it has no permanence; it is only fashionable; it acts out a part and holds the stage, but it is without real being. Once a person realizes this, how foolish it is to join in with this "flick," which is projected on such a shaky screen. There is something better in Christ.

Paul warns his readers not to be "conformed" (NASB) to this age. The word means to be poured into the mold of something and thereby to shape the outward appearance, to rubber-stamp something. Phillip's oft-quoted translation has: "Don't let the world around you squeeze you into its own mold." Or in keeping with our previous thought it may be translated, "Stop letting this age give you your lines in its flick."

But Paul does not stop with the negative as do so many Christians. He goes on to admonish them that they should allow the new age of the reign of God to break into their lives and "transform" (literally, metamorphose) them. Paul's word here is the same term found in the "transfiguration" of Jesus (Matt. 17:2). He uses the word to describe the "changing" of believers into the image of Christ by the Holy Spirit as they reflect the glory of Christ (2 Cor. 3:18). This is no mere imitation of Christ, but the outworking of the divine presence and power in the life. That the "mind" needs "renewing" shows how radically different Paul's idea of the mind is from Greek thought, which exalted the mind to almost divine status. The mind here, however, implies much more than human intellectual activities. It refers to the deepest springs of human existence and includes our affective, willing, and knowing faculties.[4]

The purpose or goal of this constant renewal of the mind is that you might "approve what God's will is" (v. 2). To "test" does not mean to test whether God's will is good or bad, but it means to "test" or examine with a view to "approve" the will of God. In the consciousness of a person who is being transformed by Christ's Spirit, there lies the possibility of actually recognizing and doing the will of God in every human situation (Eph. 5:9–10).

This challenge of the apostle, on the one hand, indicates that "so far from being an unfallen element in human nature," the mind "needs to be renewed. . . . On the other hand," this latter clause in the verse "indicates the dignity of the individual Christian [who is] called on . . . to exercise a responsible freedom." Likewise, it is a strong refutation of every form of church government that would "reduce the Christian lay[person] to a kind of second class citizenship" in the local church (Cranfield, 2:610).

In the examining and affirming of what is actually the will of God, the believer will also discover that it is precisely equivalent to the "good," to the "pleasing," and to the "perfect" in God's eyes in each situation. By following out these terms in

Paul's usage, a further clue can be obtained as to what precisely constitutes the moral will of God.

Here then in the first two verses is Paul's way of restating Jesus' call, "If anyone would come after me, he must deny himself and take up his cross and follow me. For whoever wants to save his life will lose it, but whoever loses his life for me will find it" (Matt. 16:24–25). There will be found a constant tension in the Christian life between the present age in which we live and the age to come which has, in some measure, through the Holy Spirit already broken into our lives. There is a wrong way of staying in the world, just as there is a wrong way of fleeing from it.[5]

Christianity is change—radical, revolutionary change at the center of human consciousness. Paul's thought strikes devastatingly at every form of Christianity that is stagnant, complacent, proud of its accomplishments, or not radical enough to stand in judgment over every aspect of its relationship to the current age—whether political, social, personal, or ecclesiastical.

THE CHRISTIAN COMMUNITY 12:3–8

In the practical outworking of our deeply personal relationship to Christ, we will be confronted immediately with the fact that Christianity involves a people. One cannot be Christlike alone. Every Christian is united inseparably to all Christians in the one body in Christ (vv. 4–5). Paul, in an epistle to the Corinthian believers, has already elaborated more fully on this thought (1 Cor. 12).

Furthermore, this section of Paul's letter illustrates the outworking of the first principle of Christian ethics stated in verse 2. Such may be the force of the word *for* at the beginning of the paragraph. One of the characteristics of this age that Christians are not to copy is pride (v. 3). Pride always has reference to others and must be seen as one of the prime roots of dissension. Paul may have had some knowledge of one group of Christians in Rome who thought they were better than others (11:18–21; 14:1–4). So he exhorts, "To every one of you: Do not think of yourself more highly than you ought, but rather think of yourself with sober judgment, in accordance with the measure of faith God has given you" (v. 3).

Humility, contrary to general opinion, is not assuming the least role, or taking the lowest notch on the totem pole. Rather, humility is an attitude and action that results from taking an honest look at where we best fit into the whole of God's work as He has determined by His gifts to us. Paul himself, for example, exercised his gift as an apostle by exhorting the Roman Christians, prefacing his exhortations with the words, "Because of the grace God gave me" (15:15). Pride assumes or desires more prerogative than God has given to us. It is an exaggerated self-esteem. False humility, on the other hand, tends to assume a lesser role than the Lord has assigned. Therefore, Christians are to "have sound judgment" (v. 3 NASB) or to hold a balanced viewpoint of their harmonious contribution to the whole body (vv. 4–5).

The "measure of faith" (v. 3) certainly should be understood as the same as "gifts, according to the grace given to us" (v. 6) and corresponds to Paul's similar statements about gifts in 1 Corinthians 12 and Ephesians 4 (so Luther and Schreiner). Gifts of the Spirit are given to every believer. These spiritual enablements are differentiated and yet interlaced within the church so that there is a preservation of the beautiful relationship of the uniqueness of each individual contribution together with the importance and necessity of the community of the redeemed for the mutual edification and maturing of each individual person (Eph. 4:13–16).[6]

Individual Christians must not then think of themselves as the whole church but as petals to the flower. In realizing this truth I must constantly affirm two things: (1) I, or my group, do not have all the truth or all the gifts, and (2) the other person or group may have truth and gifts I do not have. So to be whole I must have fellowship and dialogue with all true Christians worldwide (and in history).

Paul enumerates seven such gifts in this passage. The list should not be thought of as exhaustive or without special significance in Paul's mind with respect to the Roman Christians' needs and problems.[7] It is interesting to ask why no special "charismatic" gifts (other than prophecy) are mentioned as they are in the Corinthian correspondence (1 Cor. 12; 14). It is tempting to answer by stating that these other gifts were not being abused in the Roman churches as in Corinth.

Prophecy is mentioned first (v. 6). In the other lists of gifts "apostle" takes preeminence even over a prophet (1 Cor. 12:28; Eph. 4:11). Because no apostle had apparently yet ministered to the Roman Christians (15:20), Paul may omit mention of it. The prophetic gift in both the Old and New Testaments involves the receiving of a message from God and communicating it. Frequently, but not always, the prophet predicted future events (Acts 21:10–11) as well as gave the Word of God for the contemporary situation.

The church stands in need of this ministry today. Those who can sensitively discern the movement of God in contemporary events and are able to apply the biblical revelation dynamically to our times may be modern-day prophets, such as the late Francis Schaeffer. Of course, their words are not infallible and must always be evaluated critically in the light of Scripture (1 Cor. 14:29), especially by those who have the gift of "distinguishing between spirits" (1 Cor. 12:10).

The prophet is to use this gift "according to the proportion of his faith" (Rom. 12:6 NASB). This expression might well mean that the prophet must speak in agreement with the faith, that is, Scripture doctrine. However, it is better in the context to understand the exhortation as a further subtle reminder by the apostle that the prophet is not in pride to go beyond his appointed authority, but should exercise the gift in exact agreement with the divine grace of enablement that has been given. The same warning would hold true for the other gifts as well. Those who minister their gifts should be neither negligent nor pretentious.

The next gift mentioned is "service," or ministry (v. 7 NASB). This gift should not be thought of as one involving merely a call to be a preacher or missionary but means all forms of service, especially to the needy (Rom. 15:25, 31; 2 Cor. 8:4). It may also refer to the deacon's work (Acts 6:1–3; 11:29; Phil. 1:1; 1 Tim. 3:8, 10, 12–13). This gift and its ministry should not be regarded as less spiritual because it deals with material needs. A man or woman (Rom. 16:1) may give full time to such services without coveting higher or allegedly more spiritual ministries (1 Tim. 3:13).

"Teaching" (v. 7), such as Paul has given in this letter to the Romans (Acts 13:1; 15:35), involves more systematic explanation and application of Christian truth than mere preaching. Although all prophetic preaching contains explanation (1 Cor. 14:1–5, 20–25) and all teaching should have contemporary application, the prophet is more concerned with proclaiming a direct word from God to the immediate historical situation, whereas the teacher will explain and relate this word to the rest of Scripture and its great themes. The effective ministry of the Word of God needs both gifts. If they are not found in one person, and it is rare that they are, then provision should be made for multiple public ministries.[8]

As for encouragement (v. 8), Paul may have reference either to the gift of ministering consolation (Gk. word is the same) to those in affliction or to the gift of exhorting the congregation to arouse their spirits and encourage their hearts toward God and His will. Both aspects are related. Have you ever left the presence of a Christian, saying to yourself: *Oh, how thankful to God I am for that person's life; how glad I am to be a Christian!* I believe this is the ministry of exhortation that we all need in a day of recurring waves of less-than-zealous Christianity.

The one who gives ("contributing to the needs of others") is to do it "generously," or more likely, with "unmixed motive of the heart" or "sincere concern" (TDNT) (2 Cor. 8:2; 9:11, 13; 11:3; Eph. 6:5; Col. 3:22). Though it is possible to understand Paul's words for "liberality" to mean to distribute "liberally," the idea is more that gifts of money given by the individual to the needy should be for the single purpose of showing deep concern and expressing Christian love in meeting the needs of those lacking and not to gain merit before God or status before others. So hidden from others' eyes should these deeds be that Jesus said, "Do not let your left hand know what your right hand is doing" (Matt. 6:3). How different this sounds from so much Christian giving where everyone knows who the liberal donors are! In fact, if they were unrecognized, the money would probably not be donated. I am reminded in contrast to this of the cornerstone plaque affixed to a large building complex now used by a well-known Christian organization in California: "Purchased by a Christian and donated to the glory of God."

Next, Paul refers to those who "lead." The Greek word for lead *(proistami)* used here may also mean "to care for." That "leading" and "caring for" are dual meanings for the word is explained by the fact that caring for the needs of people in the early church was the obligation of the elders or leading members (1 Thess. 5:12; 1 Tim. 3:4–5; 5:17). The emphasis is not so much on authority or power as on pastoral care.[9] Jesus emphasized this aspect as the chief role of a leader (Luke 22:26). Caring for the flock is to be done with "diligence" or zeal, which may explain why a special recognition for this diligence is recommended by Paul elsewhere (1 Tim. 5:17).

Finally, one who "shows mercy" as the expression of the Holy Spirit's gift should do these deeds cheerfully and brightly. Calvin's remark captures the spirit of the exhortation: "For as nothing gives more solace to the sick or to any one otherwise distressed, than to see men cheerful and prompt in assisting them; so to observe sadness in the face of those by whom assistance is given make them to feel themselves despised.[10]

Though it is extremely encouraging in our day to find so many individual Christians exercising a variety of Spirit-ministered gifts, it is sad to see so few Christian churches that provide any planned structure in the church meetings for the spontaneous ministering of gifts to one another. To counteract this deficiency, one church in the 1970s was a pioneer in holding a Sunday evening meeting called a Body-Life service. After nearly a thousand people would pack into the Peninsula Bible Church in Palo Alto, California, the leader would get things started by saying, "This is the family, the body of Christ. We need each other. Let's share." One after another, persons all over the auditorium would stand and speak. A divorced mother of three told how God put food on the table that week. A glassy-eyed girl requested prayer for her older brother who was blowing his mind with LSD and would not stop. The leader asked a former "acid head" to go stand by her and lead out in prayer for the brother. A woman gave the keys for the family's second car to a student who had expressed a need for transportation for work. Other needs, insights, helps, prayers, comfort, and good news would be shared, and at times laughter, applause, or hushed moments of anguish could accompany the events. When the offering was taken, those in need could also take from the plate up to ten dollars![11]

Somehow I believe that example must have come closer to the New Testament meaning of the gifts than most of our churches have experienced.

THE LAW OF LOVE APPLIED 12:9–21

At this point, Paul seems to change the subject matter and offer a number of ethical injunctions or general rules for Christian conduct.[12] Each command appears permeated by the underlying principle of showing love first to Christians (vv. 9–13), and then to all, even to those who treat Christians as their enemies (vv. 14–21). In this section as well as the following, Paul seems to be integrating and applying Jesus' teaching found in the Sermon on the Mount (Matt. 5–7) as well as selected Old Testament ethical injunctions. Two main overarching principles govern Christian conduct: love and peace. In these exhortations, there is really no system of ethics propounded, but nevertheless all of life comes under the direction of the renewed mind in Christ (v. 2). Little comment is needed except at certain points in the exposition.

Paul heads the list with love, as he does elsewhere (Gal. 5:22). If love is true and genuine and not just a put-on or facade, then everything else to which Paul exhorts the church will follow. The great identifying mark of the Christian lifestyle and the final compelling apologetic for Christianity is the love that Christians have for one another (John 13:34–35). This love must be especially visible to the world. One area of acid test is the way we behave toward other Christians who differ with us. We must truly regret our differences that cause friction among us and must show a costly love by practicing consciously our love for each other regardless of the inconvenience or loss to us personally or to our group.[13]

"Hate [shrink back from] what is evil; cling [stick in total devotion] to what is good" (v. 9) underscores the dual nature of the world in which Christians live. Christian love must at times constructively negate some things in the world and affirm others. Furthermore, this love should embrace fellow Christians as if they were members of the same family with all its emotional and affectionate ties (v. 10). Genuine love for others in our common family in Christ will incite us to "be devoted to one another" or to take the lead in honoring the other before any honor comes our way (v. 10), each being readier than the other to recognize and honor God's gifts in a brother or sister (Eph. 3:8). This exhortation can have tremendous healing effects in the fractured church of today, especially if we will apply it to groups of Christians other than our own and in honor prefer them above ourselves!

Verse 11 contains three exhortations that seem to relate to the problem of Christian apathy. "Never be lacking in zeal" relates to Christian enthusiasm in using God's gifts to multiply His harvest (Matt. 25:26–27; 2 Tim. 1:6–7). The same warning against discouragement appears elsewhere (Gal. 6:9; Heb. 12:3). To uncover this problem, the question could well be asked: Are there any issues in my life that I am concerned about? Have I ceased to get excited over anything anymore?

"Spiritual fervor" surely relates to both the former injunction and to the following command to serve the Lord. The inner human spirit of the Christian is surely "set aglow" by the fire of the Holy Spirit (Acts 18:25 NASB). Translate therefore, "Be aglow with the Holy Spirit" (not as NIV, "spiritual fervor"). The final order concerning "serving the Lord" suggests how this zeal is to be channeled to avoid apathy in our Christian lives. When Christians become overly depressed in any type of work or service, and zeal ebbs, it may be due to the fact that the priority of the Lord's service has slipped from their minds. These are general exhortations designed to keep God's people from indolence and apathy.

Three further brief commands are linked together in verse 12: "Be joyful in hope, patient in affliction, faithful in prayer." Power for living now lies in the direction of the Christian's future hope (8:18–27). Because God has granted to us in His promises such a strong vision of His future kingdom and the resurrection, our present lives are to be lived as if this kingdom had already arrived.

Such living in hope will bring a radical criticism and judgment upon the present world order and result in the world's reaction and very often persecution. In these afflictions the believer must be steadfast and not relinquish his trust in God. No greater resource for strength in trials and joy in his hope can be found than in prayer, which should be entered into as serious work, as part of the battle of spiritual warfare.

Being "faithful in" prayer emphasizes the persistence in prayer that distinguished the prayers of the early Christians from the merely religious performance of prayers of some contemporary Jews and of the pagans. "Devoted" to prayer catches well the force of the Greek word, which means to stick diligently with something and attend to it (the same word is used in Luke 11:1–13; 18:1–8; Acts 1:14; Eph. 6:18; Col. 4:2). The word is used by Paul to refer to the activity of tax collectors in 13:6! This should alert us that prayer is central to the Christian life and is not automatic, but must be deliberately and consciously pursued.

Paul continues with the exhortation about "shar[ing] with God's people who are in need" (v. 13). The force of the verb denotes "partaking of" the needs of brothers and sisters in Christ. We are to feel a oneness, as in the same family, with those who suffer afflictions and deprivations for the name of Christ. When we truly follow this exhortation, it will be natural for us to also *meet* those needs if it is in our power.

If, on the other hand, these needy Christians come to us, we will receive them with open homes and hearts. "Practice" hospitality does not quite catch the more intensive force of the Greek verb, which means "to actively pursue." Christian hospitality demands a special effort that goes beyond the mere inconvenience of hosting non-Christians or even Christians; we cannot choose our time or our guests. Hospitality in the early church was a prime example of "sharing with God's people who are in need" (see also 1 Tim. 3:2; Titus 1:8; Heb. 13:2; 1 Pet. 4:9). Perhaps we should see the test of this ministry today in terms of whether our homes are open to the minorities and socially disenfranchised of our society. Hospitality should not be seen as a gift that some Christians have and others do not, but rather as a command to all Christians while recognizing that some provide models for the rest of us.

In verse 14 the character of thought abruptly changes. That there is a change can be noted for two reasons. First, the subject changes from general exhortations or commands stressing mainly relationships of Christians to other Christians to admonitions dealing with the Christian response to non-Christian attitudes and actions. Also, the grammatical structure of these verses changes from Greek participles to imperatives and infinitives.

"Bless those who persecute you; bless and do not curse" (v. 14) reminds us definitely of our Lord's words (Matt. 5:44; Luke 6:28). Such a response demands the exercise of radical Christian love expressed toward those who have made themselves our enemies by persecuting us. To bless means more than mere words because the utterance must come from the heart and will be followed by the appropriate action as occasion affords. When we "rejoice with those who rejoice; mourn with those who mourn" (v. 15), we as Christians identify with others in our common humanity as fellow human beings. We must and should be truly able to empathize with them after the example of our Lord (Luke 15:1–2). The early church Father, Chrysostom, poignantly observed how much easier it is to weep with others than to rejoice with them. It is at the point of our sorrows and joys that we are most deeply ourselves. At this point the Christian is to identify in love with others.

In verse 16, Paul continues by admonishing Christians to cultivate a loving harmony and practice of humility in the company of non-Christians. "Do not be haughty in mind, but associate with the lowly" (NASB) is a difficult passage and unfortunately ambiguous in the Greek. Does the "lowly" (NASB) refer to others or things? If the latter, then the thought is that we are not to cherish selfish ambitions, but to give ourselves over to humble tasks (Phil 4:11; 1 Tim. 6:8–9). If "lowly" refers to persons, then the sense is that we are to give ourselves over to association with the less attractive, more lowly people in the world. There is no final way to decide between the two views. Both are worthy Christian goals. In either case, one line of thought would lead to the other.

The force of the exhortation "Do not be wise in your own eyes" is that we must not be conceited (Prov. 3:7). Such words strike at the very heart of an opinionated person who cherishes his own ideas and judgments as if they themselves were the absolute truth and refuses to acknowledge the opinions and thoughts of others. Furthermore, we should not be misled by our own preferences, which often incline toward that which flatters our pride, namely, the distinguished and brilliant. There is a way of clinging to the truth that is no more than a way of clinging to oneself.

Finally, in verses 17–21 of the chapter, Paul interacts more specifically with the question of Christian response to hostility from non-Christians (though some Christians might also be in view). As in the teaching of Jesus concerning nonviolence and nonretaliation (Matt. 5:38–42), Paul's concern is with the question of the proper Christian's and the church's response. In chapter 13 he will consider what response toward hostility and evil is correct for civil authorities.

Love will never retaliate or "pay back" (NASB) blow for blow for harm done (Prov. 17:14), but on the contrary will "be careful [take thought] to do what is right [Gk. means "good"] in the eyes of everybody" (v. 17). Christian conduct should be recognizably commendable before non-Christians (2 Cor. 8:21; 1 Thess. 5:15). Many Christians today, in contrast, are far more concerned with how their behavior strikes their Christian friends than whether it is acceptable to non-Christian moral sensitivities.

This rule of behavior does not mean that Christians will turn to the world for their norms of conduct, but in seeking the will of God for each ethical situation, they will consider what is right and just "in the eyes of everybody" as part of the basis for their decision (v. 17; see also v. 2). In practice, believers must weigh the consequences of whatever action they take against the effects of the testimony that results to the nonbelieving community for or against the Christian message (Matt. 5:16; 1 Cor. 10:31–32). This principle takes into account that God's law in some sense is recognizable in the hearts of all persons, however dimly they might perceive or recognize His norms as they formulate their concepts of right and wrong (Rom. 2:15). The Christian, however, is always to obey God's law instead of human law wherever conflict arises (Acts 4:18–20).

By so acting, the interests of peace and goodwill are promoted (v. 18). There is, however, a qualification: "If possible, as far as it depends on you," or if the possibility of peace can be brought about by you. Peace cannot be secured at the cost of God's truth, or His commands, or if others refuse to cooperate (Matt. 10:34–36; Luke 12:51–53; James 3:17). Christians should do everything in their power to be the reconciling salt in the hostilities between persons in the world. If conflict arises where the Christian is involved, let it only arise because of the Christian's stand for the truth of God and His justice. Strife or conflict should never be sought or initiated by the Christian.

In verses 19–21 the apostle answers a possible objection to his peace way of life (v. 18). Someone might say, "Won't this approach play into the hands of evil persons, favoring their schemes and allowing them to go unchecked in their wickedness? Wouldn't it be better to set them straight, send them a message forcefully, and put an end to their injustice?" Paul says no! The essence of sin in human relations is for individuals to assume the place of God and take justice or retaliation into their own hands. We cannot presume to do this, because not only are we limited in our information and understanding, but when our own personal interests have been hurt we will invariably distort justice in favor of our own selfish concerns without regard to the other. If we are honest, what we want is revenge (retaliation), not justice.

Therefore, Christians must not try to "get even" with other persons who have wronged them. Instead we must commit ourselves in trust to the administration of God's justice upon the unjust person, that is, the wrath of God (2:5, 8; 3:5; 5:9; 9:22). God's wrath is being presently directed toward evildoers both directly (1:18–25) and perhaps indirectly through the civil authorities (13:4, "wrath") and will be completely manifest in the future final judgment (Rom. 2:5–6; Rev. 20:11–15). We should be reminded that the wrath of God of which Paul speaks is "the wrath of God which was revealed in its full awfulness in Gethsemane and on Golgotha as the wrath of the altogether holy and loving God" (Cranfield, 2:647). Paul quotes Deuteronomy 32:35 to support this principle of nonretaliation, which should be the absolute rule of God's people.

But the Christian must do more than be passive toward personal animosity; we should also take positive steps to manifest that we do not harbor vengeance against the offender. While we do *not* pay back evil for evil, we *do* pay back good in return for the harm: "If your enemy is hungry, feed him; if he is thirsty, give him something to drink" (v. 20). Here Paul seems to call to mind Jesus' admonition to love the enemy (Matt. 5:44 and Luke 6:27), but he actually quotes Proverbs 25:21–22. "Burning coals on his head" is understood by some to refer to coals of divine judgment (hence a way of ultimately getting back at the other, Schreiner). Others see the sense as the fires of shame and remorse burning the conscience of the offender and hopefully bringing about repentance and reconciliation to the offended (Moo). By following this unnatural but loving course of action, Christians will not be conquered by evil persons in their pursuit of promoting peace (v. 18). We will instead conquer such evil fostered against us by good (acts of love) toward the evildoer, more than we could through acts of vengeance (v. 21). Thus evil is more permanently dealt with when the hearts of evildoers are changed and their resentment overcome than if they were merely brought to justice. This is the secret conspiracy of love that subverts evil and leads to the transformation of sinners. It may also be the case that each act of love shown by a believer toward an enemy that is resisted and spurned and does not evoke repentance will be a coal of divine judgment at the last day.

There is another consequence of refusing to take vengeance. Cranfield says, "The Christian's victory over the evil consists in his refusal to become a party to the promotion of evil by returning evil for evil and so becoming himself like the evil man who has injured him, in his accepting injury without resentment, without allowing his love to be turned into hate or even only weakened. . . . By so doing he will be sharing in the victory of the gospel over the world and setting up signs which point to the reality of God's love for sinners; he will be living as one who is being transformed by the renewing of the mind" (2:650).

THE CHRISTIAN AND CIVIL AUTHORITIES 13:1–7

It is important at the first in this highly controversial passage to establish the link, if any, with the preceding section. This teaching on government appears somewhat abruptly (without connecting particle) between two exhortations pertaining to the exercise of Christian love and peace (12:9–21 and 13:8–10). Arguments can be advanced for a *logical* connection with the preceding in either the idea of "revenge" and "wrath" (12:19 with 13:4); or with the thought of not being conformed to the world or any of its institutions (12:2); or as answering the problem as to whether the Christian is to view the state as evil because it renders evil for evil, which the Christian is not to do.

Although these logical connections may not be absent, they are largely matters of conjecture. Actually the local historical conditions in Rome itself may have had more to do with the inclusions of this section on civil authorities than the previous subject material. Such a view would also be in keeping with the more spontaneous nature of the exhortations in chapters 12–16. In any case, we should not think of this section on civil government as a parenthesis in his exposition.

Adopting the historical explanation may be better for several reasons. In the first place, there is good evidence that, at the time Paul wrote Romans (early A.D. 57), considerable hostility was mounting between Rome and the Jews. In A.D. 49 the emperor Claudius finally had to expel all the Jews from Rome due to the continual disturbances and riots caused by one Chrestus (or Christ).[14]

A further inscription of the times may show that this trouble was caused by the preaching of the resurrection of Jesus in Rome by believing Jews and the countercharge of unbelieving

Jews that the body of Jesus was removed from its tomb by the disciples (Matt. 28:11–15). This tomb robbery allegation could explain why the trouble occurred in Rome in connection with "Chrestus" between Jewish Christians and non-believing Jews and also why Claudius wrote an ordinance about this same time (curiously found in Nazareth) forbidding tampering with graves on punishment of death.[15]

In addition, Jewish revolutionary activities (by zealots) against Rome during this period are well-known. Because Jesus was a Jewish Messiah, the Roman government was likely to suspect all followers of Jesus as having revolutionary tendencies. Therefore, any insubordination to the authorities among groups of Christians could be interpreted as a revolutionary threat to Roman rule on the part of the whole Christian movement.

Furthermore, there is evidence that due to either pagan or Jewish backgrounds certain Christians entertained perverted theological notions of Christ's kingship and lordship and its relation to the kingdoms of this world (see Matt. 22:17).[16]

Was obedience to Christ as King compatible with obedience to the civil institutions? This question also involved the further problem of the extension of Christian liberty under Christ's lordship to include freedom from all other authorities of any kind (1 Pet. 2:13–17).

In the actual text of 13:1–7, four general principles concerning the relationship of the Christian to government can be summarized: (1) There is a binding Christian responsibility toward the authority of the governing rulers as well as toward the authority of Christ; (2) human government is a divinely appointed institution; (3) the purpose of government is twofold: to promote the good in society, and to restrain and punish criminals; and (4) proper and conditional loyalty in general to the government and support of its need should be the correct attitude of every Christian.

The chief theological problem of this section is the question of whether civil authority is under the direct lordship of Christ. If so, then government can be responsive to the claims of Christ and His love; if not, then it is an illusion to seek to bring government into the service of Christ's kingdom.[17]

More specifically, Paul first states in verses 1 and 2 that all Christians ("every person" NASB—v. 4 limits Paul's address to believers, though nonbelievers are no less responsible) with no exceptions are to be obedient to the "governing authorities." They are to do this because all past rulers ("no authority except from God") and present government officials ("those which exist" NASB) have been appointed by the will of God (Dan. 2:21; 4:17, 35; John 19:11). Furthermore, to resist government agents in the discharge of their duties is to resist the command of God and incur, therefore, God's judgment ministered through the penalty imposed by the authorities (Rom. 13:2).

The "authorities" are most certainly the government officials in the Roman commonwealth.[18] At the time of Paul's writing (early A.D. 57), Nero was emperor of Rome (A.D. 54–68). Though it is true that Nero was cruel, lustful, and murderously vicious, yet he had the aid of two provincials (Burrus and Seneca) who were relatively honest and promoted a model government during the first five years of Nero's reign (during the time Paul wrote this letter). It is amazing that the apostle wrote these words on obedience to government after being himself recently mistreated by the Roman authorities at Philippi (Acts 16:37). Peter also wrote much of the same kind of exhortation to Christians later in the reign of Nero (1 Pet. 2:13–17, c. A.D. 64). "Will bring judgment" means they shall receive judgment from the rulers, not eternal damnation (Rom. 13:2).

Paul goes on to describe the reason that the punitive power given to the civil authority can be used (vv. 3–4). God has appointed government officials to a twofold duty that reflects the general purpose of the state: (1) Government must not destroy or subvert the good of society but protect and promote it: "do what is right and he will commend you" (v. 3); "for he is God's servant to do you good" (v. 4); and (2) the civil power must deter crime and bring to punishment those who foster evil in society: "for he does not bear the sword for nothing. He is God's servant, an agent of wrath to bring punishment on the wrongdoer" (v. 4). Christians who do good and not evil should have no fear of the civil powers.

"Praise" from the ruler (v. 3 NASB) simply implies approval

with no necessary reward involved. Evangelicals could do better in emphasizing this theme rather than always stressing the punitive aspect of government. "God's servant" (two times, v. 4) refers to the discharge of God's appointed civil authority (vv. 1-2) and has no reference to the salvation of the ruler. Such a term strongly counteracts any tendency to attribute evil to the existence of the state per se, as some are advocating in our day. That the ruler is a minister of God "to do you good" argues that governments exist for the good of the Christian community, as well as for the non-Christian (v. 4). The state, then, is not just an entity for unbelievers, but God's grace to the church is in some measure mediated through its protection and good benefits. This should not be overstated or overlooked.

Does the "sword" that rulers bear refer to more than the mere symbol of authority and also suggest their right to wield it to enforce justice, and if need be to inflict death (Matt. 26:52; Acts 12:2; 16:27; Heb. 11:34, 37)?[19] "For nothing" means for no purpose or for no use. The ruler does not wear the sword for effect merely, but he may also use the authority it represents in administering "punishment."

The ruler is further described in this service to God as an "agent of wrath" (Gk. *ekdikos*, note that this is the same root Greek word as "avenge" *[ekdikēsis]* in 12:19). The expression may mean simply "agent for wrath" (Käsemann). The word Paul uses here *(ekdikos)* is related to the word for justice or vindication. It is not clear if "wrath" here means God's wrath (12:19) or simply human wrath (Schreiner, *Romans*). In any event, the human ruler's coercive action in restraining evil and punishing (exercising retributive justice) those who practice evil is linked in some manner to God's agency and will in human societies.

We understand from this that the government ruler has authority from God to promote the good and punish evil as God's own servant in these civil matters. Such recognition lays a twofold moral obligation upon Christians to comply with civil authorities (v. 5). First, because to resist civil authorities by doing evil would incur their "wrath" (punishment) or force, which, as we have argued, is in fact linked to God's judgment upon evil. Second, our "conscience" toward God would smite us because we have violated His ordained authority over our lives in this area.

The Christian conscience is to be developed by God's Word as understood in the community of faith, by His Creation order, and by the promptings of the Holy Spirit. Therefore, whenever the civil power commands us to violate God's will, we must refuse on the same grounds of conscience toward God (Acts 4:19–20; 5:29). Peter says, "Submit yourselves for the Lord's sake" (1 Pet. 2:13). It is this matter of conscience toward God that leaves open the possibility of resistance and even disobedience to government.

Finally, Paul pushes one step further and suggests that because government is ordained by God, the Christian should participate in its continued existence by supporting the various financial needs of government, by paying taxes, tolls, duties, assessments, and by giving respect for officials as servants of God (vv. 6–7). Recent studies have pointed out that these types of commands to do good to the civil society are a reversal of the "benefactor concept." Rulers, or for that matter, even masters of slaves, were viewed by the society as "benefactors" toward those whom they ruled or controlled. Following Christ's teaching (Luke 22:25–27) believers were to become the benefactors to their rulers and masters by serving them in the name of Christ, thus radically reversing the benefaction convention. The good it dispenses will be for the "welfare of the city." Through "a critical engagement in the existing *politeia* the church is to take the lead in doing good; it is to claim the role of 'the powerful'; but it is to do this by means of service in humility."[20] This benefactor concept cannot be eliminated from the passage but should not be limited to it (Moo).

"Giv[ing] their full time to governing" (v. 6) is the same word *(proskartereo)* used in 12:12 for Christians being "faithful" in prayer. If Christians would exercise the same intense concern over prayer that, say, the Internal Revenue Service does over collecting our taxes, no telling what might happen in today's church! "Taxes" are the direct taxes such as income and real estate tax (from which Roman citizens were exempt), while "revenue" refers to indirect taxes on goods such as sales and custom taxes. This description in no way limits or justifies a particular form of tax or the amount assessed.

It seems clear that Paul's position on the relationship of the disciple of Christ to the governing authorities is the same as that of Jesus. Both are opposed to the zealot's revolutionary concept. In his oft-quoted words, Jesus deftly balances the two authorities, "Give to Caesar what is Caesar's, and to God what is God's" (Matt. 22:21).

Paul's theological position concerning the civil authorities leaves several contemporary questions unanswered. We can do no more here than attempt a passing comment or two.

What Is the Best Form of Government?

Paul does not commend or condemn any particular form of government, nor does the rest of the New Testament. From a Christian perspective, any form of government is better than anarchy and as such is worthy of our proper and conditional loyal support. We must remember that Roman government, with its wedding of the pagan gods and emperor worship, presented no more of a special problem to Christians in the first century than would living as a Christian under an atheistic form of secular government or an Islamic state today.

It should also be noted that Paul didn't know about participatory democracies or republics, since Rome did not allow all of its subjects to vote or run for office or participate in decisions that affected the people. If such had been Paul's situation, he might have exhorted much more of a positive involvement in government than simply paying taxes and complying with the rulers. Which form of government is better than others must be settled on the level of historical, political, and economic theory interfaced with a theological interpretation of Scripture's underlying political principles, but not directly on specific biblical passages.[21]

Should Government Policy Ever Be Criticized?

Is it possible to be properly and conditionally loyal to the civil authorities in obedience to Romans 13 and at the same time be critical of certain acts or policies of government officials? Apparently Jesus felt free to criticize not only the Jewish civil leaders (John 18:23), but also the Roman ruler Herod Antipas in referring to him as the "fox" (Luke 13:32). Paul likewise accused one of the members of a grand jury, who commanded him to be hit on the mouth, of being a "whitewashed wall," although he apologized when he learned that the man who issued the order was the high priest (Acts 23:1–5).

These examples are few but are sufficient to show that the principle of a critical attitude toward certain evil acts and policies is not foreign to Christianity. Such criticism should always be aimed at improving and not subverting the government or aimed at questioning whether a particular officer rightly represents a government. The Christian must say both yes to the state and no to the state. A Christianity tied too closely to the civil authorities soon finds itself being used as a tool to sanction the particular policies and acts of a government that uses the church to win citizen approval.

WHAT ABOUT CIVIL DISOBEDIENCE?

It is clear that the New Testament teaches that obedience to God always takes priority over obedience to the government regardless of the consequences (Acts 4:19–20; 5:29). Although a direct command of the government to disobey a direct command of God—say, in the case of idolatrous worship—presents little moral problem, the question arises whether resistance and even disobedience to the government may be the right action when our conscience toward God dictates to us in less direct matters. For example, Paul apparently resisted, or even disobeyed, the Roman official's command to leave prison secretly because he judged that he had been treated unjustly by the Philippian civil authorities (Acts 16:35–40). We don't know, but the text does not mention that he had a direct command from God not to leave prison secretly.

There are many vexing questions in regard to civil disobedience, and conscientious Christians have been divided over this issue down through history.[22] This much can be said. Paul does not qualify his request for obedience to the civil powers in Romans 13. However, he does indicate that the proper role of government is in promoting good and punishing evil, and he refers to the role of "conscience" toward God in our actions. It can be assumed that if either of these two conditions are not met there may be ground for resistance or even disobedience. The state is not absolute in its demands over us, nor is it infallible or always on the side of justice. The question of when and how the state should be resisted or disobeyed will never find unanimous consensus among Christians. The question must be constantly studied and discussed as we bring all of our decisions to the bar of careful scriptural examination and Christian conscience. Whatever action is taken must be responsible and conscientiously fully Christian with a willingness to submit to the government's punishment for such disobedience.

SHOULD A CHRISTIAN EVER PARTICIPATE IN POLITICAL REVOLUTION?

This question is extremely important in a day of worldwide revolutionary movements, especially among young people. Political revolution is a more extreme form of civil disobedience directed at the destruction of the established structure of a particular form of government and the ultimate replacement of it by a new form of rule. Paul does give instruction as to what a Christian should do when a revolution has occurred: He should "submit himself to the governing authorities" (13:1). At what point this new government is the "governing authority" he does not discuss, because such discussion lies more in the area of moral and political thought than theological direction for Christian behavior.

Furthermore, Paul indicates that the ideal government functions as God's servant when it promotes good and resists evil (13:3). If, in the judgment of a majority of its people, the existing government is largely suppressing good and promoting evil, has the civil authority abdicated its divine orders and thus proven no longer worthy of the Christian's obedience?

Whatever our answer to these vexing questions for the Christian conscience, it must be affirmed that because our ultimate (though not exclusive) loyalty belongs to the kingdom of God, we can never be identified totally with either a proposed revolution or the established form of government powers. Our position in Christ will lead us to be critical of, but not aloof from, all human movements. There can be no "Christian" revolution. "Sometimes the Lord of the world speaks more audibly out of prison cells and graves than out of churches which congratulate themselves on their concordat with the State" (Käsemann). One should also realize that much of the revolutionary movement in our times arises from a Marxist philosophy of history and not a Christian worldview. Does not Jesus' teaching and model lead Christians to condemn violence in all of its forms? This would still leave open the possibility of Christians acting responsibly in nonviolent ways to replace an existing totally corrupt government.

DOES PAUL ADVISE THE CHRISTIAN TO GO TO WAR?

It should be clear from what has been said on the exegesis of the text of Romans 13:1–7 that Paul is not talking about whether governments have the divine right to wage war or not. The "sword" is the right to punish offenders of the civil government. To some this implies but does not directly teach that the government may use violence including lethal force to put down evil. This however is disputed by others. Even granting that government has the authority to use violence, the question is whether this right also extends to punishing evildoers who assault the government from without (national or civil wars). A yes to this question can at best be only an inference from this passage and not a direct teaching.

From very earliest times, the church has been divided over whether killing in warfare under obedience to one's government constitutes a violation of Jesus' teaching on love to the enemy and of the sixth commandment against killing. One group of Christians (pacifists) sees such violent killing as disobedience to God's will and refuses to participate; another group (believers in a just war) argues that governments must from time to time defend themselves in punishing the evildoer through warfare and have therefore a right to expect their citizens to obey and bring the offenders to justice by whatever means are necessary.

We allow that Paul does seem to consent to the legitimate use of force by the civil ruler within his own realm, yet he does not directly forbid or justify killing in warfare. This difficult question must be settled by bringing other factors to bear, including scriptural principles (Old and New Testament) and moral concerns. If I as a Christian agree that obedience to the state involves participating in a justified war, that does not relieve me of the responsibility to bring appropriate moral criticism to bear on the military activities of my country. On the other hand, if my conscience toward Christ leads me to refuse military service, I must resist in a manner that will not subvert the other functions of the government. Also, I must show that my position is contributing to the good of the society in a fully responsible way.

FURTHER INSTRUCTIONS ON LOVE, VIGILANCE, AND HOLINESS
13:8–14

In this section, Paul shows how the great command of Christ concerning love relates to the divine commands under the old covenant. He argues that the old and the new are mutually complementary, the former hinting of the latter, and the latter revealing the former (vv. 8–10). At the close of the chapter, Paul turns to exhortations to holiness motivated from a consideration of the nearness of Christ's return and the consequent urgency to act (vv. 11–14).

In verse 8 Paul calls upon Christians to "let no debt remain outstanding," which is understood by some to refer back to verse 7 concerning paying our taxes or other obligations to government. In any case, this exhortation refers to unpaid debts and not to borrowing money (Exod. 22:25; Matt. 5:42; Luke 6:35). All of our obligations are to be paid up except one: the perpetual debt of Christian love to one another. This sole perpetual obligation is not at variance with or neglectful of the obligations of the divine moral commands of the Mosaic Law, because "he who loves his fellowman [neighbor] has fulfilled the law." The neighbor (v. 9), who often becomes the one like-minded to ourselves, is defined by the word *another* in verse 8 as "the other one who is different" from us (Gk. *heteros*). This guards Christian love from mere mutual admiration.

In verses 9 and 10, Paul explains further the connection between the Mosaic Law and Christian love. He cites the following commandments of the Mosaic tables as the epitome of the law (the order varies somewhat): adultery, killing, stealing, and coveting (lust). He says that these and any other commands of God (positive and negative) are summed up in the statement, "Love your neighbor as yourself" (v. 9, from Lev. 19:18; Matt 22:39–40). Paul's point simply is that the essence or chief point of all the commands is to promote loving action toward the other person. He is stressing that law and love serve one and the same end, to do no harm to the other person (v. 10). Morality is based on non-malevolence following Aquinas (J. Porter, *Moral Action*, 51–52).

To pit love against law as some have done in our day is to miss Paul's whole point.[23] Where love prevails the things that the law forbids do not occur (see Gal. 5:23). Note carefully that the apostle does not institute a new legalism of "love-righteousness" to merit justification as the situation ethicist seems to do, but in Paul's teaching the fulfilling of the law through the Spirit is a valid divine expression of love for the neighbor. Since the law required love to the other person, Paul teaches that "love is the fulfillment [or fullness] of the law" (v. 10). It is only love that makes the law fulfill its purpose. The Christian who walks continually in love fulfills all the demands of the law.

The thought changes in verses 11–14. The apostle turns to a final ethical exhortation pertaining to the urgency of adorning the life of holiness in Christ. Verse 11 gives a further reason for doing all the exhortations in chapters 12 and 13; it is the kind of "time" we live in. The word Paul uses for time (Gk. *kairos*) means not chronological succession of time but kind, season, or quality of time. In the New Testament, it often has an eschatological usage (Mark 13:33; Luke 21:8; Acts 1:7; 1 Thess. 5:1; 1

Tim. 4:1; 1 Pet. 1:5; Rev. 11:18). According to the New Testament, we are living in the eschatological "last days" (Acts 2:17; 2 Tim. 3:1; Heb. 1:2; 1 John 2:18), not chronologically but qualitatively. This "last days" kind of time began with the first coming of Christ and continues until His second coming. "Last days" are the days of the imminent consummation of all things and the manifestation of our full salvation (Rom. 8:23) in the kingdom of God (the coming of the "day" into the world). Each day brings us closer to this consummation.

Because we live on the edge, or brink, of this new day, our conduct must be in keeping with this momentary end event. We must wake up and not live or "sleep" (NASB) as if the character of the time were different (Matt. 24:42–44). Christ's coming was always "imminent" to the church, not in the sense that it was soon to happen, but from the standpoint that nothing major needed to occur before Christ could return. Paul and the early church (as in every generation) may have thought the coming was soon (1 Cor. 7:29–31); they may have even later revised their estimate (2 Tim. 4:6–8), but they still maintained their view of imminence. They believed that Christ might still come at any moment (Rev. 2:25; 3:11; 22:20). "The point of this sentence was to underline the urgency of the need to awake: the time of opportunity for faith and obedience was for Paul and his readers the shorter by this lapse of time. . . . It may further be said that the very transcendent importance of the expected Event itself lends significance to each passing moment and period of time" (Cranfield, 2:682).

Since the character of the coming consummation is "light" and "day," the proper response is to live in the light as if the day had already dawned ("properly," v. 13 NASB, really means "appropriately"). This requires arousing ourselves and putting off the night clothes of darkness: "orgies and drunkenness . . . sexual immorality and debauchery [moral corruptness] . . . dissension and jealousy" (v. 13). Finally, we are to put on the "day" clothes consisting of the "armor of light" (v. 12), which Paul elsewhere states to be faith, love, and hope (1 Thess. 5:8–9); or goodness, righteousness, and truth (Eph. 5:7–10)—weapons for conflict against the forces of spiritual darkness. The figure of changing clothes is, in good Hebrew tradition, an appeal to make an inward and spiritual change (Isa. 61:10; Zech. 3:3).

But nothing is so inclusive as the word in verse 14: "Rather, clothe youselves with the Lord Jesus Christ" (see Gal. 3:27). To put on Christ means to live in conformity to His mind and will (12:2), which is the natural outworking of our identification and union with Christ in His death and resurrection (6:1–10). "It means to follow Him in the way of discipleship and to strive to let our lives be molded according to the pattern of the humility of His earthly life" (Cranfield, 2:688–89). To "make . . . provision for the flesh" (NASB) is to make plans for satisfying the selfish and sinful desires of flesh. John's emphasis is the same when he says, "We shall be like him. . . . Everyone who has this hope in him purifies himself, just as he is pure" (1 John 3:2–3).

Historically, some importance can be attached to this section in that the great theologian, Augustine, was led to a personal acceptance of Jesus Christ on the basis of these last two verses as he tearfully meditated under a fig tree (*Confessions,* Book VIII).

It is sad to find in our day that much "prophetic" teaching and preaching stresses the chronological timetable approach and lacks the true sense of the apocalyptic force of the Pauline and New Testament emphasis.[24] And yet this later type of preaching is greatly needed in today's apathetic and morally weak Christian church.

CHRISTIAN FREEDOM AND CHRISTIAN LOVE
14:1–15:13

With the previous section Paul has concluded a series of ethical injunctions relating to personal, church, world, state, and Christian holiness. In chapters 14 and 15 (first part) the thought changes to a consideration of a special problem existing in the church due to the diverse cultural backgrounds of certain converts to Christianity. The problem may have been especially intensified by the presence in the church of Rome (also at Corinth, 1 Cor. 8–10) of both Jewish and Gentile Christians. The Jewish Christian minority in the church may have been reluctant both (1) to give up certain ascetic rules such as to eat no meat (Rom. 14:1–2) and to drink no wine (v. 21), and (2) to give up some of the Jewish feasts and fasts (v. 5). However, there is no evidence that these people were exclusively, or even primarily, Jewish in background.

This problem over religious and cultural background in the churches of Rome and Corinth should not be confused with the more serious problems involving certain Judaizing teachers at Galatia (Gal. 5:2), or the Jewish Gnostic teachers at Colossae (Col. 2:16–17, 21). These latter cases involve doctrinal distortions and warrant no toleration on Paul's part, whereas the Roman problem calls for a sympathetically patient attitude from the apostle. Furthermore, the problem at Corinth of eating food and drink sacrificed to idols does not seem to be the same issue dealt with here in Romans, even though both issues resulted in an unchristian spirit of alienation. Paul exhorts Christians to walk in love toward others who differ with them in this matter (14:15).

These chapters have special pertinence to Christians today who have different opinions over the religious and moral significance of certain practices that are not specifically mentioned in the Bible. To see exactly how Paul deals with these problems is of the utmost importance to us in preserving the love and unity in the Christian family.

More specifically, in the church at Rome there was a group that, because of religious conviction and conscience, wanted to refrain from the eating of certain foods (meat and wine, v. 21) and to consider "one day more sacred than another" (v. 5). It should be clear from what follows that Paul is not talking about any specific commands of God or biblical prohibitions such as adultery, lying, and idolatry. The argument was over the use of certain material things and the observance of social and religious customs. This group was considered "weak" by the majority in the congregation who had no qualms of conscience in these matters.[25] The problem then was how the church should respond to this minority opinion.

We are not told why this group held these opinions. However, there is good reason, based on the similar problem in

Corinth (1 Cor. 8–10), to believe that those who abstained from meat and wine had associated those substances with their former idolatrous worship and drunken life. The "day" problem, on the other hand, might be related to Jewish Christians who felt compelled to continue the observance of the Sabbath day (Saturday). Paul clearly agrees with the majority that the scruples of the weak are baseless. He is convinced, out of his relationship to Christ, that "no food is unclean in itself" (v. 14). The apostle thinks these things are of small matter to Christian faith, but because the problem has threatened the unity of the church, he must deal with it at length.

THE PRINCIPLE OF MUTUAL ACCEPTANCE (14:1–4)

What should the majority in the church do? The answer is clear. They who are strong should "accept" (welcome, accept fully) the weak (v. 1). Even though the weak in faith have qualms about certain matters, they are full members of the body of Christ and "God has accepted him" (v. 3). But the strong should not receive them for the purpose of debating and changing their practice over their scruples ("disputable matters," v. 1). An attitude like this on the part of the strong would only fan the problem into a larger fire of division. Instead, there should be mutual acceptance of each other without either snobbery on the part of the strong or criticism on the part of the weak (vv. 3–4). It should be to the glory of the church that we accept one another fully as we are without trying to press one another into one particular mold. Any such forced conformity is expressly forbidden in these exhortations.

THE PRINCIPLE OF INNER MOTIVATIONS (14:5–9)

In verses 5–8, in contrast to petty divisions over social and religious customs, Paul stresses what really is important in the Christian life. Whether we eat meat or do not eat meat is incidental. What is important is the inward motivation of our actions. We are to develop personal convictions before the Lord on everything we do: "Each one should be fully convinced in his

own mind" (v. 5). In the following verses (6–9) appears one of
the strongest passages in the New Testament on the lordship of
Jesus Christ over the individual Christian's life ("Lord" occurs
seven times). Both the strong and the weak are motivated out of
devotion to Christ in their behavior, which is evidenced in that
they both "give thanks" to God for what they allow or abstain
from (v. 6). In verses 7 and 8 there is further emphasis on the
possession of the believer by Christ and the consequent attitude
of the Christian toward the issue of his whole life and toward
the issue of his death. We no longer live to ourselves but we live
to Him who died and rose again that He might be our Lord in
life and our Lord in death (v. 9).

THE PRINCIPLE OF NO PRESUMPTIVE JUDGMENT (14:10–12)

When either the strong despises the weak, or the weak condemns the strong, one has presumptively judged the other. All
judgment in these matters must be left to the Lord Himself who
alone will know whether or not the motivation behind our
actions was indeed to honor Him. In another place, Paul can say
that though his conscience is clear, he cannot even judge himself
until the Lord's verdict is in on the last day (1 Cor. 4:3–5). Here
Paul appeals to Isaiah 45:23 to support his point of the future,
universal judgment of all believers (v. 11). In that day we will
not be held accountable for others, but we will only be responsible for ourselves to Him alone—"each of us will give an account
of himself to God" (Rom. 14:12; 1 Cor. 3:11–15; 2 Cor. 5:10).

THE PRINCIPLE OF THE LIMITATION OF FREEDOM IN CHRISTIAN LOVE (14:13–23)

Paul now turns to exhort the strong concerning the conduct
that their love for the weak demands. When the strong use their
freedom, they are not wrong in their position (v. 14), but they
must never consciously allow their freedom to jeopardize the
spiritual life and growth of a brother or sister in Christ, or
worse yet, threaten another's eternal salvation. Though nothing
(material) is evil (unclean) in itself, it may be viewed as evil by a

person whose mind is more influenced by his cultural background than by the truth of God's good creation taught in Scripture (Mark 7:15).

One of my young daughters brought home the suggestion from school of how an avocado seed could be put in a glass of water to sprout and then subsequently planted. In a week or so, we noticed a strong, repulsive odor coming from the kitchen. After much looking, we found the source. Right, it was the avocado seed, which had rotted and become rancid. Mother threw out the seed and thoroughly scalded the pretty, flowered juice glass. But until this day no one in our family will drink anything out of that glass. It is perfectly clean, but in our minds it is so associated with the rotten avocado seed that we cannot comfortably use it any longer.

The real issue revolves around the meaning of the "stumbling block" or "obstacle" (vv. 13, 20–21). What is it that strong Christians create for the weak by the use of their freedom that causes the weak to "be distressed" (grieved or sorrowed, v. 15), destroyed or caused to stumble (vv. 15, 20), and even condemned (v. 23)? The language Paul uses seems much too strong to refer simply, as it is commonly explained, to the displeasure felt in the heart of the weak when they see another Christian doing something they believe is wrong. Rather, the weak must in some way be emboldened by the behavior of the strong to actually do something against their conscientious conviction of the good, and thus their conscience is violated and "hurt" over their own sin. Because such an action is done not out of faith but against their faith, it brings God's judgment into their life and ruins their relationship to Christ (v. 23).

The strong, then, must consider the gravity of the consequences toward the weak of their behavior. If they fail to take thought in this manner for their fellow Christian, they are not walking in responsible love, and thus they sin against Christ (vv. 15, 20). Note that the stumbling block is not the mere displeasure that other Christians may have over my behavior, but the temptation for them to go beyond what their faith approves and to sin by abandoning their convictions. They have done this thing not to please Christ, as I have done, writes Paul, but because of desire for pleasure or convenience. The weak have misunderstood my behavior.[26]

But what about the freedom we, the strong in faith, have in Christ? If we accommodate our behavior to weaker Christians, won't we have to give up our freedom that Christ wants us to exercise? Furthermore, shouldn't the Christian show his freedom to the world and thereby show his faith? Paul says that the faith that we (the strong) have, we are to keep between ourselves and God privately (v. 22). And it is not the display of our freedom that commends our faith to the world, but our practice of responsible love (John 13:35). We are God's representatives to the world, not in matters of freedom over food and drink, but in matters of the kingdom of God. The kingdom is God's rule over us. What are the issues, then, of this kingdom? Paul answers, "righteousness, peace and joy in the Holy Spirit" (v. 17). One who is thus emphasizing the justice of God in life's human relations and peace and who thrives on the inner joy produced by the Holy Spirit has found the really important essence of Christianity before God and others (v. 18).

THE PRINCIPLE OF LIVING TO PLEASE OTHERS (15:1–6)

Not only are the strong to walk in responsible love for their weaker brothers and sisters, but they are to help them by bearing (along with) their weaknesses (infirmities) even when it is distasteful, "and not just please ourselves" (15:1–2 NASB). The example of Christ provides Paul with further reason to support his exhortation (v. 3). The whole human life of Jesus is summed up as a willing humiliation whereby He Himself bore the reproaches of the ungodly against God (Ps. 69:9). Paul's point seems to be that whatever inconveniences or reproach the strong may have to endure in order to please their weaker brothers and thus edify them, it can never compare with the inconvenience and reproach that our Savior endured in order to bring us eternal benefit.

Such Scriptures as Paul has been quoting provide the Christian with instructions in "endurance" (steadfastness) and "encouragement" (v. 4). Just how this is related to the context is not clear. Perhaps Paul means that by learning from the Scriptures that God is aware of our reproaches and lot and that He supplies what we need to be steadfast, we have hope (encouragement) in His ultimate plan and providence. In any case, the character of God is found in the Scriptures (such as Psalm 69:9), which strike the note of hope in those who hear them speak (1 Cor. 10:6, 11).

Finally, by relying on such graces that come to us from the God who is revealed to us in the Scriptures, we can glorify God for His mercy to us with a united voice of praise free from condemning attitudes toward one another (15:5–6). Rather than critiquing each other and being perpetually suspicious of one another, we ought, according to Christ's will for us, to seek together the glory of God in all our relationships.

CHRIST AND THE GENTILES (15:7–13)

These verses reflect again the fact that there was racial and ethnic prejudice in the church at Rome. Jewish believers could not overcome their backgrounds of discrimination against the Gentiles. Accustomed to thinking of non-Jews as "sinners of Gentiles" and "dogs," Jews, even though affirming Jesus as Lord, still could not accept their Gentile brethren as fully as they did their own. Paul speaks sharply to this issue and encourages them to put away all such attitudes and actions. He says, "Accept one another, then, just as Christ accepted you, in order to bring praise to God" (v. 7). You are to treat others, no matter how different they are from you, in the same way Christ treated you. There can be no racial, ethnic, or gender discrimination among God's people where this truth is taken seriously and obeyed (Gal. 3:28).

Turning to the ministry of Jesus, Paul asserts the reason that Christ confined His labors to the Jewish people. It was not because of favoritism, but for the purpose of fulfilling the ratified oath, covenant promises made to the Jewish patriarchs (v. 8). "Circumcision" was the covenant seal given to Abraham and his descendants in hope of the realization of the promise of a seed in whom all the world would be blessed (Gal. 3:16;

4:9–31).

Furthermore, contained in the original Abrahamic promise was the promise of universal blessing to all people (Gen. 22:17–18; Gal. 3:8). Therefore, Christ's ministry to the "Jews" (lit. "circumcision") was not only to prove God's faithfulness to His Word but also that "the Gentiles might glorify God for his mercy" to them also (v. 9). Paul proceeds in verses 9–12 to string together Old Testament quotations that predicted the blessing of the Gentiles as Gentiles together with Israel, both in covenant relationship to God (v. 9b from 2 Sam. 22:50 and Ps. 18:49; v. 10 from Deut. 32:43; v. 11 from Ps. 117:1; v. 12 from Isa. 11:10). Paul certainly saw no theological teaching in the Old Testament that made any distinction between Jew and Gentile when both are in Christ. The Old Testament itself actually predicted the mutual acceptance of both on equal footing before God.

Finally, verse 13 forms a beautiful cornerstone to this whole section dealing with the relationship of Christians to one another. It is Paul's prayer for all believers that with the divine supply of joy and peace supplied to them through their continued faith, they might be strengthened by the power of the indwelling Spirit so that they can abound in the hope of their future final salvation.

In our day, the church urgently needs Paul's insights and admonitions in this section. Whereas a large segment of Christendom seeks unity on a false basis, we who confess Jesus as Divine Lord divide ourselves from one another over the slightest differences. In many evangelical churches the weak have gained control and through extrabiblical rules and restrictions have rejected the strong from membership. Racial prejudice in varying degrees still abounds in many of our churches today.

Nevertheless, wherever Christians have been enabled to overcome the barriers that divide them, there is found the greatest testimony to the living Christ among His people. This is the Christian church's greatest glory. Not that it can penetrate to the most orthodox interpretation of Scriptures, though it is important to know what Scripture teaches, or delineate the best expression of what it means to have a Christian testimony today, but the church's greatest glory is that, in spite of strong differences among us, we can fully accept one another *even* as Christ also fully accepted us. It is not that the whole church holds one opinion, but that it follows one purpose and with one mouth of praise glorifies God.

From this section (14:1–15:13) we learn that faith-living for the Christian means doing whatever we do in conscious honoring of the Lord (14:6). Sin in these areas, on the other hand, consists not in breaking the traditional taboos but more in a betrayal of our own faith convictions (14:23), or in causing other Christians to stumble by luring them through our liberty to go against their own faith convictions (14:15), or by passing any presumptive judgment on another Christian in any of these areas (14:10–12). Finally, the real glory of God is manifested when we fully accept each other in spite of these strong differences in convictions (15:7).

NOTES

1. Paul may not mean to exclude the self or person from his use of *body*, but there is no warrant to follow Bultmann and others here to see only the self. We are whole beings from the biblical view, including the body as a prime ingredient; so Ernst Käsemann, *Commentary on Romans*, trans. Geoffrey W. Bromiley (Grand Rapids: Eerdmans, 1978), 327; Robert H. Gundry, *Soma, in Biblical Theology, with Emphasis on Pauline Anthropology* (Cambridge: Cambridge Univ., 1976).

2. F. J. Leenhardt, *Romans* (London: Lutterworth, 1961), 303, cites some examples of the word from Hellenistic Jewish texts where it denotes what is interior, what concerns the deepest part of our being, in contrast to what is formal, external, or theatrical.

3. C. E. B. Cranfield, *A Critical and Exegetical Commentary on the Epistle to the Romans*, The International Critical Commentary, 2 vols. (Edinburgh: T. & T. Clark, 1975, 1979), 2:601.

4. See Harry Blamires, *The Christian Mind: How Should a Christian Think?* (Ann Arbor, Mich.: Servant, 1978).

5. One good modern exposition of discipleship is Dietrich Bonhoeffer, *The Cost of Discipleship* (New York: Macmillan, 1949). One does not have to agree with all of Bonhoeffer's theological conclusions to reap a rich profit from his understanding of obedience to God. A more recent statement is

Dallas Willard, *The Spirit of the Disciplines: Understanding How God Changes Lives* (San Francisco: HarperSanFrancisco, 1988).

6. Cranfield has a slightly different interpretation of the "measure of faith." He believes it refers to what we all hold in common with others in Christian faith, namely, that we are all sinners under the judgment of the Cross and we are all likewise the objects of God's undeserved and triumphant mercy in Jesus Christ (*Romans*, 2:615–16; Moo also). While possible, this view does less justice to the context (so Schreiner, *Romans*, 652).

7. One should study more than a single tradition in the interpretation of the gifts; e.g., John Walvoord, *The Holy Spirit* (Wheaton, Ill.: Van Kampen, 1954), chaps. 19–20; and Donald Bloesch, *The Reform of the Church* (Grand Rapids: Eerdmans, 1970), chap. 9 form a good comparison; more recently, the charismatic view has been defended extensively by Gordon Fee, *The Empowering Presence: The Holy Spirit in the Letters of Paul* (Peabody, Ma.: Hendrickson, 1994).

8. Cranfield, again, prefers to understand "according to the standard of faith," v. 3 ("measure of faith") and gives it this sense: "The prophets are to prophesy in agreement with the standard which they possess in their apprehension of, and response to, the grace of God in Jesus Christ—they are to be careful not to utter (under the impression that they are inspired) anything which is incompatible with their believing in Christ" (2:621); also Moo. Käsemann thinks all this is too subjective and instead believes Paul is referring to some traditional Christian confessions of faith that formed the standard (*Romans*, 341–42). Schreiner, however, has in our opinion the better understanding, which links this verse with the "measure of faith" in v. 3 and refers it to the *quantity* of faith each prophet has received to exercise his or her gift within the bounds of God's will (*Romans*, 656).

9. TDNT, 6:702.

10. Cited by John Murray, *Epistle to the Romans*, 2 vols. (Grand Rapids: Eerdmans, 1959), 2:127.

11. Edward Plowman, *The Jesus Movement in America* (Elgin, Ill.: Cook, 1971).

12. The series of imperatives in English, "abhor," "cleave," are participles with imperative force in Greek and probably follow the Rabbinic Hebrew use of participles for expressing, not direct commands, but rules and codes (see C. K. Barrett, *The Epistle to the Romans* [New York: Harper & Row, 1957, rvsd. 1991], 239). If this is a correct explanation of the linguistic phenomenon, then these commands could represent a Semitic source originating in a very early Jewish Christian church.

13. Francis A. Schaeffer, *The Mark of the Christian* (Downers Grove, Ill.: InterVarsity, 1970); see also the penetrating analysis of Vincent Brummer, *The Model of Love* (Cambridge: Cambridge Univ. Press, 1993) who defines Christian love as "fellowship love," where we identify ourselves with others by treating their interests and their claims as our own.

14. C. K. Barrett, ed. *The New Testament Background: Selected Documents* (New York: Harper & Row, 1956), 14. Acts 18:2 records that the Jew Aquila and his wife, Priscilla, were expelled by Claudius from Rome. They were probably Christians before they met Paul.

15. Ibid., 15; also E. M. Blaiklock, *The Century of the New Testament* (London: Tyndale, n.d.), 42. The inscription was discovered in 1932.

16. See H. P. Liddon, *An Explanatory Analysis of St. Paul's Epistle to the Romans* (Grand Rapids: Zondervan, 1961), 246, for illustrations from Jewish and Ebionite sources to the effect that government authorities were the expression of the evil and devilish power of the universe.

17. Cranfield following Calvin argues the former view (2:653–55), whereas Käsemann following Luther argues the latter view (*New Testament Questions of Today,* trans. W. J. Montague [Philadelphia: Fortress, 1969], 205–7). The resolution of this question has an effect on the way Christians see their relationship to government and politics. For example, Käsemann rejecting Calvin's (and Cranfield's) view can then state the Lutheran conviction that: "He is Kyrios, however, in a peculiar hidden-ness, so that the assault of grace upon the world is borne forward by the gospel concerning him and by the servanthood of the community and no corner of our earth is left free from the demand and the promise of that same grace. To speak of Christ's universal sovereignty otherwise than in this relation to the word of preaching and the servanthood of the community can only be to come once again under the spell of enthusiasm."

18. Although Oscar Cullmann (*The State in the New Testament* [New York: Scribner's, 1956], 93ff.) has shown that philologically the word "powers" or "authorities" in Paul's writing has a dual reference to both angelic powers and government rulers (see Col. 1:20; 2:15), it does not seem to fit the evidence in this passage. See Murray, 2:252ff, for criticism of Cullmann; now Cranfield also has agreed that Paul has only civil authorities in mind (2:659), and Käsemann, *Romans,* 353.

19. According to some, the "sword" is the power possessed by all higher magistrates of inflicting the death penalty for certain crimes and is known technically as *jus gladii* (Tacitus, *Histories,* 3:68, cited by C. K. Barrett, *The Epistle to the Romans* [New York; Harper & Row, 1957], 247); Cranfield disagrees and argues that the *jus gladii* was the right to condemn to death a Roman citizen serving in the military under one's command. Rather, the "sword" refers to military power, that is, one is armed, is able to employ

force to quell resistance (2:667). Neither too much (the right of govern-ments to wage wars against other countries) nor too little (mere symbol with no reference to the just use of force) should be read into the word "sword" here. It is also possible but less probable that Paul means simply the small "dagger worn by the Emperor as *Imperator* [commander in chief]" (Cranfield, 2:667).

20. Philip H. Towner, "Romans 13:1–7 and Paul's Missiological Perspec-tive," 168–69 in *Romans & The People of God*, Sven K. Soderlund & N. T. Wright, eds. (Grand Rapids: Eerdmans, 1999); also Bruce W. Winter, *Seek the Welfare of the City* (Grand Rapids: Eerdmans, 1994).

21. See Oliver O'Donovan, *The Desire* of *The Nations: Rediscovering the Roots of Political Theology* (Cambridge: Cambridge Univ. Press, 1996).

22. Daniel B. Stevick, *Civil Disobedience and the Christian* (New York: Seabury, 1969). Stevick argues that the scriptural ambiguity on this ques-tion has pervaded the church from earliest times to the present; more recent-ly Stephen C. Mott, *Biblical Ethics and Social Change* (New York: Oxford Univ., 1982), 167–91. Mott is more open to civil disobedience and to a jus-tified revolution. For a less open view see Carl F. H. Henry, *A Plea for Evan-gelical Demonstration* (Grand Rapids: Baker, 1971), 91–106. Francis A. Schaeffer argued for civil disobedience in *The Christian Manifesto* (West-chester, Ill.: Crossway, 1981).

23. Joseph F. Fletcher, *Situation Ethics* (Philadelphia: Westminster, 1966), 69–75. Fletcher's strong antithesis between law and love violates Paul's whole emphasis and lies at the heart of Fletcher's strong relativistic love-only ethic. As Edward L. Long Jr. has noted, Fletcher's approach borders strongly on a new legalism that has replaced the old Pharisaic "works/righ-teousness" with the new "context/righteousness." (See Paul Ramsey and Gene H. Outka, eds., *Norm and Context in Christian Ethics* [New York: Scribner's, 1968], 281ff.). Today, thankfully, this perspective of Fletcher seems to be diminishing among Christian ethicists of all types who regard the necessity of love working together with principles, or law-commands or some framework as an essential part of moral action. However, there is still a populist mind-set that continues to embrace elements of situationist ethics.

24. The prophetic or eschatological may be distinguished slightly from the apocalyptic by understanding the prophetic to be viewing the future from the standpoint of the present, whereas the apocalyptic views the present from the ground of the future. This is often overlooked. The NT has both perspectives, but most preaching on prophecy today reflects only the for-mer. A return to the more biblical view could have great significance, espe-cially to more apathetic forms of Christianity in our day. (See Carl E. Braat-en, *Christ and Counter-Christ* [Philadelphia: Fortress, 1972]).

25. Cranfield makes an important observation we should remember: The strong in faith in the sense that they did not have scruples over wine and Sabbath day observances and so on "were actually exceedingly weak in basic Christian faith—so weak in it that they were prepared to risk the spiritual ruin of a brother for whom Christ had died for the sake of a mere plate of meat (14.15, 20)" (2:698).

26. Cranfield agrees and says: "What Paul has in mind (as the sequel makes clear) is not merely the weak brother's distressed feelings (a serious thing though they are), but something much worse, the actual destruction of his integrity as a Christian by his being led by example or social pressure into a deliberate violation of what he believes to be the will of God" (2:714, n. 3); see also Calvin, *Institutes,* III 19:1–5, 7–13 for a strong exhortation not to lose Christian freedom for the wrong reasons.

THE CLOSING

15:14–16:27

Paul is now finished with the main body of his letter. The remainder of the materials entail words of a more personal nature, including his purpose in writing, encouragement, commendations, greetings, a final warning, and closing doxology. Our treatment will be brief, simply calling attention to some of the more significant features.

PAUL'S REASON FOR WRITING 15:14–21

In this section, Paul very tactfully relates his purpose for writing to the Romans. His somewhat bold letter to them was penned not so much to instruct them in new truth or to spoon-feed them, for he concedes that they were knowledgeable and able to instruct each other (v. 14), but to strongly remind them of those well-known truths and their implications (v. 15). This apostolic ministry to the Roman Gentiles is viewed by Paul as a "priestly" service to God. He offers up the evangelized Gentiles as his sacrificial offering (v. 16). This is a beautiful thought. Paul views his service in the gospel as an act of worship.

The apostle ascribes the glory for what has been done and said by him solely to Christ, though he has reason, humanly speaking, to be proud of his work (vv. 17–18). Christ's working through Paul also included miracles ("signs and miracles") as means of the Spirit's powerful attestation of the truth of the gospel (v. 19; see also 2 Cor. 12:12; Gal. 3:5; Heb. 2:4).

"From Jerusalem . . . to Illyricum" (Dalmatia, northwest of Macedonia) sets the eastern and western limit where Paul had planted the gospel thus far in his ministry (v. 19). His activity was aimed at, though certainly not limited to, territories where no church was established (v. 20). This type of ministry Paul sees as a fulfillment of the prophecy of Isaiah (52:15) in foretelling of those who, though ignorant of the Word of God, would hear of the Messiah and respond (v. 21).

PAUL'S PERSONAL PLANS 15:22–33

Paul planned to go to Spain and make a stopover in Rome en route (v. 24) after he had taken a special financial gift to the church in Jerusalem sent by the Christians in Macedonia and Achaia (v. 26). Like his statement in 1:13, he again assures them of his interest in visiting them even though until now he has been unable to come because of the busy schedule in fulfilling his primary evangelistic calling. He would, however, come and fellowship with them, and allow them to send him on his journey to Spain. Missionary and church were closely bound together.

Paul also takes time to describe the significance of the gift from the Gentiles to the Jews at Jerusalem (vv. 25–27). Because the Jews were the original stock of the Abrahamic covenant blessings, Gentiles who have become partakers in these "spiritual" blessings rightly feel an obligation to share with the Jews their "material" blessings (v. 27). The gifts are a seal and a fruit of the love and bond that exists between these Christians though they live in different parts of the world and are different culturally. Theologically, the acceptance of such a gift from Gentiles by the Jews at Jerusalem would confirm the full acceptance of Gentiles into the family of God. Hence, his concern in the next paragraph for the Jews' acceptance of the gift.

It is noteworthy how Paul regularly solicits the prayers of

believers for his special needs and circumstances. He realizes that faces unfriendly to the gospel of Christ await him in Jerusalem. How much he needs the prayers of the saints for deliverance and prayer that the Jews would accept the Gentile gift and that at last he might indeed visit the Romans in God's will (vv. 30–33)! Paul trusted the Roman Christians and put great confidence in them.

It is instructive to trace the answer to Paul's prayer. Part of Paul's prayer was answered just as he prayed by the joyous reception he received in Jerusalem (Acts 21:17–20); part was not answered exactly as he wished in that he was seized by the unbelieving Jews (though not harmed) and yet delivered from them by the Roman cohort (Acts 21:27, 32); part of his prayer was answered differently than he planned in that, although he went to Rome, he went under arrest (Acts 28:16); and part was answered much later in his life when he was released from prison and apparently completed his tour to Spain on a final missionary journey (1 Tim. 1:3; 2 Tim. 4:13; Titus 1:5; 3:12).[1]

COMMENDATION OF PHOEBE 16:1–2

On the northeastern side of the city of Corinth lay one of its ports, the city of Cenchrea. From a church located there came Phoebe, who is described as a "servant" (Gk. *diakonos*) and a "help [lit. protectress, patroness] to many people," including Paul (v. 2). She may have been quite wealthy and socially prominent.

It has been traditional to explain Paul's calling Phoebe a "servant" (Gk. *diakonos*) of the church as a quite general reference to her nonofficial service to the church (see discussion at 1:1). But for a number of reasons it is better to refer the expression to the office and ministry of *deacon* to the church (not *deaconess*). Elsewhere, when Paul is talking about persons connected with specific church functions, the word *diakonos* means a church leader, a deacon (Phil. 1:1; 1 Tim. 3:8, 12). Cranfield concludes: "We regard it as virtually certain that Phoebe is being described as 'a (or possibly 'the') deacon' of the church."[2] In any event she *is* a *leader* in the church at Cenchrea. The word "help" (Gk. *prostatis*) in verse 2 is found only here in the NT and its sense is not entirely clear. Its choice here by Paul at least affirms that Phoebe has some position, wealth, and independence. However, since the word is found eight times in the Greek OT (LXX) and thirteen times in the first-century Jewish writer Josephus, in each of the twenty-one cases with reference to a person who holds a publicly recognized service-oriented leadership role, the word may be stronger than simply a benefactor. The word however does occur eight times in the LXX (Gk. OT) and in every instance it refers to a person who carries an officially recognized, public leadership role. It is also used by Josephus twenty times and it refers to a wide variety of leadership functions. This word seems to convey the idea of servant-leadership since it is contrasted in several of the references to a tyrant's rule. Its choice here by Paul seems to clearly affirm that Phoebe has not only some social position, wealth, and independence, but that she is recognized as an official leader in the church as well.

Apparently Phoebe carried the letter of Paul to the Romans, and chapter 16 formed a necessary letter of commendation for her to the Roman Christians (2 Cor. 3:1).[3] This woman among a number of others like Priscilla (v. 3) has been immortalized in the Christian tradition because of her deep dedication to Christ and the service she faithfully rendered in the gospel ministry. Here is also one more glimpse into the radically transforming power of Christ to change a woman from paganism (Phoebe: "goddess of the moon") to a devoted and highly notable servant of Jesus Christ. Note also here and in the following verses the number, roles, and the very high place women hold in the Christian mission. At least nine women are addressed in verses 1–16, and they are called "fellow workers" (or partners), not maidservants!

HELLOS TO PAUL'S FRIENDS IN ROME 16:3–16

This section is a greatly neglected portion of Scripture, yet it provides a fascinating historical picture of the composition of a typical demographic crosssection of an early first-century Christian church—perhaps the only one! Chrysostom (d. 407) comments: "I think there are many, even some apparently good commentators, who hurry over this part of the epistle because they think it is superfluous and of little importance. They probably think much the same about the genealogies in the Gospels. Because it is a catalogue of names, they think they can get nothing good out of it. People who mine gold are careful even about the smallest fragments, but these commentators ignore even huge bars of gold!" (*Homilies on Romans*, 30).

There are no less than twenty-seven different people greeted by Paul from all walks of life and background, together with general greetings to the households of Aristobulus and Narcissus. Some are Jewish-Christians, (Priscilla and Aquila, vv. 3–5), some names are Greek (Aristobulus, v. 10, Junias, v. 7), others Roman-Latin (Rufus, v. 13; Urbanus, v. 9), no less than ten are women (Mary, v. 6; Junia[s], v. 7, Julia, v. 15), some sisters (Tryphena and Tryphosa [twins?], v. 12), a mother is mentioned (v. 13), prisoners (v. 7), relatives of Paul (vv. 7, 11), a family of a deceased man (Narcissus, v. 11), and so on. Some were no doubt wealthy and noble; others were poor and slaves.

What does Paul say about these believers in Christ? He commends Priscilla and Aquila (Acts 18:1–3) for their service and courage in risking their lives for him (Rom. 16:3–4). Note that the wife, Priscilla, is named first (cf. 2 Tim. 4:19). Sometimes she is listed in the reverse order (1 Cor. 16:19). Epenetus receives the title "dear friend" because he was the first convert from Asia (v. 5). Mary's hard work and industry are recalled (v. 6). Two Jewish believers, Andronicus and Junia[s], who knew Christ even before Paul was converted, are referred to as "outstanding among the apostles." A number of recent commentators hold strongly to the view that Junia[s] was a woman, not a man (Junia). That she and Andronicus were "outstanding among the apostles," according to their view, does not mean that they were merely "respected by the apostles" (i.e., the twelve, so TLB, though no other English translation that I have seen, and only Murray among the modern commentators). The phrase instead means that they were outstanding in the group that was known as apostles. The term *apostle* in the NT can have a wider use than just the twelve disciples and seems to refer to those who are sent to preach the gospel (Acts 14:4; 1 Cor. 9:5–6; Gal. 1:19; 1 Thess. 2:6). In the modern debate over women's leadership in the church this point is minimized by male leadership advocates and emphasized by inclusive leadership advocates. At any rate, there has been a modern interpretive debate on Junia(s).[4] Apelles is "approved in Christ," perhaps through trials (v. 10).

Rufus (v. 13) may well be the son of Simon of Cyrene who bore Jesus' cross (Mark 15:21). If so, it would show why Mark specifically mentioned his name and would further connect the gospel of Mark with Rome. He is called "chosen in the Lord" not because he was chosen to salvation, but because he was selected for some special honor unknown to us to which he was called by Christ. Rufus's mother became mother also to Paul in some way. Paul may have lost his mother through death or because she never became a Christian. Perhaps Simon, the father, was saved, then the mother and the whole family.

In verse 14, Paul greets five men and a group who were with them. Could this be some type of early all-male Christian commune? Believers are further exhorted to greet one another with a "holy kiss" (Rom. 16:16; see also 1 Cor. 16:20; 1 Thess. 5:26; 1 Pet. 5:14). Such a warm Christian token of love is conspicuous by its absence in the modern Western church.

In summary, we might learn some important things about effective Christian service from this chapter. First, Paul was interested in people. To him Christianity was persons following Jesus Christ. He may have had a long prayer list. Paul's commendations seem to highlight faithful labor as the predominant quality (Rev. 2:2). He commended those he worked with and constantly held them up for recognition (12:10). Note also the near equal balance in numbers, and the high place of women in the service for Christ. Finally, remember that the gospel of Christ when faithfully proclaimed and taught bears fruit in the lives of all kinds of people. This section illustrates in living stories the truth of Romans 1:16, "The gospel . . . is the power of God for the salvation of everyone who believes."

A FINAL WARNING
16:17–20

Before Paul's concluding remarks, he pauses to issue a direct warning against fellowshiping with those who taught doctrines contrary to the original apostolic teachings (v. 17). It is not exactly clear to whom Paul has reference. These deceivers may be the same crowd that created a problem for the churches of Galatia (Gal. 3:1; 5:7, 20), Philippi (Phil. 3:19), and Colossae (Col. 2:20–23). "Serving . . . their own appetites [lit. belly]" (Rom. 16:18) probably does not refer to their physical appetites for food but their own self-centered, lustful living and preoccupation with food laws (James 3:15; Jude 19; also Phil. 3:3–4; 1 Cor. 6:12–13).

This heretical group should not be confused with the "weak" Christians of chapter 14 whom Paul exhorts to "accept" into the fellowships. It is vital to note this distinction lest we be "marking" fellow Christians who have different opinions as "deceivers." The "unsuspecting" (NASB) are those who do not suspect any deception and therefore uncritically soak up the false teaching to their own harm.

Yet Paul is not insinuating that the Romans had actually fallen prey to this teaching; rather, he commends them for their obedience and faithfulness (v. 19). Nevertheless the apostle wants them to be alert to deception—"wise about what is good"—and uninvolved with any heresy or evil practice— "innocent [inexperienced] about what is evil" (v. 19). This is a tremendously needed balance in our lives: to know the good well enough to do it and to know enough about error to be warned of its presence (e.g., drugs, demonism, occult, nationalism, materialism, oriental mysticism, and so on), so that we may avoid experience with those things that damage our persons and hinder our relationship with God. Grotius paraphrases, "Too good to deceive, and too wise to be deceived."

Verse 20 contains an allusion to Genesis 3:15. It is Satan who causes these heresies and allures people into their evil consequences, but it is God who, in the soon coming of Jesus, will deal the final death blow to Satan's activities. The hope of the final overcoming of all enemies of Christ sustains believers in their present battle against these forces (1 Cor. 15:25–28).

Hellos from Paul's Companions in Corinth 16:21–24

Timothy is well-known (Acts 16:1–2). Lucias, Jason, and Sosipater were probably Jewish relatives of Paul (see 16:7). Tertius (v. 22) wrote the letter in the sense of serving as Paul's secretary *(amanuensis)*, which was the apostle's custom (1 Cor. 16:21; Gal. 6:11; Col. 4:18; 2 Thess. 3:17). Gaius hosted not only Paul but the whole church at Corinth in his house! He must have had much but he also used it for the Lord. Gaius may be the same individual referred to elsewhere as Titius Justus (1 Cor. 1:14; Acts 18:7; 19:29).

Erastus is called the "treasurer" (NASB) of the city of Corinth. He must have been a prominent man in Corinth. These men were usually slaves, though wealthy (Acts 8:27). In 1931, a Latin inscription dated A.D. 50–100 was found at Corinth bearing the name of Erastus, the city Aedile (treasurer?), who in exchange for his appointment paid himself for the paving of this street. Scholars are now generally agreed that this inscription most probably refers to the same man Paul mentions.[5] The repeated benedictions in verses 20 and 24 are by no means scribal slips but fitting endings for each section.

The Doxology
16:25–27

Such a long doxology is not unfamiliar in the New Testament (Heb. 13:20–21; Jude 24–25), though it is not customary for Paul. It is a superb summary of the main notes of the epistle and in perfect harmony with its contents and with the teaching of other Pauline letters (Eph. 3:20; 1 Tim. 1:17).[6] In particular, the significant strands of chapter one are picked up and reiterated in a beautiful concluding praise to God Himself.

The apostle begins with reference to the strengthening power of God granted to believers and resulting from the ministry of Paul's preaching of the gospel of Jesus Christ (1:11). This gospel of Paul's is in fact a "revelation of the mystery hidden for long ages past" (lit., in eternal times). On Paul's use of the term "mystery" see discussion at 11:25. Here the content of the mystery is much broader. It is not certain whether by the expression "for long ages past" Paul means "since the creation began" (see 2 Tim. 1:9; Titus 1:2) or "in the eternal times of God." Perhaps the term means "times reaching back to eternity."[7] In any case, the mystery of the gospel of Jesus Christ, God's Son (Rom. 1:3–4), which was kept quiet in the past, is now fully revealed to all people: "But now is manifested" (v. 26 NASB).

Paul links this present gospel revelation to the "prophetic writings." How the mystery, which has been hid in the past, can now be revealed in Scripture, which has been known for centuries, presents a problem. One solution posits the view that the phrase "Scriptures of the prophets" (NASB) refers to the New Testament prophets and the apostolic Scriptures (2 Pet. 3:16).[8] Yet it is difficult to maintain this view in light of Paul's abundant quotation of Scripture in Romans all taken only from the Old Testament; the parallel in 1:2 certainly refers to the Old Testament; and in light of the early date of this epistle (before A.D. 60) very little New Testament Scripture would have been written. It seems best to maintain a tension between what was revealed in promise in the Old Testament concerning the gospel and which belonged primarily to Israel and what is now revealed in history in Jesus Christ and by the command of the eternal God made known (and thus given) to all peoples. This mystery is not an esoteric phenomenon that is the property of an elite few, but God commands that the knowledge be given without distinction through the Scriptures to all people in order to bring them to the "obedience of faith" (NASB) in Jesus Christ.

Paul began his doxology with an address to the one who is able to establish us; and now, after contemplating the tremendous mystery of the gospel, he closes by turning to the "only wise God" (v. 27). To this God of unfathomable wisdom, the One who has revealed the mystery of His plan for the salvation of the whole created order effected through Jesus Christ and the Spirit, Paul can only attribute eternal glory.[9] Amen!

Thus, as the epistle began with the promise of God (1:2–4),

so it ends with the glory of God. The letter is perhaps the greatest treatise about God that has ever been written.[10]

NOTES

1. This is based on the inference that these letters were written after Paul's release from his first imprisonment and refer to places not mentioned in Acts as related to any of his first three missionary journeys.

2. C. E. B. Cranfield, *A Critical and Exegetical Commentary on the Epistle to the Romans*, The International Critical Commentary, 2 vols. (Edinburgh: T. & T. Clark, 1975, 1979), 2:781; that such an office was an early appointment of women to assist other women in their "visitation, baptism, and other matters" (Schreiner, *Romans*, 787) lacks any early supporting evidence. The later development of a deaconess order cannot be read back into the NT.

3. See Introduction for a discussion of the problem of whether chapter 16 was part of the original letter.

4. See Cranfield (2:788–89) for support for both that Junia[s] is a woman and that she is also an apostle. No reliable person took the name "Junia[s]" to be that of a male until Aegidius of Rome (13th cent.). Then a split developed (some holding it as male, and some as female). Finally, in the modern period until recently it was held unanimously to refer to a male. Now almost all commentators and articles argue for a return to the earlier position of Chrysostom (A.D. 407) that he is in fact a she: "It was the greatest of honors to be counted a fellow prisoner of Paul's. . . . Think what great praise it was to be considered of note among the apostles. These two were of note because of their works and achievements. Think how great the devotion of this woman Junia must have been, that she should be worthy to be called an apostle!" Chrysostom, *Homilies on Romans*, chap. 31; see also Richard S. Cervin, "A Note Regarding the Name 'Junias' in Romans 16:7," NTS 40 (1994): 464–70. In summary Cervin argues: (1) The name is Latin and quite common; (2) It is clearly a feminine word/name; and (3) the expression "among the apostles" is best understood as a reference to Junias as an apostle.

5. H. J. Cadbury, "Erastus of Corinth," *Journal of Biblical Literature* 50 (1931): 42–58; the inscription reads: "ERASTUS PRO: AED: S: P: STRAVIT" ("Erastus, Commissioner for Public Works, laid this pavement at his own expense"). The inscription is still at Corinth on the roadway (Cranfield, 2:807–8); another Corinthian Erastus inscription is also now known found in 1960 (see Andrew D. Clarke, "Another Corinthian Erastus Inscription" *Tyndale Bulletin* 42.1 (1991): 146–51.